GLOBAL FINANCE
AND FINANCIAL MARKETS

A MODERN INTRODUCTION

GLOBAL FINANCE
AND FINANCIAL MARKETS
A MODERN INTRODUCTION

FERDINAND E. BANKS
Uppsala University, Sweden

World Scientific
Singapore • New Jersey • London • Hong Kong

Published by

World Scientific Publishing Co. Pte. Ltd.

P O Box 128, Farrer Road, Singapore 912805

USA office: Suite 1B, 1060 Main Street, River Edge, NJ 07661

UK office: 57 Shelton Street, Covent Garden, London WC2H 9HE

British Library Cataloguing-in-Publication Data
A catalogue record for this book is available from the British Library.

GLOBAL FINANCE AND FINANCIAL MARKETS: A MODERN INTRODUCTION

ISBN 981-02-4326-X
ISBN 981-02-4327-8 (pbk)

Printed in Singapore by World Scientific Printers

For Christian Otto, Claudia Soleil, and Beatrice Gunilla

Foreword

"**Victory begins here**", read the sign over the gate at Fort Jackson, South Carolina, when I passed under it many years ago. For those persons who are interested in learning about and perhaps playing a role in the great world of global finance, the same thing might apply to this book. My basic intention in this short text is to introduce many categories of readers to real-world financial markets and practices, and to help make it possible for them to follow *all* the financial commentary in the press, in other books, on the radio, and on television. Former president Lyndon Johnson once said that "international finance is a mystery to most men and women", which is true, but it will not be true for those persons who read most of this book.

I have taught from previous versions of this book in Sweden, Australia, France, Singapore, and at the business school of Charles University, Prague; and I am convinced that it contains materials that will be useful to all levels of readers. The first thing I want to emphasize is that this is a book on international finance, and not international micro and macro economics. Its purpose is to assist readers in analyzing and thinking about real-world financial markets, and that *especially* includes persons who are using it for self study, and as a review. I had as my "models" for this project "Alexander" in Michael Lewis' book *Liars Poker*, and "Thomas" in Nancy Goldstone's *Trading Up*. These were the kind of people who were dedicated to the pursuit of excellence, and for better or worse have made the international financial community a place where high salaries, high bonuses, and even higher levels of competition are the rule. Everyone who wants to can match their knowledge, providing that they learn two things: concentration and patience.

And now an important observation is necessary. Great care has been taken to keep the mathematical content of this book at the level of simple algebra. In principle, there is nothing in this book that will exhaust the mathematical resources of a first year economics student in a Swedish university, and much of the book contains no more than secondary school algebra. This book also says something about the lecturing style that I adopted early in my teaching career. It is based on a combination of the methods introduced at the Ecole Polytechnique (Paris) by Joseph Fournier, and those which have been employed at the United States Miliary Academy at West Point. At the present time the term that would be used to describe these methods is *interactive teaching*. Exercises are worked at the board by teams of three or four students, who then discuss their work, and answer both my questions and those of the remainder of the class. It is for this reason that no answers are provided in the book for the chapter exercises. Of course, most of the exercises are easy, and their purpose is to build rather than undermine self confidence. Readers should also be aware of the survey foremat of the first and last chapters. These chapters are designed to get everyone into the "swing" of international finance.

In preparing this book I want to thank, first and foremost, the many "kulls" of international economics students at Uppsala University who have been subjected to my polemics and rather special vocabulary through the years; and before them my students in mathematical economics at the University of New South Wales (Sydney), the Technical University of Lisbon (Portugal), and the African Institute for Economic and Development Planning (Dakar, Senegal). Here I must single out the brilliant linguist Ulf Carlander and express my gratitude once again for the invaluable help he gave me with the first version of the book, and the same applies to my colleague Ann-Sophie Djerf. I also thank Shadi Amin, my daughters Amelie and Madeleine, my colleagues Åke Qvarfort and Pebbe Selander, and my personal trainer Thomas Banks for their assistance. All mistakes are, of course, my very own, and let me apologize to those colleagues whose work could not be cited in this short book.

Finally, I would like to thank my own teachers. My decision to teach is the result of having the good fortune to hear a few brilliant lectures at an impressionable age. The first of these was by S.I. Hayakawa at Illinois Institute of Technology (Chicago), and in case anyone is interested, its title was "When is a square not a square". The most important, perhaps, was by a captain in the US Army at Camp Gifu, Japan — at that time home of the 24th (US) Infantry Regiment. His message was that real intelligence consists of looking at and/or listening to, and trying to remember everything that takes place around you. Thinking about it also helps. I would also like to take this opportunity to thank my teachers at Roosevelt University (Chicago), and the University of Stockholm.

Finance — like the universe itself — might be described as following Nils Bohr's quantum law: there is no precisely determinable objective universe — the universe exists only as a series of approximations. At the same time though, mainstream finance suggests that objects on a human scale generally obey several well-defined (i.e. classcial) laws of causality. The most provocative of these laws is that they prefer more money to less, regardless of the amounts under discussion. Virtually every millionaire will tell you without hesitation that a million dollars isn't what it used to be! Whether this attitude makes the present subject more or less interesting for the individual student is left for that person to decide for himself/herself.

Let me close by reminding readers that the time you spend learning the definitions in the glossary is one of the best investments that you can make. Most of these definitions are in the test, of course, and in teaching finance, after we have covered about half of the book, I will use a few minutes of every class session for students to demonstrate their familiarities with these expressions, with the empahsis on speed. Finance is a serious business, and you should do everything humanly possible to put yourself in the path of some of the serious money associated with it.

Contents

Chapter 1

The World of Money

As indicated in the preface, my intention in this book is to prepare readers to analyze and explain real-world financial conditions and transactions. I have taken great pains to keep this work squarely on the plane of reality, because I think that in economics and finance more attention needs to be paid to history and "politics", and somewhat less to mathematics and certain esoteric theoretical considerations.

Yes, algebra is important for the study of finance, and later in this book it is freely used; but first and foremost I like to regard finance as the physics of economics, and feel that it is one of the few areas in economics where it is possible to come into contact with, and often practice, the kind of genuine scientific thinking that we too often fail to encounter in much of the economics curriculum. As odd as it may sound, learning to handle scientific concepts does not necessarily mean being overexposed to advanced mathematics. For instance, Albert Einstein, Enrico Fermi, and Richard Feynman — Nobel Laureates in physics — made a point of using as little mathematics as possible, although they had plenty at their disposal.

Of course, when the humorist P.J. O'Rourke writes that "We don't need to know math to understand economics ..." then our immediate reaction should be to ponder the identity of the "we" to whom he is referring. Perhaps it is the famous Mr. O'Rourke himself, although this would undoubtedly come as a surprise to almost every serious student of economics between the ski slopes of Northern Sweden and the Capetown (South Africa) naval yard who perused Chapter 6 of that gentleman's book "Eat the Rich" (1998).

Before completing this prologue, I would like to assure all readers that they will know a great deal about the financial structure and logic of the world in which they live well before they finish the last chapter of this book. In fact, it could happen that they will have a considerable amount of knowledge about this subject by the time they complete the first (non-technical) part of the book, and if they do not feel like confronting the algebra in later chapters right away, they can read the first four chapters again, and also Chapter 9. As you will ultimately find out, becoming conversant with the materials in those five chapters, as well as a few topics from the other chapters, could turn out to be an excellent career move. See also Marc Levinson (1999).

I. Money and Interest

The purpose of this chapter is to provide an overview of some important topics in money and finance. It is also designed to give readers an introduction to the rather special vocabulary of financial markets. This aspect of the present book is extremely important, and possession of an extensive financial vocabulary is something that you will find enormously valuable in many professional and social situations. This is an important reason for studying the glossary. To begin, let us consider the four most important functions of money. Money is a means of exchange, a measure of value, and a store of value. Whether it is satisfactory in these functions — especially the last two — is a much debated question, but there do not seem to be any alternatives. Particularly annoying is money's performance as a store of value, since inflation has occasionally eroded the value of many national currencies to an alarming extent. Money is also a unit of account.

If we consider the position of the US dollar after the Second World War, then the dollar was the international unit of account because other governments used it to define their exchange rates; the means of exchange, because it was universally acceptable for the payment of international debt; and an international store of value, since foreign exchange reserves were mostly held in dollars. The term dollar is derived from the word "thaler", which is a monetary unit introduced in Joachimstal (Czechoslovakia) in 1518. The dollar became the official US currency unit in 1793, and was defined as being worth eight Spanish "reales", represented by the symbol

/8/. This symbol later became a "$". One year earlier, in 1792, the first securities were traded on Wall Street (New York).

That was the past, and now for the present. The dollar enters one side of 90% of the world's interbank foreign exchange transactions, and 90% of the international trade in commodities is priced in dollars. Moreover, as Steve Hanke (1999) surprisingly notes, 40% of Japan's manufactured exports, and 70% of its imports are invoiced in dollars, not yen.

During a large part of the post World War II period, inflation has turned out to be a tenacious economic dilemma for the governments of many countries. Inflation is particularly malignant for individuals with a fixed income (such as pensioners), but even employers in most countries — who tend to find rising prices a comfort much of the time — have come to regard inflation as a nemesis: when prices go up, their employees often insist on compensatory rises in pay, and occasionally they or their unions are strong enough to obtain them.

At the close of the 20th century, it became clear that inflation was extremely important for both bond and stock (or share) market values. (Note: bonds refer to corporate or government debt, while stocks — or equity — refer to ownership.) If the price of goods and services shows a tendency to rise, then purchasers of bonds might require higher interest rates in order to refrain from present consumption to the extent that they continue buying the same or an increased amount of these securities. And if interest rates rise then, *ceteris paribus* (i.e. all things remaining the same) shares lose some of their attraction. The reason is that the desirability of a financial asset depends on its yield (or return) and its risk. If bond yields increase (via a rise in interest rates), then — ceteris paribus — many investors might consider it prudent to substitute bonds with their (supposedly) guaranteed yields for some of the riskier shares in their *portfolios* (i.e. collection of assets). There have also been occasions when shares became slightly less attractive, and nervous investors rushed to the conclusion that there was considerable trouble ahead. If these and then other shareholders begin selling shares, and this behavior accelerates, then eventually we could be faced with the kind of stockmarket "meltdown" in which a huge amount of investor wealth is decimated.

A short digression on the concept of yield might be desirable before continuing. An asset's yield can be calculated from the receipts and costs resulting from its possession during a specific interval. If these receipts and costs can be valued in some monetary unit, then the *value* of the yield can be determined. (For example, if you buy a bond today for $100, and obtain $109 in a year, then the nominal (or monetary) yield is 9%. The cost (= principal) is $100, the interest income is $9, and at the end of the year the purchaser obtains the principal + interest.) But it is also possible to think of the yield in terms of satisfaction, or *utility*, as with a durable good (such as a washing machine, or TV set). The concept of utility is also useful in describing or comparing situations in which uncertainty is present. For many persons, a guaranteed return of 9% has a higher "utility yield" than a highly likely but still uncertain return of 10.5%.

Labor markets have been "tight" in the US during the late 1990s, and a great concern was that this would lead to higher wages and salaries, which in turn will be transformed into higher prices, with the next step being higher interest rates and the possibility of a traumatic stock market "correction". Of course, there are economists claiming that a new paradigm (i.e. pattern) now prevails in countries like Sweden and the US, with high productivity increases restraining inflation, and thus justifying the lower yields on stocks that, ceteris paribus, might result from having to pay more for these assets. (The capital gain on a share costing $50, whose price increases by $5, is 10%; while a $5 price increase on a $100 share yields only 5%. But once again, it has been contended that investors might be willing to accept modest yields if the inflation rate is low.)

In considering the foregoing argument, readers should be aware that we have touched on the difference between money income and real income. Money income is the compensation received by an employee in money, while real income is (in theory) the compensation in goods. Quite simply, if the price of goods and services rises faster than incomes, then real incomes decrease, and the amount of goods (and services) that can be purchased — even with a rising income — decreases. This is one of the reasons why, when consumers see that prices are rising, and/or they expect that prices will rise, they might demand higher interest rates on bonds, and higher yields on shares, before they are willing to postpone consumption.

By way of clarifying this matter, consider the following example. Suppose that you have a certain income, and your tastes are such that you only consume that wonderful Swedish delicacy, sill chutney. If the price of sill chutney is unity (p = 1), and the rate of interest is 10%, it means that if you save 100 dollars, then after a year you receive 110 dollars (= 100 (1 + r) = 100(1 + 0.10) = \$110). If there is no increase in the price level, then with this money you can consume 110 units of sill chutney. The real interest rate, which is a commodity rate of interest, is 10% (= (110 − 100)/100) × 100%), which happens in this case to be the same as the money rate of interest. But suppose that with the same savings and interest rate, the price rises by 5%: from p = 1 to p = 1.05! Your 100 dollars still grows to 110 dollars under "the force of interest", but you can only consume 110/1.05 = 104.76 units. The real rate of interest is therefore only {(104.76 − 100)/100} × 100% = 4.76% ≈ 5%. More generally, if we call g the inflation rate, and r_m the money rate of interest, then the (approximate) real rate of interest (r_r) is $r_r = r_m − g$. If you are concerned with real as opposed to money (or nominal) rates of interest, and you hear on CNN that labor markets are "overheated", or the money supply increased by a large amount, then you might expect an increase in the rate of inflation, and thus a (ceteris paribus) decline in r_r.

It is virtually impossible to overestimate the value of being able to reason in both real and nominal terms. Debtors, for instance, are quite partial to allowing inflation to reduce the real value of their debts. Here I think immediately of student loans in Sweden. More relevant, governments with long-term nominal debt (e.g. governments that have much of their outstanding debt in long-term bonds) might be tempted, in theory, to inflate in order to erode the real value of their obligations. (Of course, the US has a huge national debt, but has shown no sign of encouraging inflation.)

If you read the financial pages of your local newspaper, or watch TV, then you know that the stock (or share) market often assumes that if there is inflation, then an increase in the (money) rate of interest (r_m) will follow; and as you will learn later, it might lead to a decrease in the demand for shares.

Inflation is the rate of increase in the price level. In the above, the price of sill chutney this year is unity, and 1.05 next year, and so the inflation rate is $[(1.05 - 1.00)/1] \times 100\% = 0.05 \times 100\% = 5\%$. It sometimes helps to differentiate between *ex-ante* (before or expected) and *ex-post* (after or realized) entities. In the present exercise, in theory, it might be better to speak of the expected inflation rate, and write $r_r = r_m - E(g)$, where E is called the *expectations operator*, and thus E(g) is the expected inflation rate: bond buyers might demand higher interest rates because they *expect* inflation to increase, and without these higher rates their increase in purchasing power in the future due to saving is judged inadequate for the sacrifice of present consumption. Similarly, deflation is the rate of decline in the price level, which can also be considered ex-ante and ex-post. *Disinflation* is a slowing down in the rate of inflation.

Interestingly enough, the UK government's use of indexed debt in the 1980s helped reduce interest rates because it increased the credibility of the government's anti-inflation intentions, and as a bonus the fall in interest rates reduced borrowing costs. (Indexing a loan to inflation means e.g. that (interest) payments are tied to price increases. Similarly, pensions in many countries are tied to the inflation rate.)

A popular definition of inflation is "too much money chasing too few goods". In the last years of the 20th century, we have seen large increases in productivity that have raised the output of "goods". Technology has been important, along with changes in work habits and income distributions, although it is not easy to confirm the economic relationships at work here.

A symbol that you will need later is Δ (i.e. "delta"), which in words is interpreted as "the change in". In the calculation above of the inflation rate we could have written $g = [(p_{t+1} - p_t)/p_t] \times 100\%$ which in turn can be written $g = (\Delta p/p) \times 100\%$. Δp is then $(p_{t+1} - p_t)$, which means "the change in p". In the example $\Delta p = 1.05 - 1.00 = 0.05$, and $\Delta p/p$ is a *rate*!

Exercises

1. In Switzerland, accounts owned by foreigners sometimes carry a negative rate of interest. What does this mean for the real rate of interest? Can you figure out why the Swiss impose this arrangement?
2. Market "watchers" and financial analysts are interested in things like the money supply, and capacity utilization in industry. Explain why!

3. Redo the exercise immediately above in the text, only taking the price rise as 10%. In words, what does $\Delta X/X$ mean? $\Delta X/\Delta Y$?

II. The Markets for Money

The definition of the money supply is important. The narrowest money-supply measure is the monetary base, or M0. This consists of currency and bank reserves. Next comes another narrow money stock (called M1 in the US, or sometimes "transactions money") consisting basically of currency (which is about 25% of the narrow money stock in the US) and demand (or checking or current) deposits in financial institutions. Checks can be written against these demand deposits, but conventionally they pay little or no interest. However, in the US, it is possible to transfer checking account balances above a certain amount to interest bearing savings accounts via ATS (Automatic-Transfer Savings) accounts, and a transfer can take place in the other direction via NOW (Negotiable Order of Withdrawal) accounts. Accordingly, in the narrow money supply, demand deposits should be replaced by checkable deposits, which includes ATS and NOW accounts, and also the accounts supporting credit cards and travellers checks.

Electronic currency in the form of debit cards and stored value (or "smart cards") can in theory be issued for virtually any amount. The most sophisticated smart cards contain a computer chip, and they can be loaded with digital cash from its owner's bank account. As an aside, readers might like to know that coins are believed to have originated in Lydia, a Greek city-state (about 700 BC), while paper money is thought to have been introduced in China during the Ming dynasty (1368–1399 AD).

Why this emphasis on the "narrow" money supply (e.g. M1)? The answer is that when market watchers and financial analysts in the US were routinely obsessed by the weekly announcements of money supply statistics, they inevitably focussed on M1. The point was to outguess other players as to how the market reacts to changes in M1. Needless to say, an adverse reaction in the US can have serious consequences for many other countries.

There is also a broad money stock which comprises such things as savings and time deposits. This broad money stock operates on several levels, and is where we introduce expressions such as M2, M3, and so on. Something that needs to be mentioned here is that during the period when monetarism was taken seriously — where monetarism as a concept merely means a steady growth in the money supply, and (in theory) hands-off management by the authorities — one of the major problems was deciding "which" money supply was applicable for this steady-growth treatment, and/or which money supply analysts should be scrutinizing.

One of the difficulties here, according to Charles Goodhart — a former advisor to the Bank of England — is that when an economic indicator becomes an instrument of government policy, the behavior of this indicator shows a tendency to change from its pre-governmental policy status. This is called "Goodhart's Law", however what it amounts to is a very rough adaption of Heisenberg's "Uncertainty Principle" in physics. This principle has sometimes been interpreted to mean that the close observation of certain aspects of a phenomenon can lead to an inaccurate perception of other aspects of the same phenomenon. The well known trader Bruce Kovner feels that applied to financial markets it says that the closer a price pattern is observed by speculators, the greater the likelihood that false signals will be generated. (Literally, the Uncertainty Principle maintains the impossibility of satisfactorily measuring both position *and* velocity of an elementary particle: measuring the velocity perfectly means that the particle could be anywhere.)

Ordinary persons have a number of ways of saving money. They keep it in a cookie jar or mattress, put it in financial institutions (such as banks), buy financial assets such as bonds and shares, and so on. As a matter of definition, bonds originate in the debt market — since they are usually the debt of corporations or government; while shares (i.e. stocks) indicate ownership, and are called equities. Bonds are often called fixed income securities, since unless things go drastically wrong, the owner will always get a certain amount of money at regular intervals over the maturity of the bond, and/or the face value of the asset at the maturity or expiry date, unless the bonds are "callable". If not callable, then e.g. 30-year bonds "pay-off" after 30 years; but if callable the earliest date at which they can be called is clearly specified. Both bonds and shares are called securities, although a security is usually defined as a promise to pay a specific sum of money on a specific future date! A share does not usually make this promise.

Persons or institutions that are not so ordinary, such as multi-millionaires and pension funds, also occasionally use banks, and they definitely buy bonds and stocks, but in addition they have the option of purchasing certain money market assets that are specifically tailored for big-ticket savers. Among these assets are Treasury bills (T-bills), which are usually short-term (three to six months) government securities that tend to be denominated in amounts that are beyond the reach of small savers. These bills make just one future payment. Bills of longer maturity are designated zero-coupon bonds, and they too promise just one payment. Conventional bonds promise a series of payments, often every six months, and a payment of the principal (i.e. the face value of the bond) on the maturity date. Short maturity bonds — one year or less — are often called notes.

Certificates of deposit (CDs) are a favorite of institutional investors in the US. These are fixed term deposits that are issued by almost all the major commercial banks, and can be resold in a secondary market. (The market in which these assets are issued is called a primary market. The same thing holds for other financial assets that can be traded — i.e. bought and sold — after they are issued.) The money market includes the commercial paper market, which has become extremely important in the US. Commercial paper usually takes the form of an unsecured short-term (30–60 days) promissory note that is issued into the money market, where it is sold at a discount to its face value. Often it is associated with a back-up (bank) credit facility that can help with funding in case of a liquidity problem at the time the paper falls due.

There is also the market for bankers' acceptances (i.e. debts between companies), where banks "accept" bills of exchange, and lend to creditors (expecting to receive their money later from debtors); and the very important federal funds market in the US, and the inter-bank market in the UK, where banks with a surplus of reserves lend them to banks that do not have enough. Although it seems odd, huge sums of money are loaned overnight, and in the US, overnight federal funds represent the shortest-term security that is actually traded. The reserves mentioned here are liquid assets necessary to support bank lending. (An asset can be defined as anything that has economic value!) Interest rates on these and other financial assets are published daily in the *Wall Street Journal* in the "Money Rates" column.

In talking about bank reserves and the unexpected liquidity problems that are implied by the presence of large overnight loan markets, it is interesting to note the launching in Europe of US-style liquidity funds for institutions. The logic here is simple. There are hundreds of billions of dollars in "cash" — i.e. mostly short-term bank deposits — being held by e.g. pension funds and large corporations. (UK pension funds traditionally hold about 4% of their assets in cash.) If a part of these went into e.g. Merrill Lynch Mercury Funds, they could earn at the present time about 15 basis points (i.e. 0.15%) more than bank deposits. These liquidity funds channel their money into highly liquid assets (such as government bonds), and the clients of these liquidity funds can obtain cash in currency or deposit form almost as easily as they can withdraw money from an ATM.

Access to the money markets has increased for small savers due to such innovations as money market mutual funds, that combine the resources of small savers into amounts that are large enough to purchase the most expensive shares, bonds, and other assets. The purchase of such items is an integral part of the process known as disintermediation, in which banks can be bypassed, and financial assets obtained directly from their issuers. Similarly, borrowers can obtain money by issuing bonds rather than by borrowing from banks. Of course, it often happens that it is less expensive for large corporations to borrow from (a syndicate of) banks than to issue bonds.

In the US at the beginning of the 21st century, commercial banks' share of total financial assets has fallen to one-fifth from about half in 1950, while half of all households own shares directly, or through mutual funds. Internet brokers now give their customers access to several hundred mutual funds which do not require entrance or exit costs. This "depot-trade" is often financed by the funds themselves because it relieves them of a part of their administrative work. They merely levy a small fee on the amounts being managed.

A well known fund of this type in the US is Charles Schwab's highly successful "One Source", where customers are offered a choice of several hundred no-commission mutual funds that are without transaction or redemption fees. Instead there is a moderate flat fee that is tied to the value of the assets under management. This is a typical no-load fund, as compared to funds where a fee or commission must be paid in order to become a member. Professor Burton Malkiel once remarked that on the average the performance of these two types of funds were about the same, and as a result he always shopped in the no-load market. Why buy something that you can get free, he asked, although even among the very sophisticated denizens of high finance it is quite normal to encounter or to hear about persons who insist on paying for a free lunch.

Two other fund categories can be mentioned here — open end and closed end funds. In the first shares can be redeemed at any time, at a price that is tied to the asset value of the fund. The shares of the fund represent a proportionate ownership in a portfolio of assets held by the mutual fund. At any time a shareholder can buy additional shares from the fund, or cash in (i.e. redeem) shares in the fund at their net asset value. In the closed end arrangement, shares are neither issued nor redeemed after the initial offering. The buying and selling of these shares takes place in the stock market from a fixed amount of equities at prices determined by supply and demand. Closed end funds are in the minority.

Globally, there were thousands of mutual and other types of funds in existence as the world entered the 21st century, many of them highly specialized to regions and/or concepts, such as East Asia, Latin America, Eastern Europe, emerging markets, etc. Included in this roster of mutual funds are index funds which, since they match market averages, literally allow investors to buy a "market": for instance, it is possible to "buy" the Dow Jones index, which is a collection of 30 industrial shares that supposedly measures the performance of the entire US share market; or the Standard and Poor's (S&P) 500, or whatever. In the US, 20 cents of every retail dollar going into mutual funds goes into index funds, where "retail" means that institutional savers (such as pension-funds) are excluded. (In the UK, however, by 1999 about 10% of pension-funds' money was invested in index funds, as compared to 4% in 1993.) This type of investment, which is sometimes called a "no brainer", routinely yields higher returns than those registered by all except a handful of superstar investors — mostly high-profile finance professionals. In fact I have never heard of a time — in either the US or the UK — when, on the average, index funds did not achieve palpably superior returns to a very large majority of managed funds. This does not mean, however, that fund managers and brokers are an endangered species, since their highly specialized knowledge and experience is often worth a great deal to prospective investors.

As compared to money markets, bonds and shares are issued in capital markets. Most persons are familiar with stock markets, but they seem unaware that bond markets can be much larger. During the last year of the 20th century a few starry-eyed stock-market watchers have been claiming that in the next century, stock market valuations will explode upwards, and as a result virtually no price is too silly to pay for an equity that has something to do with the Internet or mobile telephony. Consequently, bonds and bond funds should be imbibed in the smallest possible doses.

According to Jeremy Siegal, author of the influential book "Stocks for the Long Run", if your ancestors in the US had invested a dollar in gold and a dollar in stocks in 1802, then in 1997 the gold "play" would have been worth $0.84, and the stocks $558,945. All this is very well, but one of the things I hope that you learn from this book is to be careful where analytical evidence covering centuries is concerned. If you had bought $100 worth of stocks at random on 1 January 1920, with the intention of holding them for a decade, then when you sold them on 1 January 1930, you might been able to buy enough apples to join the hundreds of destitute war veterans selling that delightful fruit on street corners in New York city. On the other hand, if you bought a hundred dollars worth of gold on 1 January 1970, then if you sold it a decade later, it would have financed a pleasant week of skiing at Sun Valley (Idaho), or a long stay at Miami Beach. As they say on The Street: "No, Virginia. Now is not the time to turn your back on the bond market!"

In the US, the derivatives (futures and options) markets for bonds is huge. London is much more important for the trading of such things as Eurobonds than for its excellent stock market facilities, even taking into consideration the modernization and computerization of the London stock exchange in 1986 in an operation that was termed the "Big Bang". (The Big Bang was immediately preceded by the Financial Services Act, which was mostly concerned with curtailing the regulation of financial markets.) Interestingly enough, London is not generally considered to be a really dominant center for such things as the issuing and trading of corporate bonds, even though London (and not Tokyo or Frankfurt) is the second most important global financial center (after New York), and will probably be the financial capital of the European Union (EU). Frankfurt has recently developed high hopes of overtaking London in the not too distant future, especially after its Eurex Exchange surpassed the London International Financial Futures and Options Exchange (LIFFE) in trading the 10-year (German) Bund Futures Contract, which in financial prestige is at least the equivalent of a futures on the US 10-year T-bond (i.e. Treasury bond). "At least" because the underlying fixed income security, the Bund, though issued by the German government, is the benchmark (i.e. reference or standard) bond for the 11-nation Euro-zone bloc.

Regrettably, one swan does not make a summer, and although LIFFE considered the Bund to be its pride and joy, London's stock market has twice the market capitalization of Frankfurt's. Three times the number of overseas banks are associated with the London market, along with a few battalions of highly successful risk takers and top traders, and it has a long and successful risk taking tradition. In addition, Frankfurt does not have a good reputation where that elusive quality known as "openness" is concerned: it was not until 1995 that insider trading was formally outlawed.

When a firm has a high ratio of debt to equity (i.e. ownership), it is called highly leveraged in the US, and highly geared in the UK. 1987 and 1988 were years in which leveraged buyouts (LBOs), often financed by junk bonds reached a new peak. What we usually have here are arrangements in which various investors buy junk bonds — which are more formally known as "below investment grade" or "high risk" securities — and thus become lenders to the buyers of a firm. If lucky, the new owners (who are sometimes called "raiders", if the projected takeover is "hostile"), obtain uninhibited access to the firm's cash flow. The problem is that equity in the taken-over company is literally swamped by new debt, which in theory will be repaid out of higher profits obtained via more efficient management and higher productivity, and/or, in the best of all possible worlds, an upswing in the business cycle.

Needless to say, the business cycle often turned in the other direction, which caused a serious problem for many employees of the taken over firms — though not those who had come on board wearing golden parachutes; and in a number of cases the additional debt had to be serviced by the sale of physical assets, and contracting for even more debt.

There has been a fairly high default rate on junk bonds, and a brief period in 1990 when the US Congress apparently forced at least some financial institutions to dump their junk portfolios. The junk bond market in the US crashed in the mid-nineties, however it appears to be gathering momentum once again. As will be noted later, Europe is developing an attachment to junk bonds. A main factor here is that junk *spreads* — i.e. yields in excess of those available on top-grade securities of the same maturity — are higher than at any time since 1985. Firms that are threatened by takeovers are also prone to float junk bonds in order to secure the financial capital that will enable them to buy a controlling share of the outstanding equities of these endangered firms. (Financial capital is stocks, bonds, etc used to finance the acquisition of physical capital!)

The term often used to describe this defensive ploy is "greenmail". Another self-defense mechanism is the "poison pill". What happens here is that the threatened firm gives all shareholders except the "raider" the right to buy new shares at a large discount. This makes purchasing enough shares to complete the takeover too expensive. Another nice term is "White Knight". This is a (possible) rival bidder who is preferable to the original predator.

There has been a great deal of discussion about the takeover mania of the 1980s, and one theory is that if it were justified — and this is a big if — the justification must turn on boosting the price of the stock of the target companies to a level that is closer to the fundamental value of the underlying assets. As Tobin and Golub (1998) point out, ordinary investors may have detected the same undervaluations, but could not take advantage of them until many more ordinary investors agreed (and presumably began to purchase these stocks), or a takeover materialized.

III. Banks, Bankers' Banks, and the Euromarket

Banking is an art, or science, that reportedly had its roots in ancient Egypt or Assyria, although modern fractional reserve commercial banking seems to have had its origins in Italy in the 15th century. But there are other types of banks. Investment banks, for instance, specialize in raising money for businesses via bond and stock issues, giving advice, and like the larger commercial banks they are active traders in various financial markets. Investment banking can be a very good business, although stunning miscalculations occasionally take place: in 1998 Credit Suisse First Boston lost an entire annual profit (more than a billion dollars) on some bad investments in Russia, and they were not alone. The fixed income division of Goldman Sachs also lost a billion dollars in the same country that year, and a year later lost something approaching 100 million on a bet involving the spread between government bond yields and the yield on another financial asset: this spread widened instead of narrowing, as predicted by Goldman Sachs experts. (However, as far as I can tell, Goldman Sachs is rated the top investment bank in the world at the beginning of the 21st century.)

Many investment banks function as underwriters. They guarantee the corporate or government borrower a price for their securities, and then sell them to the public at whatever price they will bring. This takes both capital and nerve. Japanese investment banks were originally called securities houses, because of the importance placed on underwriting.

Asset management — which involves "looking after other peoples' money" — is another major activity of investment banks. It is considered less glamorous than the multibillion-dollar merger and acquisition (M&A) deals that you can hardly avoid reading about these days, but the fee-based income that it generates is less volatile than the profits realized from the heavy trading of financial assets. For instance, in 1997 Morgan Stanley's net income from asset management was reportedly $400 million, although Switzerland's UBS — with well over $1 trillion under management — still leads the world in this field. The "other people" mentioned here include high-net-worth individuals, corporations, and many pension funds.

Another type of bank is the merchant bank, which was orginally a British phenomenon. In some respects they resemble investment banks, but they tend to be much smaller, and occasionally they take deposits — but mainly from important customers. They are, however, very fond of giving expensive advice to rich clients; acting as intermediaries in complicated business deals; trading large amounts of currencies, and in the 1980s became heavily involved in the leveraged buyout game. Something that should be appreciated here is that in the US, the Glass-Steagall Act of 1933 separated investment banking from commercial banking, but this act recently became history. There are some observers who claim that repealing the Glass-Stegall Act will pose considerable financial dangers to the entire US economy, because it will mean a huge displacement of liquidity from the commercial banking system to the investment banking community. This might also be the place to mention such institutions as "private banks", whose principal activity is managing the portfolios of wealthy clients (i.e. making investments for these clients), and the French banques d'affaires. The latter are similar to merchant banks, but often use their own money to build up a portfolio of shares.

The student of finance should be aware that in the United States, "merchant banking" is the designation of an activity within investment banks, and in this context explicitly means investing the firm's own money in things like mergers and leveraged buyouts. Once it was said to be Wall Street's "hottest" profit center, although it is ridiculed by some observers, who say that when a high level of risk is present, it is always best to use the money of outsiders. These same observers, however, do not ridicule proprietary trading. This is when the bank uses its own money to trade currencies, futures, options, etc. For example, at Salomon Brothers — one of the largest investment banks — bond arbitrage was the leading money maker, although at least one merchant bank — Barings (of London) — unfortunately collapsed due to the misfortunes of one of its ace foreign exchange and derivatives traders. Goldman Sachs is constantly boasting of its M&A and its asset management skills, however about 40% of its revenues originates in its trading rooms.

A very different type of institution is the central bank. Every country has one of these, and the Swedish central bank (the Riksbank) is the oldest (1668). The British central bank (the Bank of England) is second in longevity, dating from 1694. Central banks manage the money supply, and often they help ensure that governments have the finance they need: both the Swedish and UK central banks seem to have been established to help their governments fund various military adventures. In the United States, the chairman of the central bank (The Federal Reserve System) has occasionally been called the second most powerful man in the country. Managing the money supply, and setting interest rate policy are traditionally the most important functions of central banks; and the recent hue and cry about making central banks independent of governments is intended to remove these institutions from the control of governments and politicians, and thus prevent them from being too aggressive in the expansion of the money supply when the economy is weak and unemployment is high.

When government spending exceeds tax reviews, the difference is covered by borrowing. Government bonds are then sold to private individuals or institutions, both domestically and abroad. Japan, for example, has bought huge amounts of US debt. There was a time, however, when central banks bought a great many government securities, paying for them with newly printed money, and thus increasing the money supply. This is known as "monetizing the deficit" or, less politely, "printing money".

The newly formed European Central Bank, for instance, is a highly independent institution that places the fight against inflation first on its agenda. Many people in the Scandinavian countries are not enthusiastic about a brand of economic policy whose main concern is not the suppression of unemployment; but as they will almost certainly find out some sweet day, once you sign on with this particular bank, it will not be easy to sign off. In addition, something that seems to have been forgotten is that perhaps the worst inflation in modern times took place in Germany (in 1922–1923) when the central bank of that country was completely independent of all external supervision.

The Euromarket is based on cross border banking, and features such things as the depositing of dollars in various European banks, and the lending by these banks of dollars in the Eurocurrency market (which features "short-term" debt); or, e.g. the issuing of dollar denominated Eurobonds in e.g. London. This is "long-term" debt, where long-term usually indicates a maturity of over one year. To be precise, Eurocurrency markets are defined as banking markets located outside the legal jurisdiction of the authorities who have issued the relevant currencies: e.g. Euromarks are deutschemarks (DM) held in e.g. Rome or Paris.

Some investigators say that the beginnings of the Euromarket can be traced to the Cold War, when the Russians and Chinese ostensibly deposited dollars in West European financial institutions for trade purposes. At the same time that regulations on interest rates in the US (e.g. Regulation "Q") discouraged dollars that were earned abroad from returning to the United States, British banks were put in a position where it became highly profitable to lend dollars: in the UK the government placed severe restrictions on the lending of pounds, but financial institutions were left to their own devices where the lending of dollars was concerned.

Between 1965 and 1995 the rate of growth of the Eurodollar market was 22% (gross). Pilbeam (1998) gives as the main reason for the success of the Euromarkets their comparative advantage due to a minimum of regulation (as compared to banking practices in the US or Japan). Thus they could pay a higher rate for deposits, while charging a lower rate for loans. The difference between these two rates is called the *spread*, which is also the name for the difference between the bid (or buying) and ask (or offer) price of a financial asset. At your local bank you can always view the spread for various currencies, and occasionally they are very large. (Ask, or offer, is the selling price.)

The Eurobond market specializes in syndicated loans where many banks form a syndicate for the purpose of raising a large sum of money for a single borrower. Syndicated loans are still about 50% of the long-term capital raised on international markets, where international markets means capital raised across international borders: e.g. bonds issued in Stockholm and sold internationally. In 1998, financial institutions collected at least $6 billion in fees for arranging syndicated loans. Behind this figure is a new wave of corporate consolidation and reorganization.

Traditionally, one of the banks will be the lead manager for the syndicate. The first of these Eurobond operations involved the well known London merchant bank S.G. Warburg "leading" a 15-million-dollar issue, with Banque de Bruxelles SA, Deutsche Bank AG, and Rotterdamsche Bank NV as co-managers. (If you are curious about the composition of syndicates, then you can examine a "tombstone announcement" in e.g. *The Wall Street Journal*. These announcements have to do with completed deals.) There were 60,000 bonds with a face value of $250 each, and carrying a fixed coupon of 5.5%. As it happened, this issue — whose emission date was July 15, 1963 — was subjected to the interest equalization tax of 15% imposed by President Kennedy the same year on the purchase price of foreign bonds. This tax was designed to make bonds issued in Europe less attractive to US investors, and therefore relieve pressure on the US balance of payments (and the value of the dollar) caused by what the Kennedy government regarded as excessive capital outflow.

At the present time many Eurobonds are priced in terms of LIBOR — the London Interbank Offer Rate — which is the (loan) interest rate quoted each other by the best London banks. (There is also something called LIBID — the London Interbank Bid Rate — which is the rate bid to attract a deposit.) Eurobond loans can be fixed rate or floating rate, where floating rate usually means that the interest rate paid by the borrower is adjusted every three or six months with reference to some index. In discussing bonds, the expression maturity often comes up. The maturity is the "running time" of the bond, and the maturity date is the date when the holder of the bond should receive the principal or face value of the bond. Please remember too that there is a huge secondary market for bonds, and during the last ten years there were periods when higher profits could be realized by trading bonds than by speculating in stocks. (Tom Wolfe's "master of the universe" in his virtuoso novel "Bonfire of the Vanities" was a Wall Street bond trader.) How were these profits realized? Quite simply by having the acumen to know when certain bonds are underpriced, buying them, and waiting for the good news to appear in the form of a decline in interest rates: a fall in interest rates is tantamount to a rise in bond prices.

It is useful to distinguish between so-called "foreign bonds" and Eurobonds. An example of foreign bonds would be German bonds issued in the US, and denominated in US dollars: like other foreign bonds issued in the US, they are called "Yankee bonds". Another example is Swiss bonds issued in Japan, and denominated in yen. (These bonds are designated

"Samurai bonds".) On the other hand, Eurobonds are bonds denominated in a currency that is different from the currency of the country where they are sold — such as dollar denominated Eurobonds in London. Finally, Dragon Bonds are listed and promoted in Asia, while *Eurocurrencies* are foreign currencies deposited in banks outside the home country (of the currency).

An important feature of Eurobonds is that for the most part they are bearer bonds, which means that unlike e.g. Yankee bonds, they are unregistered, and mere possession amounts to ownership. They are therefore very attractive to bond thieves (as in the Donald Westlake novel "Cops and Robbers"), and persons with a strong preference for anonymity, such as tax avoiders. (On this point it should be noted that Eurobonds are not subject to a withholding tax. The market is "telephone intensive", with London being the hub. Investors simply give brokers details of the bonds they desire to purchase.) Two famous bond offerings took place in 1984, with Sweden making a 500-million-US-dollar floating rate placement in the Eurobond market. These bonds had a 40-year maturity, which at that time was the longest in Eurobond history, and carried a semiannual interest rate of LIBOR + 0.125%. On the emission date of the bonds, LIBOR was 10.4375%, and thus over the first six months after their issue the bonds yielded approximately $(10.4375 + 0.1250)/2 = 5.2812\%$. In the second six months, their yield was increased or decreased if LIBOR changed.

Similarly, in 1984, the World Bank emitted US$250 million of ten-year floating rate notes on which the interest rate was 35 basis points (= 0.35%, since one basis point is equal to $1/100 = 0.01\%$) above the money-market yield on prespecified US 91-day treasury bills. Interest, in this case, was paid on a quarterly basis.

IV. A Simple Case Study

One of the most brilliant essays of L.J. Davis (1983), winner of the 1982 Gerald Loeb award for distinguished business and financial journalism, is called "The Road to West Jockstrap", and concerns the decline and fall of the Penn Central Railroad. All this took place at the end of the 1960s, and the story of that misadventure has been repeated many times since in other commercial and government undertakings. One of the things that we find in most of these melodramas is the irresponsible optimism of many directors, CEOs (chief executive officers), chairmen and chairwomen of the board, and other persons and personalities with an almost psycotic belief in their ability to strike bargains with fate.

What happened with Penn Central was the arrival on the scene of a new CEO with a plan to make railroad history by combining the tracks, terminals, etc. of the two largest railroads in the American Northeast — the Pennsylvania, and the New York Central — which would then be designated the Penn Central. The theory was that if things went well, it could be operated at a level of profitability well above that prevailing in the not very profitable railroad business. Needless to say, financing investments of the type alluded to above required obtaining access to huge amounts of money.

According to Davis, there was an extremely heavy reliance on bank loans, the sale of a great many bonds, a major resort to commercial paper, and perhaps the first large scale tapping of the Euromarket by an American firm. Something else of importance was the ambition of the chairman of the board of Penn Central to make this railroad a part of a conglomerate. Briefly put, a conglomerate involves bringing under single ownership all types of companies. The *modus operandi* is to buy anything that is profitable. The two great conglomateers of the 1960s were Charles Bludorn — Viennese born, but fluent in American profanity; and James Ling of Texas. Both came crashing down when the banks started calling in their loans, which was also the eventual fate of Penn Central. Another interesting example was the brilliant Palestinian refugee Yusef Beidas, with properties in New York, London, and Paris under management. His mistake was to put too much short-term money into property that was not liquid, and because his personal chemistry was not always congenial, the Lebanese Central Bank and some of Beirut's financial community apparently conspired in his downfall.

One of the reasons that Penn Central chose to rely so heavily on bank loans was that some of the officers of that firm were able to convince the directors of many large banks that they were becoming involved in a very profitable project. The same story was true of many of the property loans of the 1980s and early 1990s, when many top bankers seemed to have completely lost their sense of perspective.

In 1968, Penn Central received permission from the US government's financial regulators to sell 100 million dollars of commercial paper, and later was able to increase this amount to 200 million. The broker for this frivolous undertaking was Goldman Sachs, one of the great New York investment houses; however, in the end, the cachet of their distinguished intermediary did not amount to the proverbial hill of beans, since most purchasers of this paper ended up receiving 20 cents on the dollar.

Now for the Euromarket. In the late 1960s, the Euromarket was just getting up steam, and European banks were filled with dollars looking for borrowers. Furthermore, the directors of many of these banks were not particularly skilled in handling greenbacks, and so they were often prepared to lend to any organization with a recognizable name, whose CEO had a pleasing personality. In the transaction being discussed here, Penn Central had the distinction of employing a lawyer who, somewhat later, allegedly attempted to defraud the United States Navy; but it is also possible that Penn Central was too early out where the Euromarket was concerned. Had they been on the borrowing side of this market after it started receiving large injections of OPEC cash (i.e. petrodollars), they could have borrowed any amount they wanted, and forgotten about such things as commercial paper.

Why did the bandwagon come to a screeching halt? If we exclude bad management, and bad luck in the form of a regulatory structure that was guaranteed to make the railroad business a lost cause, the answer might be that Penn Central was burdened with too much short-term debt. Davis apparently believed that short-term debt can be converted to long-term debt by simply "rolling it over" — i.e. paying off the outstanding indebtedness with new loans; but clearly new lenders with the required amount of naiveté become progressively more difficult to find.

When Penn Central's severe financial defects were fully digested by interested parties, the institutional insiders (e.g. mutual funds) unloaded well over a million shares of Penn Central equity, with the last increment being divested just a day before the firm officially confirmed the rumors that it was bankrupt. In July 1968, Penn Central stock had sold for 85.5 dollars/ share, and by the time bankruptcy was declared — which was June 20, 1970 — this price had touched 11 dollars. Apparently, some of the directors of the firm, while loudly proclaiming the soundness of their organization, began getting rid of their shares as soon as they first got wind of how things might turn out. Many of the smaller stockholders received nothing, because in their capacity as "owners" of the firm, they could only legally lay claim to what is left after all debts are paid. As they soon found out, Penn Central's creditors (e.g. bondholders) took just about everything.

It is also astounding to realize that many of the small equity owners, as well as some of the large, sincerely believed to the last minute that the US government would not permit one of the most important transportation networks in the US to fail. As things turned out, they believed incorrectly,

Davis states that the Penn Central collapse triggered a three-billion-dollar selloff of commercial paper. Exactly what he meant is difficult to say, but a possibility is that when more than 80 million dollars of Penn Central paper went bad, it soured the market on all assets of this description, and where this kind of paper could be traded in a secondary market, it was immediately unloaded for whatever it would bring, which wasn't much. Here we have a situation that will become familiar to readers: markets suddenly becoming illiquid, which in this case meant a pronounced absence of buyers! What happened next was that the Federal Reserve — the US's central bank — declared itself the "lender of last resort", and made it clear to the (several thousand) members of the Federal Reserve System that the Fed's "discount window" would be open indefinitely. ("Discounting" — or "rediscounting" as it is often called — means the lending by the central bank to commercial banks, and usually at a relatively low rate of interest.) In addition, the famous — or infamous — Regulation Q, which limited the interest rates on deposits in domestic US banks was relaxed, which attracted more money into the banking system.

Finally, let me mention that an economist who has become a kind of saint in some quarters, Frederich Hayek, would have declared the above cited behavior by the Federal Reserve to be irresponsible and economically unjustifiable. As it happens, however, if the authorities had remained passive, there could have been a nation-wide financial panic. The same applies to the near collapse of the "hedge" fund Long Term Capital Management (LTCM) in the late 1990s. That firm, whose own capital was five billion dollars, had borrowed approximately 125 billion from institutions like Chase Manhattan. Had nature been permitted to take its course, the macroeconomic consequences could have been calamitous.

V. Financial Market Structure, and Final Remarks

The London stock exchange traces its origins to a coffeehouse club of brokers in the 1760s, although the oldest stock exchange is probably Hamburg (Germany), which dates from 1538. A common name for the stock exchange in France and Northern Europe is "bourse". This expression goes back to a commodity exchange in Bruges, Belgium, founded in 1360 in front of the home of the Chevalier van de Buerse.

In speaking of stock exchanges (or bourses), we think of a certain way to do business — a way that is quite different from selling pizzas at the nearest one-stop pasta emporium. Leon Walras, who could probably be called the grandfather of mathematical economics, observed more than a hundred years ago that "The more perfect competition functions, the more rigorous is the manner of arriving at value in exchange. The markets that are best organized from the competitive standpoint are those in which purchases and sales are made by auction, through the instrumentality of stockholders, commercial brokers, or criers acting as agents who centralize transactions in such a way that the terms of every exchange are openly announced, and an opportunity is given to sellers to lower their prices, and to buyers to raise their prices".

If we take a careful look at modern exchanges, we see what Maureen O'Hara (1995) calls four "categories" of players. We can start with order submitting customers; then brokers who transmit orders, and almost in the same category dealers, who often trade for themselves, but who might also handle the orders of customers. These are sometimes designated broker-dealers. Finally, there are the specialists or market makers, who usually post prices for one or more assets that they are prepared to buy or sell.

The US Commodity Exchange Act of 1974 defines a market as meeting the public interest if it satisfies three requirements: reliable price discovery, broad-based price dissemination, and effective hedging against price risk. In my own work on energy, I have taken a particular interest in the last of these, and come to the conclusion that often it is incompatible with the first: the use of exchange traded derivatives (or derivative products, as they are sometimes called) will often — but definitely not always — provide effective hedging; while the derivative product that is sometimes the most suitable for hedging purposes, swaps, does not provide a high degree of price discovery (because swap rates are usually not made public).

Of late, there has been a tendency to play down price discovery in the name of transparency. Ostensibly, in a world where information is generated faster than the managers of many exchanges thought was possible, such things as trading by open outcry are viewed by the new generation of screen warriors and their gurus as reactionary nonsense. They are not concerned with how prices are formed, but with their visibility. The ultimate goal is fully electronic exchanges and, worldwide, only a few of these.

Some simple exercises follow. Please remember that the purpose of these is not to trip you up, but to increase your self-confidence. I can recall a member of my platoon telling me that when he left the army, he was going to return to school. As he put it, "the more I know, the better I feel". Testing your knowledge with simple exercises that you learn to answer without hesitation will eventually help you to feel better than you have ever felt.

Exercises

1. Make sure that you know the meaning of the terms merchant bank, merchant banking, proprietary trading, capital market, fixed-income securities, "big bang", real rate of interest, secondary market, disintermediation, money market, disinflation!

2. Distinguish between real and money wages; and real and money incomes! Construct a numerical example involving 15% inflation, and if you can, put this illustration in algebraic (i.e. symbolic) form!

3. In the basic course in economics, many students come to the conclusion that central banks can stop inflation any time they please by simply raising the rate of interest. At times this might be true, but there might be costs involved. Discuss this issue!

4. In the light of the discussion in this chapter, why might foreign investors be worried if the inflation rate in the US began to escalate?

5. Suppose that on Jan 1, 2002, you look in the paper and see that your government has just issued a batch of 30-year bonds with a 10% rate of interest, and with a face value of $1,000. They will also guarantee that the central bank will completely suppress inflation. If you buy a $1,000 bond on that date, then you will obtain $100 on Jan 1 of the next 30 years, and your $1000 at the end of 30 years (along with the final payment of interest). This seems like an attractive proposition, and so you buy a bond. At the beginning of the following week, you look in the paper and see that the interest rate on a new issue of 30-year government bonds is 20%, but you suddenly find that you have financial problems, and instead of buying another bond, must sell the one you have in the secondary market. Are you in trouble? (Hint: the person to whom you sell the bond will continue to obtain the bond yield (or return) of $100/year.) Ignore the fact that the bond is now a week old, and the purchaser is one week closer to collecting his or her first $100!

VI. Appendix*

All discussions marked with an asterisk (*) can be skipped if the reader desires. Of course, as you may remember, the only technical materials in this chapter concerned the real rate of interest, and the algebra involved was the kind that you were introduced to in a late course in primary school, or an early course in secondary school. The same is true here. To be exact, we saw that the real rate of interest (r_r) could be written $r_r = r_m - E(g)$, where r_m is the money (or nominal) rate of interest, and $E(g)$ is the expected rate of inflation.

Suppose that we have two countries, Japan and the US. For Japan, this expression would be $r_{rj} = r_{mj} - E(g_j)$, and for the US, we have $r_{r,us} = r_{m,us} - E(g_{us})$. Now, in case a couple of charming and well spoken young people appear at your door to interview you for a 150,000 dollar/year in the financial district of Chicago, and the question of interest rates pops up, you can begin your presentation by saying that a number of theorists like to claim that while money interest rates are different between countries, real interest rates "tend" to even out. Thus, we would have from this hypothesis $r_{mj} - E(g_j) = r_{m,us} - E(g_{us})$, which can be solved to give $r_{m,us} - r_{mj} = E(g_{us}) - E(g_j)$. Accordingly, you would conclude your presentation by suggesting that on the average, differences in nominal interest rates — which are often considered the principal cause of capital (i.e. money) flows between countries — might be caused by differences in inflationary expectations. Whether the interviewers buy this or not, and whether you get your job, remains to be seen, but you can thank them warmly for joining you in your humble abode on the South Side, and after they leave, return to the study of this book. As an aside, you might point out that exchange rates are also influenced by inflation and/or inflationary expectations.

"On the average"? Your visitors turn at the door, and in a not so polite tone of voice ask you what a concept like "average" is doing in an interview where precision is supposed to be the keystone. The correct answer on this occasion is that the great English mathematician Bertrand Russell once said "Although this may seem a paradox, all science is dominated by the idea of approximation". The implied approximation here is that "on the average" this hypothesis will be useful to hardworking young (and not-so-young) financial market players in pursuit of their first million, and so they should not hesitate to include it in their intellectual armory.

Exercises

1. What is the bid rate? The offer rate? The spread?
2. There seems to be a great deal of pressure at the present time on pension fund managers to replace some of the bonds in their portfolios by stocks. Why? What do you think about this?

3. Portfolio managers in the US probably prefer a strong appreciation of the US dollar to a strong depreciation. Why?

4. What are "spreads"? Give two examples! What is Goodhart's Law? What is "monetizing the deficit"? What is a bearer bond?

5. *Asymetric information* means that one party does not know enough about the other party to make accurate decisions. *Adverse selection* is the problem created by *asymetric information* before a transaction occurs, while *moral hazard* is the problem created by asymetric information after the transaction occurs. Think about and discuss these terms in relation to loan markets.

If you had no trouble with this chapter, then let me suggest that you examine Chapter 9. That chapter is another non-technical survey that is designed to cover some last minute developments. Let's take a few more exercises.

6. In a formal sense, the first banknotes were issued by the Bank of Sweden in 1661; but earlier, banknotes were 'invented' by goldsmiths in the UK. Explain how this invention could have come about.

7. There is a common belief in finance that in every market there is a fool. Comment! Warren Buffett has apparently said (according to Michael Lewis) that any player unaware of the fool's identity is probably filling that role himself. (The definition of a fool is someone willing to trade an asset for less than its worth, where its worth is determined by the person who valued it properly.) Is this science or nonsense?

8. Pension schemes have traditionally involved pay-as-you-go arrangements, with current employees being taked pay current pensioners. The theory now being offered in many countries is that pre-funded individual pensions are better, where employees have an account in which money must be saved — and therefore invested — until retirement. Comment on these approaches, and what they could mean for the holding of financial assets.

Chapter 2

Banking and Banks

Just before beginning this chapter, I examined a number of finance books in order to get some idea of what they have to say about banking. This project did not take long, because with the notable exceptions of e.g. Frederic Mishkin (1998) and Stephen Valdez (1997), most of them seemed to barely touch on the subject. Imagine my surprise, because international finance is one intellectual discipline where there is no substitute for at least a modest insight into the mechanics and structure of banking.

Banks are at the heart of the global financial system, and since one of the features of the 21st century will be a steady growth in cross-border banking and mergers, the importance of these institutions can only increase. It was a group of large banks that provided the hedge fund Long Term Capital Management (LTCM) with $125 billion in loans, and had Chairman of the Federal Reserve, Alan Greenspan adopted a take-no-prisoners attitude when LTCM's bets went sour, all the financial markets in the US might have been sent rocking on their heels. The international repercussions of such an event should be obvious, which was probably one of the things weighing on the Chairman's mind when he helped to organize a 3.6 billion dollars rescue package by 14 financial institutions. On an even less cheerful note, after a financial crisis in 1998, Russia defaulted on $32 billion-worth of restructured debt known as PRINS and IANS. Much of this was held by commercial banks, although it appears that a few American hedge funds — which employ some of the best analytical minds in the financial world — were also the proud owners of some IOUs that originated in Moscow. The latest round of negotiations over this debt has resulted in an offer from Russia to back the debt with a "sovereign guarantee", on the condition that they will be allowed to write off up to 40% of its face value. Just in case, though, they have launched a 30-year Eurobond.

The initial topic below will be commercial banks of all descriptions (i.e. "deposit" banks), but attention will also be given to investment and merchant banks, "private" banks, and finally the World Bank and the International Monetary Fund (IMF). Readers who have completed the first (or basic) course in economics might regret the absence of T-accounts, but given the varigate backgrounds of the audience that I hope to reach with this book, they do not fit into the exposition. A thorough insight into the economics of money and banking can be found in Mishkin (1998), while readers who want banking combined with macroeconomics in an innovative and exciting way are referred to Miller and Upton (1974). The appendix to this chapter makes a few comments on laundering and hiding money.

Commercial banks, or "banks of deposit", probably came into existence in the Venice of the 13th century, and were followed by similar institutions in Genoa, and later in the Po Valley. (Bank-like institutions may have existed in the Middle-East hundreds of years earlier, and even before that in China.) When money lending came into its own in London, the street on which many financial institutions were located was named Lombard Street, referring, of course, to Lombardy. According to the *Economist* (April 10, 1993), "modern" banking was invented in the 17th century when the Bank of Amsterdam (founded in 1609) discovered the relationship between liquidity and credit risk. If in a given period only a proportion of borrowers and depositors asked for their money in the form of cash (= silver coins at the time), then as long as borrowers repaid their debts, and depositors had confidence in the bank, that institution could create claims (e.g. loans) for more than the cash it held in its vaults. The first modern banknotes were issued by Sweden in 1661.

As the reader might guess, the *moral hazard* problem was considerable in the early days of banking. There was always the chance that borrowers might abscond, and it was not unheard of that bankers took flight if their books failed to balance. At the present time moral hazard in finance is interpreted as meaning that investors and borrowers may behave reck-lessly because they believe that governments cannot afford to allow key institutional players to get into serious trouble. More generally, moral hazard comes about when having insurance against a risk causes the insured party to take less care to avoid the risk (and its possible consequences).

Before getting down to cases, some terminology might be useful. Bank is the transformation of the French word "banc", which in this context means the "bench" where a money lender and his client sat and transacted their business. If the bank went into liquidation, then the bench would be broken: this is the origin of the word *bancorupto*, or bankrupt. The present day monetary system is one of *fiat money*, in which governments print a paper currency that is not backed by gold. In a simple world of fiat money and private (i.e. commercial) banks, with only demand deposits, the money supply (M) can be defined as M = fiat money in circulation + demand deposits at the commercial banks.

Please observe that it is the banking system that creates a great deal of a country's money supply, although the central bank — in addition to printing and issuing fiat money — has several extremely important policy functions that influence the money supply. First, it can change reserve requirements (see below), which influences the money supply by setting a limit on how much a bank can lend (and thus create new deposits). In addition, it can engage in open-market operations, which means that it can increase the money supply by purchasing outstanding government bonds with fiat money, or reduce the money supply by selling some of its holdings of government bonds to the non-bank public.

Currency-in-circulation plus bank reserves is called the *monetary base*, or sometimes *high-powered money*. Fiat money is generally the largest portion of the monetary base. We also have the expressions *outside money* and *inside money*. The stock of fiat money is called outside money, because it is determined outside the banking system; while the amount of money added to the money supply via e.g. bank loans (in that it results in borrowers obtaining deposits), is referred to as inside money. Currency in the vaults of the central bank is not money, however. It is simply brightly colored paper.

Central banks were mentioned in the previous chapter, but they do not get much attention here. Alan Greenspan (who once played jazz saxophone on the same stage as Stan Getz) is now regarded as a hero in the US because of the success of his anti-inflation policies, but many other central bank chiefs have sometimes been pilloried for their lack of imagination, and an even more deplorable lack of basic economic knowledge.

Managing the money supply and the interest rate (i.e. monetary policy) are the traditional duties of central bankers, but it has been suggested many times that fiscal policy (i.e. manipulating taxes) is more efficient than monetary policy, whose effects can take a long time to be felt. Of course, nobody really cares when growth is vigorous, and unemployment low; but when the business cycle changes direction, voters tend to become less tolerant. Moreover, the effect of monetary policy tends to be spread less evenly across an economy. Among other things, raising interest rates impacts harder on certain manufacturers, while leaving others — together with a large fraction of consumers — undisturbed. An easily read book that provides some interesting insights into central banking is White (1999), as well as the earlier mentioned book of Frederic Mishkin.

I. Commercial Banks

Suppose that you are the owner of a comfortable house on Canal Street in Amsterdam that is equipped with a large collection of durables (e.g. washing machine, big screen TV, etc). Behind your house you have an automobile (a cadillac), while anchored in front you have a speedboat — just in case. By adding up the monetary value of these and other material possessions (which includes such things as bank accounts and securities, and if relevant jewelry, paintings, etc), you obtain a figure which can be labeled the value of your assets. Then, if you subtract from this amount the non-avoidable payments on your possessions, e.g. the outstanding mortgage on your house, and the total payments remaining on your boat and car, etc, you arrive at your *net worth*. (The amount subtracted is the sum of your *liabilities*.) For example, when President Ronald Reagan first took office, it was estimated that his net worth was somewhere in the vicinity of one million dollars.

A very bad piece of news would be a severe reduction your net-worth. Suppose that the picturesque waterway just outside your house overflowed as a result of global warming, submerging your house and car, and overturning your boat. This kind of catastrophe cannot always be insured against, and so it could happen that if you make the kind of calculation referred to above, your net worth is negative — i.e. less than zero. (Exercise: take a few minutes to assign some numbers to the above assets and liabilities, so that if the value of assets fell sharply, the net worth turns negative!)

The commercial banks in Amsterdam are in a similar situation, and the same is true of those in Paris and New York. Their assets are in cash, bonds, shares (when they are allowed to buy shares), and especially loans. Paying from 2% to 2.5% interest on deposits, and then lending this money at somewhere in the neighborhood of 6% to 8% can be a rewarding pastime. Of course, the thing that has made the big difference for the major banks in the past decade is the ability to engage in the large scale trading of financial assets: currencies, bonds, futures and options on currencies and bonds, etc. In Sweden, where there are hardly any small banks remaining, some absolutely lovely profits are being registered year after year by the major depository concerns. Quite naturally, everything is relative in this old world of ours, and banks that lag behind in the profit marathon — in the sense that they do not live up to expectations — might see the price of their shares stagnate, or even decline, and perhaps the careers and incomes of some bank employees endangered. It can be mentioned that some observers claim that the stock price of individual banks reflect the risk assumed by the bank, however I doubt whether that thesis can be proved.

An asset that was not mentioned above was bank reserves. Under the Monetary Control Act of 1980, commercial banks in the US that are members of the Federal Reserve System were initially required to keep an amount equal to a fraction of their demand deposits and other checkable accounts in cash or in non-interest bearing deposits at a regional Federal Reserve Bank. (There are 12 regional banks, with the Federal Reserve Bank of New York being the most important.) Other countries have the same system, although obviously highly liquid assets such as short-term government securities and high quality commercial paper can be declared eligible to function as reserves — or to serve as collateral for a loan by the central bank. This might also be a good place to furnish a definition of liquidity: liquidity is the ease with which an asset can be turned into a means of payment, or simpler, the ease with which an asset can be bought or sold. For a market, however, liquidity signifies the ease of carrying out financial transactions.

When Japan's asset-price "bubble" was gaining momentum in the 1980s, bank loans increased by more than $1.5 trillion, largely secured by real estate: land attained a status equal to that of gold during the gold standard. If it is true that the value of land declined from $20 trillion to $8.5 trillion during the 1990s, then it is easy to understand why Japan's banking system had to go into intensive care. The fall in the price of land and other assets has probably left Japanese banks holding between a half trillion and a trillion dollars of bad debts. (A "bubble" is a price not justified by fundamentals.)

In what follows, readers should be aware that e.g. loans and bonds can often be unpredictable in value, or illiquid, and thus in theory a bank could find itself in deep trouble because of the illiquidity of its loans. This is one of the reasons for the great importance of the interbank markets and the short-term lending practiced on these markets.

The principal liabilities of commercial banks are deposits: these belong to the depositors, and banks have only borrowed them. These institutions may also have borrowed "cash" or reserves from other banks or the central bank. Finally, as before, we can define net worth as assets minus liabilities. Mishkin defines net worth as being the same as bank equity (or bank capital), but when we do the accounting we see that net worth can include loans that may or may not be liquid, as well as such things as real property, and items of this nature are of little or no use if there is a "run" on the bank, and depositors are outside the front doors with passbooks in one hand and shotguns or horsewhips in the other. This problem will not worry us too much however, although the matter of bank capital and its composition has become extremely important over the last decade. Bank failure is typically accompanied by negative net worths, and it has been said that for the US in the bad years 1931–1933, negative net worth came to about 4% of the gross national product (GNP).

Really bad news can arrive for bank managers and owners as a result of a protracted period of sloppiness in the trading room, or the accumulation of a large portfolio of non-performing loans, or perhaps something like a bond market crash. To take the first of these, I have never heard George Soros called anything except a financial genius, but even so his Quantum Fund left $2 billion on the table as the result of a bad bet on the Russian ruble. If this can happen to something that Mr Soros himself is closely involved with, then it can happen anywhere. It happened, for example, to the German Bank Herstatt in 1974, where a spell of unwise currency speculation led to a bank failure that almost caused a panic in Germany. Outsiders accused the German central bank — the Bundesbank — of sleeping on the job; but the Bundesbank helped to organize a consortium of banks that provided a rescue package for the Herstatt's creditors.

A consortium also had to be formed to save the Franklin National Bank, the 20th largest bank in the US. The problem with that bank was both unlucky currency speculation and bad loans and, perhaps most of all, the ambitions of its new owner, Michele Sindona, who might best be described as a "peekaboo finance" specialist. (Peekaboo finance is an expression coined by Naylor (1987), and it refers to the laundering of "black" money and the cooling down of "hot" money.) Sindona was almost certainly a financial genius with the innate talent to run any bank or business in the world successfully, but according to Sampson (1981) he was heavily involved with, among others, the CIA and the Mafia. After fleeing to Switzerland in order to avoid having to account for the bad debts incurred by his enterprises, he was arrested in New York, and eventually convicted of fraud and larceny. (There is a Sindona type character in the film "Godfather III".)

Herstatt and Franklin failed, but many others have been close to failure — much closer than the television audience is aware. In the future, however, it is seems likely that governments, central banks, and ad-hoc consortiums of large banks will always be available to keep the top banks from endangering the financial equilibrium of their customers, as well as the political equilibrium of the countries in which these banks are located. Take for instance, the case of Mr. Walter Wriston (of New York's Citibank) and Mr Jim Slater, who were among the major financial players of the last quarter of the 20th century. Wriston ostensibly abhorred all forms of what later came to be known as "crony capitalism", in which the movers-and-shakers — or what was known in the US "South" at one time as the "power structure" — of a community were always ready to lend each other a helping hand; and in his make-believe world the market dealt swiftly and unmercifully with enterprises that failed to make the grade. Wriston achieved instant celebrity when he stated that "banking was not about money, but about information". Later (in 1982) he wrote that "countries do not go bankrupt", although several had in all but name, and their loans were on Citibank's balance sheet where he could contemplate them morning, noon, and night if he so chose.

Eventually the governments and central banks of the creditor countries were able to smooth things out for Citibank and the other financial institutions that had gone on a lending spree when the petrodollars began rolling in, although at a cost to the taxpayers that in the end was reckoned in the billions. Wriston continued his brilliant career, and eventually retired with his reputation and his beliefs about the survival of the fittest intact.

Mr Slater was not so fortunate. He began his career with mutual funds, added a bank and insurance company, and began spinning a web of property and share speculation into which other institutions were inevitably drawn. The first oil-price shock more or less finished him off: when the world economy suddenly went flat, all those wonderful housing and office blocks developed and/or controlled by men like Slater suddenly became albatrosses around their necks. And not only their necks. Bad property loans and falling property shares threatened many so-called "fringe" or "secondary" banks, which greatly increased anxiety throughout the financial community about the condition of the flagship banks. Slater not only had to fall, but to be given a lesson. His "empire" was taken over by the Bank of England, and the great man's smiling, confident face disappeared forever from the front pages of the tabloids. Once again a rescue syndicate was cobbled together, and at least $3 billion mobilized to keep anything genuinely ugly from happening to the fringe banks or the odd major bank — such as National Westminster (NatWest) — that were in the line of fire.

If we are to draw a conclusion from the above, it might be that the enormous wisdom in the great Bill Tilden's iron rule of tennis — "always change a losing game; never change a winning game" — does not inevitably apply on Wall Street or in the City of London. The one thing that many students of the late 20th century have become aware of is that there were many outstanding and genuinely talented financial "players" who would still be riding high if they had not been so intent on making the most of a good thing, that they forgot to notice the handwriting on the wall.

By way of closing, it should be noted that the central bank of the EU has been located in Frankfurt. This is to some extent ironic, because German banks are known to be among the least profitable in the Western world. One theory as to why this is so is that they tend to ignore the modern business creed calling for deploying capital in such a way as to maximize shareholder returns. Instead, German banks pride themselves on acting as owner, adviser, financier, and watchdog to industry, which has led them to accumulate a huge stock of illiquid industrial assets. This sort of arrangement is completely outside the Anglo-Saxon banking tradition.

II. Some Basic Bank Accounting and the Basle Overtures

The purpose of this section is to give readers some practice in manipulating the key items on a bank balance sheet (or T-account), without becoming involved with the T-accounts themselves. Why this approach? The answer is to keep the exposition in this book focussed on essentials, which among other things means eliminating as many digressions as possible that detract attention from the non-bank components of global finance.

Some attention is also paid to the Basle accords or proposals, which are now applied in nearly 100 countries. The purpose of these is to ensure that banks have enough capital (i.e. highly liquid assets) available to prevent commonplace financial turbulence from turning into a fully-fledged crisis. The technique for doing this to is set aside capital in proportion to the amount and riskiness of different types of loans. Naturally, highly liquid assets tend to carry a minimum yield, and as a result many bank executives prefer to see them subordinated to more profitable investments, even if it means having to accept a much larger risk.

We can begin by once again looking at the basic balance sheet identity: Assets (A) = Liabilities (L) + New Worth (NW), or $A = L + NW$. To keep things simple, the assets will be taken as cash (CA), loans (LO), and bank reserves (R); while the liabilities are exclusively deposits (D) belonging to the non-bank public. (Hopefully, readers will recall the earlier discussion of reserves.) The point here is that bank directors make a large part of their profits from their loans, and they should make a conscious effort to limit these to high-quality assets. Similarly, the deposits they are holding do not belong to the bank, but to the depositors: they are loans from the depositors. We can summarize our analysis as $CA + R + LO = D + NW$. In what follows NW will often be called bank capital.

Now let us take the unlikely situation that all loans become non-performing, or $LO \to 0$. Since the deposits belong to depositors, they are not at the disposal of the bank, and so in order to maintain our identity, net-worth must fall. How much must it fall? Well, if the bank has plenty of reserves, and cash in its vaults, it may not have to become negative. Rewriting the above equation (with $LO = 0$) we get $CA + R - D = NW$, and if $(CA + R) \geq D$, then $NW \geq 0$. (In case you have forgotten, $\geq$ means "greater than or equal".) But obviously it could happen that $(CA + R) < D$, in which case NW becomes negative. ($<$ means "less than".) This is not good for anyone's peace of mind, because what a negative NW means is that the bank does not have enough currency to service all the depositors in the event of a "run" on the bank. Those who arrive first, and those whose total deposits are insured by the central bank or government, might be all right, but the others could be in deep trouble. In 1929, in Chicago, my father was one of the others.

Continuing this example, suppose that the net worth turns negative, and the central bank decides to lend this bank enough money so that if necessary they can provide all depositors with their deposits; and so they simply print some money and cart it down to the bank. The amount that they would lend them is $D - (CA + R)$. Some adjustments are needed for our (balance sheet) identity, and thus we get $LO + CA + R + CA^* = D + GL + NW$. CA^* is the physical currency received from the government, while GL is the amount on the promissory note of the bank (to the central bank). Remembering that in this exercise $LO = 0$, and the net worth had fallen below zero ($NW < 0$), we get $CA + R + \{D - (CA + R)\} = D + \{(CA + R) - D\} + \{D - (CA + R)\}$. The first parenthesis on the right hand side (RHS) is the net-worth, while the second parenthesis on the RHS is amount of the central bank loan.

If the reader makes the obvious cancellations in the above, he or she will see that, trivially, the balance sheet still balances. As an exercise, let me suggest that you put some numbers in the above discussion. For instance, start with LO = 1,000, CA = 100, R = 100, and D = 800, and then let all or a part of the loans go bad, or both.

Before we leave this topic, some mention should be made of the leveraging of a bank. Probably the most useful statistic in this context is the (bank) capital/loan ratio, or even the capital/asset ratio, since the largest percentage of assets by far are usually loans. During the greatest period of US bank failures in history, the 1920s and 1930s, US commercial banks averaged capital/asset ratios of about 10%. This ratio tends to be less now, because for many bank managers growth comes first on the agenda, and the key to growth and improved career prospects inevitably reduces to directing a maximum of resources into loans, and into improved technology and facilities for proprietary trading. In fact, the undercapitalization problem is so bad on the global scene at the present time that several of the largest banks in Japan have been in danger of collapsing if a relatively small percentage of their loans went bad — and they received no help, which is unlikely.

In the above example, since no loan-loss reserves are designated, the capital/loan ratio was NW/LO, while the capital asset ratio is NW/(LO + CA + R). The reader can calculate these using the figures given above. By way of completing this discussion, the two most important measures of bank profitability can be given. The first is the "return to assets" [= (net profit after taxes)/assets], and probably more important "return on equity" [= (net profit after taxes)/equity capital].

In 1988, with the stockmarket meltdown of 1987 still fresh in their minds, the Basle "club" of central bank directors — under the auspices of the Bank for International Settlements (BIS) — formed a committee from the world's banking supervisors for the purpose of drawing up a set of rules that would keep bank directors from operating with inadequate capital/asset ratios. What these rules amounted to was specifying how much in liquid assets of "capital backing" should be available.

Some observers now feel that those rules are showing signs of age, and so arrangements are being made to bring them up to date. Under the old system, bank capital was suppose to amount to at least 8% for high risk loans. Other types of loans are then "risk weighted" with respect to this 8%. For example, a residential mortgage is 50% risk weighted, and requires a capital cushion of only 4%, while loans to the governments of highly developed countries are zero weighted. Still tottering from the 1997 crisis, many Asian banks became more stringent in their lending after accumulating a stack of non-performing loans, and raised their demand for high quality bonds (which, incidentally, are items in increasingly short supply at the beginning of the 21st century).

I see no point in running this topic into the ground, but I have been told that it is worthwhile to know a little more about the subject. Suppose we take the numbers given above, which includes $LO = 1,000$, and divide these loans into commercial loans (= 600), and municipal bonds (= 400). The risk weighting on the loans is 100%, and on the bonds 20%, while cash and reserves are 'zero' weighted. *Risk weighted assets* are thus 600 × 100% + 400 × 20% = 680. According to the Basle stipulations, the minimum core (Tier 1) capital required is 4% of risk weighted (or adjusted) assets (= 0.04 × 680 = 27.2), while the minimum total capital (Tier 1 + Tier 2) required is 8% of the risk-weighted assets — or 0.08 × 680 = 54.4. (Note: loan loss reserves are a component of bank capital.)

On the other hand, even the best quality corporate loans counted as 100% risk weighted, and the capital backing had to be 8%, which did not seem logical to some experts. A point that should be kept in mind is that a bank's reserves apply to deposits, and can differ from country to country, while the capital backing being discussed here is supposed to be uniform for all banks. Stockholders' equity capital is often regarded as the most important part (or "backing") of its Tier 1 (or *core*) capital, together with preferred stock; while Tier 2 capital mostly consists of loan loss reserves and subordinated debt — i.e. debt that is serviced after depositors and other creditors have been paid.

The new proposals are intended to add "flexibility" to the system by giving more weight to the judgement of local bank management, "The Market", and external credit rating agencies. The opinion here is that the improvements in the new proposals are few, while the irregularities are many, and with the exception of some minor (but important) changes, things should have been left the way they were. Of course, the world is not becoming an easier place for bank regulators or officials and employees of the BIS. Exactly how they would keep track of the activities of e.g. the Bank of Credit and Commerce International (BCCI), whose clients may have included the CIA, and which, according to *Time Magazine* (June 29, 1991) contained a department specializing in "bribery, extortion, kidnapping, and even, by some accounts, murder", or for that matter some of the more elegant participants in the recent "bribesville" scandals in Italy, is a deep, dark mystery. To be sure, there is no reason to believe that the above named anti-social inclinations of the directors of the BCCI are factual just because they appeared in a prominent weekly, but if they are then I see no reason to place too much confidence in the capabilities of the ladies and gentlemen associated with the Basle "club" to do something about them. A similar observation applies to another former jewel in the banking crown, Crédit Lyonnais, described by *Forbes* (December 13, 1999), as "the dirtiest bank in the world". Its management went on a spending spree, and the three bailouts that were necessary in 1994–1995 cost French taxpayers 21 billion francs.

The final observation here is that proprietary trading is an off-the-balance-sheet activity. This does not mean that it is illegal, however it would not explicitly show up in the T-accounts that you manipulated in your first course in macroeconomics, although any profits generated would find a home in the asset column, and serve to boost net worth. Obviously, the money obtained from proprietary trading has been extremely helpful to managers that want to merge their banks with other institutions.

As Sachs and Larrain (1995) stress, bank regulators are not always careful in their supervisory duties. Particularly annoying is their habit of equating the market value of loans to the face value of the original loan. As indicated by the algebra in this section, it is easy for a bank that has the full confidence of its supervisors to slide into a position where its net worth is negative, and it does not have enough money to withstand a "run". As to be expected, the larger the bank, the greater the temptation to play fast and loose with loans, because in every country there are major financial institutions that cannot be allowed to fail.

In the next section, the Japanese fondness for trading loans will be mentioned. The selling of loans — and particularly Third World loans — became an important activity when a crisis involving Third World debt threatened to disrupt the international financial system during the 1980s. Banks found that an extensive secondary market was available for these tarnished assets, assuming that the price was right. It seems, for example, that Mexican debt once sold for 50% of its book value, implying that this was the percentage of its outstanding liabilities (i.e. bonds) that would eventually be honored.

Readers of *The Economist* will notice the constant reference to the "London Club", and the "Paris Club". These are simply meetings or negotiations that take place between debtors and creditors in London, Paris, or for that matter New York. Since the Paris Club is held under the auspices of the French Ministry of Finance, it has on more than one occasion been referred to as a "rich man's club".

Exercises

1. In the exercise in the text, start out with L = 1,000, CA = 100, R = 100, and D = 800. What is the starting NW? Suppose that L goes to zero. Now, what is the NW? Suppose 450 of the loans went bad. What does this make the NW?
2. Using the numbers in exercise 1, and forgetting about loans going bad, state the value of NW, loan loss reserves, core capital, and bank capital. What happens if a bank does not have enough capital to satisfy the regulators? Assume a risk weighting of 50% for loans.

III. Investment Banks and Private Banks

In Anthony Sampson's book on banking (1981), he quoted an investment banker as saying "We're very good at leading lambs to the slaughter".

Occasionally they lead themselves to the slaughter. At the time Sampson wrote his book, Barings was one of the great survivors among merchant banks. Founded in 1765 in the City of London (i.e. London's financial district), it was one of the first "merchant banks" — establishments that provide money and advice for clients, and at the same time functioned as merchants. They also traded property and commodities, and financed trade.

Barings collapsed following the creative derivatives trading of Mr Nick Leeson. According to Leeson, he was victimized by his blundering superiors, as well as senior officials at the Bank of England. This exact circumstances of this victimization were not really made clear in his book (1996), but it was enlightening to read about how easy he found it to confuse and hoodwink his superiors, even when they were sitting next to him or looking over his shoulder while he was embellishing his ledgers.

Having spent three years in Geneva (Switzerland) where persons in or near the money business know exactly who is buying or selling what or whom, I gave a great deal of thought to inserting a long discussion of this most fascinating of all branches of banking into the present work, but it would serve no purpose. With a book like Paul Ferris' "The Master Bankers" available (1984), the rest of us have very little to add. As Ferris puts it, investment bankers "are not the ones who cash checks: they are the fixers and dealers of the system". Quite naturally, in Switzerland they did both, and eventually they may be doing both everywhere else. The gigantic bank deal entered into in 1999 by Dai-Ichi Kangyo Bank Ltd., Fuji Bank Ltd., and Industrial Bank of Japan, will be accompanied by a shift of capital and personnel from traditional banking to investment banking areas. Exactly how this will work out is uncertain, since the investment banking skills of the Japanese have often been called into question. It is also interesting to note that Japanese commercial banks have developed a knack for trading loans as if they were bonds. As a result, they occasionally end up with a portfolio filled with loans that could not be sold, and which promise a great deal of trouble in the future.

This merger will create the largest financial institution in the world, with assets of more than $1.3 trillion at the beginning of the 21st century, and it may turn out to be the first step in the restructuring of the Japanese economy. Among other things it appears that the merger has greatly weakened Japan's *Keiretsu,* or "business groupings", since the manager of the Fuji bank unexpectedly announced that the merger made it impossible for his organization to continue leading the Fuyo *keiretsu*. The keiretsus function to a certain extent as industrial and commercial cartels, with an extensive cross-shareholding. Some observers see them as hand-holding, back-scratching support groups that prevent the free allocation of capital; but for decades they were viewed as one of Japan's greatest economic assets, and just recently, when the Rothschild Recovery Fund joined in the reorganization of Nikko Electric Industries, they invited some of Nikko's largest suppliers to become investors with them. This is in keeping with the keiretsu tradition.

Something that deserves mentioning is that while 5,000–6,000 jobs are expected to be eliminated in the above bank merger, this does not mean the forced removal of the same number of employees. As the head of a Japanese pharmaceutical company once said, the main responsibility of his firm was to his employees and customers, and up to now the clients of financial institutions have not indicated a strong desire for relationships with firms that elect to break with Japanese tradition. This kind of attitude seems to annoy many analysts and researchers in the US and Europe, however in the light of Japan's history and culture it makes a great deal of sense.

The blurb on the front of Ferris' book, in referring to what goes on inside the world of investment banking, uses the following language: "The deals, the wealth, the awesome global impact ..." All this and more is true. Michael Lewis (1991) tells of Salomon Brothers' top executives working out their fees for involvement in the famous RJR Nabisco buyout. Although they had not figured out exactly how much they needed to borrow to purchase the company, they knew "their fees to the last decimal place". These, incidentally, came to $1.9 billion.

Although Lewis clearly has a grudge to work off where his former employers are concerned, he did not forget to emphasize that the entire finance elite keeps score with dollar bills and not charitable endeavors, although occasionally they confuse the two. For instance, the chairman of a hedge fund which suffered heavy trading losses in 1998, once informed fellow diners at the Windows on the World Restaurant (New York) that hedge funds were a positive force in that by making money from market inefficiencies, these funds perform crucial work "from a social welfare point of view". In other words, when the gargantuan deals that investment banks and hedge funds specialize in are possible, it is supposed to indicate the likely presence of "market inefficiencies" whose elimination — through these deals — will make the world a better place. Personally, I am not 100% convinced that this is true, although it was the case in Sweden once, thanks to the Wallenberg family. Unfortunately, those days are gone forever.

This kind of logic makes it clear that investment and commercial bankers are far from interchangeable, since legitimate commercial bankers generally realize that they have a vital service to perform for their communities. To get an idea of the kind of thing that investment bankers do, we can consider the actions in the Czech Republic of Nomura Securities, the Japanese investment bank. After spending two years buying a nice share of the Czech beer industry, Nomura has decided to merge these facilities into Europe's largest brewery, and then to auction off at least a part of the new firm. Whether this deal will be a good thing for the Czechs in that it will provide them with more, tastier, and/or cheaper beer seems to be both irrelevant and uncertain.

The big three within investment banking in the US are Goldman Sachs, Morgan Stanley Dean Witter, and Merrill Lynch. The second of these originated with the merger of Morgan Stanley and Dean Witter, while the other two are on a perpetual hunt for acquisitions. Goldman Sachs is now in the process of "going public" (after a failed public stock offering in 1998), however it has found time to publish a "shopping list" that included the largest asset management operation in the UK. This was Schroder, with about $120 billion under management (as compared to Goldman Sachs' 110 billion). Exactly where Schroder was supposed to fit into the Goldman Sachs' lineup is uncertain, but while management was working that out, all the employees of Goldman Sachs, except the 221 partners, began collecting bonuses (in shares) of one-half their pay, plus amounts depending on length of service. The partners were awarded about $52 million each for keeping the faith. (See Chapter 9 for more on Schroder's final destination.)

An interesting question here concerns the exact activities of these 221 equity partners. Undoubtedly they provide an input to the firm that the managing partners, at least, feel is worth a $52 million gratuity, although at present rates of remuneration that firm — like some of the other investment banks — seems to have a problem recruiting enough capable advisors at the non-partner level. There is no point in implying that the equity partners are not making an invaluable contribution to the intellectual side of the business, however some observers have been known to say that there has never really been a shortage of fresh ideas for the operational directors and partners of the big investment banks to ponder. The basic problem has been to abandon or refurbish the many stale conceptions that are put in circulation by certain individuals close to the upper levels of international banking before they contribute to a macroeconomic debacle that affects the rest of us.

Before turning to private banks, it can be noted that investment banks, as compared to merchant banks (which in a sense are "pocket" investment banks), try to provide "one-stop" shopping for clients and potential clients, while many merchant banks still tend to specialize in giving strategic advice. Of course, since the present M&A boom — especially in Europe — offers rich rewards to all concerned, the investment banks will tend to become larger, and unless merchant bankers have lost their flair for survival, they will be wise to completely discard the idea that small is beautiful. The driving force behind the above mentioned "boom" as the 21st century opens is a corporate culture that centers on what the modern executive calls "execution". This means driving down costs (i.e. getting more work from fewer employees) in order to support the capital investment programs that underly expansion. All this speeds up industrial consolidation, and with many firms desperate to buy or position themselves to be bought, some members of the investment banking fraternity will face a brighter future than ever, especially if they maintain their desire to excel and win.

That brings us to private banks. A private bank is an institution that provides personal banking services. (In France, it is called a Banqué Privée.) These institutions cater to many different types of persons, and to quote *Business Week* (May 24, 1999), the "cream of European and American high society" occupy a special place in their hearts; but also those members of the monied minority who feel that they might have to cross a border on minimal notice, leave their country quickly by rocket ship, or who — while traveling abroad — receive a message which indicates that it would be best for their health if they elected not to use their return ticket.

Representatives of the deserving poor are unlikely to be found among the core business of private banks, since the kind of people for whom private banks came into existence require specialists who know about exchange rates, interest rates, tax laws, and asset diversification in order to relieve them of the stresses and strains of managing inheritances, bonuses, windfalls, and the like. They need urbane professionals to collect the rent on their apartments in Nice or London, and to see that fresh flowers are available in their hotel suites when they drop into Geneva for a long weekend. They need sympathetic, intelligent and discreet investment and legal counsellors with a wholehearted belief that serious money deserves serious respect. They need private bankers who are really and truly private.

The Swiss banks, UBS and Credit Suisse are reputedly the largest private banks in the world, but the undisputed personal champion where private banking is concerned was the late Edmond J. Safra. Safra was inclined to say that banking is a "simple, stupid business", and to claim that "The book on banking was written 6,000 years ago", which sounds a little off-key, but he also noted that in private banking — unlike e.g. investment banking — "it's not what money you might make, but what you might lose". (The *Financial Times*, October 9, 1990.) Since this appears to be true, some readers are almost certainly asking the question: "How do I get into this line of work"? The answer, unfortunately, is that private banking is not something that you "get into", for the simple reason that most people tend to be more careful about who handles their money, than who handles their wet raincoat. A well known joke in the Geneva banking community is that the switchboard operators at a Safra operation would answer the phone with a rather dry "hello" instead of the name of the firm: they want the caller's name first, in case that person might be inclined to interpret any familiarity as a license to seek information.

The financially powerful American Express Company bought Safra's Trade Development Bank in Geneva in the early 1980s, but apparently lost many of his clients. Safra reentered private banking in the late years of that decade, launching Safra Republic Bank with $1 billion in capital, of which private shareholders furnished 300 million. Two years later (on June 30,

1990), it allegedly had assets of $7.2 billion, of which about $1 billion could be called loans. It should be made clear though that Safra never had an aggressive attitude toward lending.

Safra eventually sold Republic to the London based Hong Kong and Shanghai Banking Corporation (HSBC) for approximately $10 billion, of which 3.3 billion was initially destined for Mr Safra's pocket. HSBC is a superstar in the world of universal banking, but it has been suggested in many quarters that they will not have Safra's aptitude when it comes to private banking. There are others who point to the $190 million in trading losses that Republic incurred in 1998 as a sign that Safra was losing his touch, but no one suggested that the managers of the Tiger Fund — the second largest hedge fund in the world — were over the hill when they lost a billion dollars in the first nine months of 1999. Private bankers generally understand — as do many of their clients — that the world economy moves in cycles, and when bad patches come along, rapid capital augmentation is out of the question, and occasionally some losses will be suffered. The key thing for clients is knowing that their assets will receive personal attention by highly qualified and discreet specialists, and will be deployed as efficiently as is humanly possible.

According to Michael Lagoupolis, senior vice-president in charge of global private banking at Royal Bank of Canada, "whether you're onshore or offshore in this business, there's still a lot of money to be made". That's putting it mildly, and is precisely why there will always be a place in *any* part of the banking world for people like Edmond Safra.

IV. Background to the World Bank and IMF

Memories are short, and sometimes too short. Something that should never be forgotten is the power of history, although Frederich Nietzsche undoubtedly had a point when he said "The future influences the present as much as the past". Such being the case, it would not be appropriate to write a finance book without at least mentioning the World Bank, and presenting a sketch of the International Monetary Fund (IMF) and its present activities. The latter organization, and its management and so-called experts, are playing a key role in global finance today. There are some very astute observers who say that the manner in which they are playing this role is counterproductive, but this does not mean that they will be closing their doors in the near future. They have always been important, and their importance seems to be increasing.

The World Bank and IMF had their roots in the economic and social discomforts and disorders of the period between the two World Wars: inflation, mistakes in the setting of exchange rates, the absence of comprehensive official lending facilities, the crimping of world trade due to various trade barriers, and so on.

The first great disaster was the German hyper-inflation of 1922–1923. An artistically bizarre rendition of this event can be found in Ingmar Bergman's film "Ormens Ägg" (The Serpents Egg), but what it involved was the following: in 1923 the price level in Germany rose by a factor of 452,999,200, with such things as postage stamps selling for millions of marks. A currency reform toward the end of 1923 brought the inflation to an end, but it was too late for the German middle class. In general their savings were wiped out, and many of them turned to the Nazi party.

It also needs to be made clear to as many people as possible, that the independence of central banks may not mean a low-inflation panacea. Germany's Reichsbank was statutorily independent when its directors took the fateful decision to flood the country with new money.

The next disaster came in 1925, when Great Britain reinstated the prewar exchange rate between the pound and gold. (Under the gold standard, some important currencies had their values officially defined in terms of gold, and convertibility was supposed to prevail between the currency and gold.) This overvalued the pound, just as the French franc was undervalued when the gold price of the franc was set too low. In both instances, it might have been wise for finance ministers and heads of state to have spent a few hours pouring over their economics textbooks, because in the UK the overvalued pound led to the general strike of 1926, which the workers lost. (Two of the most brilliant TV series of the 20th century depicted some aspects of that strike. These series are "Brideshead Revisited" and "Upstairs, Downstairs", both produced in the UK.) This loss by the "Red Team", coupled with a sudden optimism in many countries, and economic revival in central Europe, caused an economic upswing that lasted until the stock market crash of 1929. (That crash will be discussed later.)

In 1931, a notable Viennese bank, Kreditanstalt, went bankrupt. This was easily the most important bank failure of the 20th century, and in considering what took place in the next ten years, perhaps the most important of all time. Furthermore, Austria and Germany stopped payments on their debts, while the Bank of France speeded up its conversion of pounds into gold. As a result, Britain was forced off the gold standard, because convertibility between the pound and gold became impossible. By now, banks were failing all over the world — particularly in the US — and people in general suddenly found themselves faced with the unpleasant news that their politicians (and what John Wayne in the film McQ called "servants of the people") had completely lost control of the situation. In addition, to make matters worse, there were competitive devaluations by many European countries — despite which world trade stagnated, and then spiraled downward. There was also a general price level deflation taking place almost everywhere that worked to crush investment: the only rational response of business to falling prices is to reduce investment. As a result, the unemployment figure in the industrial countries often touched — and sometimes exceeded — 25%; while in the US real output fell 30% in four years, and the money supply also contracted by about 30%.

In the US, Congress gave President Roosevelt the power to begin a comprehensive tariff cutting program that was based on negotiation and reciprocal action, while in many countries public works programs were commenced. These programs were widely ridiculed in the US at the time, but in reality they occasionally achieved striking results, and this was particularly true in Germany. Apparently, however, it required the approach of another major war to pull the world out of the economic doldrums.

The wartime years need not be taken up here, but when it became apparent that the Allies had won the war — after the victories at Alamein and Stalingrad — discussions began at the highest diplomatic and economic levels about the configuration of the post-war world economy. The Bretton Woods Conference of 1944, at Bretton Woods (New Hampshire) in the US, formalized a large number of loosely conceived plans and intentions. These included establishing institutions to finance the reconstruction of Europe, beginning with the International Bank for Reconstruction and Development, which became the World Bank. Later it was decided in the US that the reconstruction of Europe had to be speeded up, and the Marshall Plan (which was formally known as the European Recovery Program) took over from the World Bank. (The World Bank presently concentrates on lending to the developing countries, and has about 2000 "experts" in the "field". Just now it seems to be lending about $30 billion/year, and claims that half of this goes to what they call "institution building, governance, multisector lending and social programs"; however the US Congress, among others, is largely unimpressed.) The Korean War began in 1950, bringing with it the Korean War "boom" that drove up the price of industrial raw materials throughout the world, and creating the kind of political climate in which Germany and Japan were encouraged to rebuild their economies as rapidly as possible.

Now we arrive at the International Monetary Fund. John Maynard (Lord) Keynes — who was the star of the conference — wanted an international central bank founded that could issue its own reserve currency (to be called *bancor*), but the US balked at this arrangement, since they assumed — and correctly — that the US taxpayers would have to finance this scheme. The prime mission of the IMF then became to help countries cope with temporary balance of payments problems without resorting to devaluations, and also to lobby for changes in fiscal and monetary policies that would improve the balance of payments of these countries. Of course, if the problem was judged too serious to be solved by borrowing from the Fund, or altering domestic economic policies, then a fundamental disequilibrium was declared by the Fund, and the country could change the value of its currency. Another organization proposed at Bretton Woods was the International Trade Organization (ITO), but its charter was not ratified by the US Senate. The present World Trade Organization (WTO) is in some sense an update of the proposed (ITO), and its brief is to promote the liberalization of trade. As the reader will soon see, the IMF has become an organization that in some ways is even more powerful than the one that Keynes thought should be brought into existence. Its power is based on its capacity to lend enormous sums of money, and to impose conditions on the recipients of these loans.

In 1947, France became the first country to draw on the IMF. One of the things agreed on at Bretton Woods was that when the pound sterling became strong enough, it would join the dollar as an official reserve currency. (An official reserve currency is one that can always be used to pay international debt.) In 1947, the UK government decided that the time had come, but as soon as *convertibility* was declared, many persons and institutions (and probably governments) in possession of pounds rushed to the Bank of England, and converted their pounds into dollars and gold. As a result, convertibility was summarily suspended. All this is mentioned because it provides an application of *Gresham's Law*, which states that bad money drives out good. If, for example, two currencies are supposed to circulate side by side, and people feel that one of them is in some way weak or defective compared to the other, then the good currency will be hoarded, and the other used for such things as paying bills. (Note: originally the pound was defined in terms of silver, and thus the designation "sterling".)

At Bretton Woods, a "pegged" exchange rate system was instituted: exchange rates were "fixed", but when severe supply-demand imbalances for a currency arose, then its exchange rate could be changed (under the supervision of the IMF). Currencies were still tied to gold, but the understanding was that the dollar was and would remain the "boss" currency, and acceptible in all circumstances for the payment of international debt. Among other things, this meant that for the system to work, the dollar must be maintained on the same "level" as gold: its exchange rate vis-à-vis gold — which was set at $1 = 32$ ounces of gold — should hold indefinitely.

Naturally, an arrangement of this type was very fragile in the long run, as Professor Lionel Triffin pointed out in his exposition of the "Triffin Dilemma". There is only a small amount of gold in the world, but virtually no limit to the number of US dollars that can be printed. Someday people would lose faith in the dollar relative to gold, and if convertibility prevailed when that day came they would go to the "bank" — i.e. the US Treasury — with their dollars and demand gold. Since there wasn't that much gold above or below the ground, the bank would initially ignore these unhappy holders of greenbacks, and ultimately devalue (relative to gold) the *numeraire* currency (i.e. the dollar). 1968 was probably the year when the handwriting on the wall was detected in wider financial and public circles, and it was also the year in the Vietnam War of the Tet offensive by the Viet Cong and the army of North Vietnam. Although a military failure, that offensive convinced the middle class in the US — and even to a greater extent in Europe — that the war was not being won. The year after Tet was the most costly of the war for the US military, and this added a sinister overtone to the changes in the international financial system that now appeared essential. Although not generally appreciated, the attempt by the US to finance that conflict by printing money rather than raising taxes put intolerable strains on the dollar, and lost for the US the sympathy of many bankers and politicians who were knowledgeable in financial matters.

In 1971, at the Smithsonian Institution in Washington, the governments of the major industrial powers agreed on a realignment of exchange rates, to include a devaluation of the dollar (against gold); and less than a year after the signing of the Smithsonian Agreement, it became clear that even more drastic measures were necessary. Those more drastic measures led — a few years later — to the end of the Bretton Woods System, and eventually the "floating" of the dollar and other major currencies against each other and against gold. Currency values were now largely determined by the market.

Under the new arrangement, exchange rates occasionally fluctuate in a manner that has nothing to do with fundamentals. This was one of the reasons for setting up the European Exchange Rate Mechanism (ERM), which was intended as a prelude to a single currency West Europe. Trying to make the ERM work cost various central banks billions, and what they lost, speculators — to include George Soros — gained. Under the Bretton Woods System, speculative capital flows were generally kept under control, but now these flows exceed by a substantial amount the demand for foreign exchange to use in commodity trade and non-speculative financial transactions. They are also the reason for the large losses that many corporations have suffered on their foreign borrowing.

At the end of 1999, rich governments' combined reserves came to $1.6 trillion, while foreign exchange trading averaged close to $2 trillion/day. Since the early 1980s, foreign exchange trading has increased by a factor of 33, while the reserves of rich countries has only increased four times. As a result, exchange rate fluctuations that are not tied to fundamentals pose a constant economic threat to the international economy. No attempt will be made to argue in favor of the EU, but the Nobel laureate Robert Mundell was essentially correct when he said that creating single currencies such as the euro will greatly reduce speculation. Speculation, however, may not be as bad as some of the problems that the EU will cause some of its members.

In 1998, a summit of the G7 (or Group of Seven leading industrial countries) met in Cologne (Germany) for the purpose of discussing a debt relief program designed to help the world's poorest countries. Twenty eight billion dollars was added to the large amount already in the pipeline, and so the debt mountain being considered was scheduled to be whittled down by almost one-half. Mr. Gordon Brown, the UK finance minister, announced that he was greatly impressed by the IMF's contribution to the project. (The IMF plans to auction off some of its gold stocks to pay its share.)

Private sector financial institutions are not always pleased by the way that Mr Brown expresses himself. Many of these claim that Brown would like to see Third World countries simply default on their debts, in order to reduce the debt-relief packages to which his country will have to contribute. Brown, of course, is outraged by these allegations, and claims that he is working for reforms and for negotiation between lender and borrower, and not defaults. The reforms to which he is referring include codes of conduct covering monetary, fiscal, social and corporate governance policies, in addition to measures to prevent economic crises, and promote financial stability.

Or, as they used to say, "pie in the sky". Obviously, no debt relief panaceas are worth the paper they are written on without durable economic growth, and neither Mr Brown or his colleagues have the slightest idea as to how to expedite this, nor do the governments of the countries that they are trying to steer down the road to self-sustaining prosperity. The correct prescription here, incidentally, turns on promoting the right kind of secondary education, which means the acquiring of technical skills that are useful for more than clearing a malfunctioning AK47 assault rifle; but the IMF and its experts never think along these lines.

Nor do they understand that the liberalized trading regimes promoted by the IMF means more imports by LDCs, and since attempts to close the trade gap through exports often encounters unresponsive markets and adverse movements in the terms of trade, maintaining growth is primarily about attracting foreign capital. As the director of the UN Conference on Trade and Development (UNCTAD) has pointed out, these capital inflows are concentrated to a relatively small group of countries, where much of this money adds little to productive capacity. By his calculations, nearly a quarter is taken out by residents, and a fifth is set aside for foreign exchange reserves.

Much of Mr. Brown's way of thinking actually fits in with the IMF's heavy-handed approach to debt reduction (and to just about everything else, since the Fund was heavily involved in the recent money laundering scandal in Russia). To qualify for debt reduction, countries must spend six years in what the IMF calls a structural adjustment program. This involves a protracted spell of belt tightening, highlighted by comprehensive privatization and deregulation, balanced budgets, currency adjustments, etc. Certainly, no realist could claim that economic growth and the eradication of poverty is possible without abandoning the losing game now being played by both the governments and people of the poorer countries, but what this presumably well meaning program will eventually do is to widen inequalities and put more pressure on the working poor. Everyone in the Third World coming into contact with the IMF is aware of that simple fact; which is why my late colleague Professor Göran Ohlin said that during one of his junkets through South America, everywhere he went he saw block letters on walls saying "Down with the IMF".

He could, and perhaps should have said much more. According to Joseph Stiglitz, a former chief economist of the World Bank, capital market liberalization has probably been the cause of three-fourths of the most recent bank exigencies in developing countries. The mechanics here are simple. Unregulated and unsupervised liberalization encourages risky but collateralized lending by banks. If something goes wrong, loans are called in, and projects go unfinished. This gives a boost to risk averseness, and the inflow of long-term capital drys up. As Stiglitz underlines, economic growth requires long-term investments (so that projects can be finished), but in a climate of uncertainty, these are quickly replaced by short-term capital movements. If asset values come under pressure, and political ambiguity enters the picture, even short-term flows can discontinue.

Another professor at Uppsala University, Stefan Hedlund, wants the IMF cut off at the knees. He quotes a *USA Today* piece claiming that the 1999 loan of $4.8 billion to Russia was disposed of in the following manner. Russian insiders got word of a possible devaluation and sold various financial assets (e.g. government notes and treasury bills) for rubles (and perhaps dollars too.) These rubles were then exchanged at the Russian Central Bank for the newly arrived dollars, and the dollars shipped out of the country — probably illegally. Eventually the ruble collapsed, and various Russian financial assets owned by some of the most prestigious financial institutions in Europe and North America augmented the long list of bad investments that distinguished the concluding years of the second millennium.

Hedlund offers as the proof of all this the fact that the Russian Central Bank's reserves amounted to 13 billion dollars before receiving the IMF's $4.8 billion, and shortly after the ruble "tanked", reserves still stood at 13 billion. The IMF has grandly announced that the missing money had nothing to do with their loan, and in all likelihood was involved in legitimate transactions (such as paying for imports), but Hedlund concludes that the use of arguments like this simply makes the Fund's directors look ridiculous.

I am not so sure. As financial markets develop, private persons or institutions take a greater interest in stocks and bonds. On the other hand, there will be little interest in these things when only a comparatively few transactors participate in financial markets. In this situation, the banking system will have an especially large role to play in the allocation of capital and the provision of liquidity, which means that the IMF — which has not only branched into dealing with pure banking and financial issues, but has displayed a more fervid taste for involvement with explicitly political issues — will roost even more securely than ever at the top of the financial world's food chain.

V. Conclusion: The One and Only Wall Street

A few years ago, when the EU began to flex its muscles, many large European banks proclaimed that ultimately they would be large enough to challenge the top US financial institutions on their own turf. They are still waiting. Today, only Deutsche Bank — and perhaps the recently merged Union Bank of Switzerland (SBU) and Swiss Bank Corporation (SBC) — look as though they can give the US giants a fight.

The basic problem is that European banks have met harder competition in their home markets; they still lack the enormous depth of US markets in which to ply their trade; and it is not certain that they have access to financial resources that are commensurate with their aspirations. Much of the stiff competition they are facing originates with US institutions, and according to an investigation made by the Stern School of Business, the relative strength of US investment banks may be increasing.

On the commercial bank side, things appear to be better for the European institutions. Internet banking is being rapidly integrated into the behavior of many bank customers, and in addition these customers and their families — and particularly their children — are prepared to increase their Internet skills.

Some large traditional banks, however, may have a problem. As compared to their highly computerized competitors, they may have large capital and personnel costs inherited from the past; however if they do not make the grade, there is plenty of scope for integration with the most profitable establishments. The most innovative banks can charge less for their services, and offer a higher rate of return on deposits because their costs are lower. The future being staked out in, for example, a country like France, turns on "home banking" as well as share market transactions built around mobile telephones and television, but there would still be a neo-traditional bank somewhere in the background, monitoring traffic, and devising new products for a mass clientiele.

Actually, it sounds better than it may be. France is not particularly Internet intensive — on the contrary. In looking at Internet penetration, the Nordic countries are far out in front, and the others well behind, however I can note that some of the plans that are being advanced in Scandinavia and Northern Europe for the trading of shares, and in particular the circulation of research and advice on share trading, have a strong air of unreality about them. Many of these plans are predicated on an unending bull market for shares, and in a declining market many small investors who have become convinced that they can manage their own portfolios because they own the latest model cellular phone, might find themselves confronted with some very uncomfortable surprises.

With all due respects, the European banks simply may not be championship material at the present time. In banking, as in sports, you can be very, very good without ever becoming the best. That little extra something is essential, and New York is still the best place to look for it.

One more observation. Finance is an activity that virtually everyone must participate in, whether they want to or not. There is no sideline. This explains the great wealth of the professionals. People with my interests and lack of commitment inevitably deploy our financial resources badly, but not the financial institutions with which I have an unavoidable contact — e.g. "my" bank. I teach finance; they practice it. For example, what I should do is to keep my deposit account at a minimum, buy more "funds" and diversify them better, learn how to use the Internet and e-mail, and so on, but for some reason I and many millions of others like me cannot be bothered. What this means is that the war between the trading rooms and executive suites of various financial institutions is not really the zero sum game that it appears to be. Instead, the professionals are competing for larger pieces of a pie whose ingredients are provided by blasé sightseers like myself, as well as those concerned citizens who have been led to believe that because they know how to use the Internet, they are ready to go to the mat with the big boys and girls.

VI. Appendix: Hiding and Laundering Money

At the last count, there were 215 banks in the city-state of Luxembourg. Luxembourg is right next door for many depositors in Belgium, Holland, and Germany; and for persons with a strong desire to conceal their wealth from the tax authorities, easy enough to reach by boat, plane, or train from the rest of Europe. At one time, Luxembourg's steel mills were the source of its prosperity, but today the finance industry has made it one of the most comfortable places in the world for its citizens. Monaco is also comfortable, and the weather is incomparably better, but King Ranier and his advisors do not encourage the financial institutions of that realm to open their doors and hearts to day-tripping middle-class depositors from surrounding countries.

In the Bahamas and Cayman Islands, banks are not particularly interested in the custom of potential clients who do not have at least 2–3 million investible dollars, but even the conspicuously poor are given a warmer welcome in these and the other tax havens than the odd tax official who turns up on a study visit. Many tax avoiders are greatly pleased by the attitude of "offshore" bank officials who assure them and anyone else within earshot that paying taxes is a private matter, and should be left up to the conscience of the individual. Of course, the most important service provided tax avoiders has come from their own governments who have hurried to open physical and financial borders in order to facilitate the advent of the new "global" economy. At the present time, for example, it is possible to have a credit card drawn on a Luxembourg bank, and deposits and withdrawals can be made via the Internet. The most recent estimate is that several trillion dollars are laundered yearly via the Internet, although this is probably an exaggeration.

The Internet has also been of great help to the money launderers in Eastern Europe and their counterparts outside those countries, although there has been so much money to launder in Russia, that primitive laundering procedures could not handle the flow. Besides, in the Caribbean and Europe the point is to cheat the tax collectors, and not make life easy for the ladies and gentlemen engaged in financing the production and distribution of "controlled substances". In the Bahamas, for example, violence and other deviant behavior accompanying the widespread availability of drugs has posed a threat to the tourist industry.

The traditional methods for laundering money introduced many years ago in the US by persons associated with organized crime are now in full use elsewhere: establish a legal business; mix legal and illegal money; enter into an "understanding" with a local business that is heavily involved with payments and receipts abroad, and then transfer money out of the country through the bank employed by this business. The final rung on the ladder is expatriating this money for legal, semi-legal, or illegal transactions or acquisitions that — if possible — yield a stream of what appears to be legal income. It is also customary to attempt to move money through as many bank accounts and countries as possible, and enormously helpful if transfers involve terminals in a CHIPS or SWIFT interface system. (CHIPS stands for Clearing House for Interbank Payment Systems, and is located in New York. SWIFT is Society for Worldwide Intertelecommunications Financial Transfers.) The annual dollar volume now being handled is well in excess of 50 trillion dollars. Clearly, locating suspicious transactions in this astronomic cascade would not be easy.

Ostensibly, there is technology available that could balk money launderers, but the opinion here is that such things as smart cards — which electronically store cash — will prove to be too much for law enforcement officials and their naïve and self-important political superiors. In the US and many other countries, most office-seekers are just as keen as the most lethargic Bahamian banker to get through life without thinking about what kind of society a high level of money laundering will eventually create.

US congressional investigators have accused financial institutions in that country of having ignored their own procedures for suppressing money laundering, and as a result may have aided corruption "abroad". The private banking division of Citibank, in particular, has apparently come under suspicion of dealing with customers who are not honest. However in prepared testimony for a Senate hearing, Citigroup Co-chairman John Reed stated that computer systems for monitoring the transactions of wealthy international clients were being upgraded. In his carefully chosen words, Citibank is "doing the work and getting results".

An exact description of "lower level" money launderers seems to be missing from the learned literature of economics, but clearly there are a great many persons who are not fond of the idea of being caught in one of those great waves of irrationality that occasionally sweep over even well managed economies, such as Germany after the First World War. The great bull market of the 1990s has made a great many persons rich or half-rich, and they intend to remain that way, even when the bubble "pops", with who knows what macroeconomic consequences.

The craziest bubble of all times was tulip mania in Holland when, for no reason at all, tulip bulbs became wildly fashionable, and traded for fantastic prices. They became even more fashionable than Internet or "dot-com" shares are at the present time. Of course, technology shares of one description or another are and always have been destiny, although perhaps not to the extent as at present, where many people realize that with diminishing supplies of minerals, fossil fuels, and even such things as water and fresh air, science and technology will have to move at top speed. In the minds of many investors, that spells bull market.

Another famous bubble that is close to the one we lived through in the last part of the 1990s was the South Seas Bubble of 1720, where enterprises that would make everyone rich were never completely described. Simply "a venture that would bring you great riches" is how the TV adverts would have read if there had been TV at the time. Even Isaac Newton was caught in that one: "I can calculate the motion of heavenly bodies", he is supposed to have remarked, "but not the madness of people". Ironically, the South Seas referred to in that bubble is the one surrounding those West Indian islands where the laundering trade has been going full blast for several decades. (Newton was rated immediately after Einstein as the scientific star of the second millennium.)

For students of US banking, the following expressions might be useful. Shell Branches or Representative Offices are offices in obscure places (such as the Cayman Islands) for the purpose of particiating in various types of highly profitable foreign business. The big advantages of this arrangement is low taxes and minimal supervision by local authorities.

There are also Edge Act and Agreement Corporations. Edge corporations are chartered under Section 25a of the Federal Reserve Act, and they permit banks to conduct international business in the United States from offices outside their home states. For instance, a Los Angeles bank may open an edge subsidiary in Miami to facilitate access to Latin American business.

Finally, International Banking Facilities (IBFs) were authorized in 1981 by the Federal Reserve to provide a largely unregulated environment similar to the Euromarket. Deposits from foreigners have no reserve requirements or interest rate restrictions, and they are exempt from deposit insurance coverage. This is a highly competitive facility that enables domestic US banks to offer attractive loan rates to foreign businesses and institutions. A similar attitude accounts for the demise of the Glass-Steagall Act. The theory here is that unless US financial institutions are given the opportunity to practice the kind of universal banking that is common in much of the rest of the world, their relative competitiveness will suffer.

Exercises

1. Risk arbitrage on Wall Street sometimes means investment banks trading in the stocks of firms that are parties to prospective mergers. One of the things that could go wrong here is that the proposed deals cannot overcome the objections of federal antitrust lawyers. What does this mean?

2. Alan C. (Ace) Greenberg, the CEO of the investment bank Bear Stearns, once told a trader: "Bobby, you haven't lost enough money lately". What could he have meant? What do you think Mr Greenberg might have said if 'Bobby' told him that a man reputed to be the greatest brain of the 20th century, John von Neumann, said that the correct way to play a game is not to win, but to avoid losing?

3. The French government is a strong believer in things French. Why didn't they declare the French franc convertible shortly after World War II?

4. As we enter the 21st century, the investment bank Bear Stearns has a reported capital of $5 billion, and an average return on equity of 21%. Explain what capital and return means in this context!

5. What is convertibility, the WTO, the G7, CHIPS, the Marshall Plan, Gresham's law, arbitrage?

6. Why did British trade unions declare a huge strike because the UK government overvalued the pound?

7. The rapid clearing of e.g. interbank payments is vital for the efficient functioning of the international financial system. Discuss! Someone has calculated that the elasticity of consumption spending to net stock market wealth is about 0.05. Comment! In the US, household equity holdings as a percent of net wealth moved from about 15% in 1990 to about 25% in 2000. Comment!

Chapter 3

An Applicable Introduction to the Stock Market

Analyzing the stock market is a serious business that is often treated too superficially, or too esoterically, in the departments of economics and finance at many universities; however the position taken here is that there are certain things that everyone should know about this market, and can learn without a great deal of difficulty. Perhaps the first thing that the reader needs to brood over is whether the *efficient market hypothesis* (EMH) is relatively efficient — that is, relative to anything else that is being offered. What this hypothesis stresses is that past stock prices — however rich in patterns they appear to be, and regardless of the computing power that is available to exploit these patterns — have no more predictive power where future stock returns are concerned than the lines on your forehead or in the palm of your hand. Personally, I find the EMH attractive, although even if stock prices do follow a *random walk*, the pecuniary advantages of sound investment advice combined with a systematic study of the stock market by the individual investor can be substantial. Of course, systematic study is the key to mastering any subject, and the most important resources that anyone can bring to this endeavor are concentration and patience.

By almost the same token, what the EMH does *not* say is that investors' knowledge and experience enables them to determine the intrinsic (i.e. fundamental) value of a stock — at least in the short run. Why should it, when many shareholders are guided by hype and hope rather than a cold calculation of what the late Benjamin Graham — the guru of value investing — called "true value", even if the general investing public were passionately interested in making such a calculation. Graham's rather casual rule for "market timing" also deserves some attention: buy stocks when they are available for less than your most comfortable estimate of their intrinsic value, and begin to think about selling when they pass that juncture. Both Graham and certain interpretations of the EMH indicate that the broad direction of the market is usually impossible to ascertain, but there are fairly long periods when this is not a very profitable tenet to keep in mind.

Earlier in this book it was pointed out that history could be as important in economics and finance as mathematics, and that includes the kind of history found in assorted dossiers and gossip columns. Since the stockmarket meltdown of 1987, various high profile economists have been hard at work trying to find an alternative approach to explaining stock prices, but as the record shows, to absolutely no avail. Chaos theory was an important candidate at one time — as absurd as it sounds; and Robert J. Shiller of Yale University — a longtime adversary of the EMH — set out about 12 years ago to quantify something called "contagion theory", which in certain contexts can be thought of as mass irrationality. The last I heard, Professor Shiller was still on the quantification trail, and it is possible that he will still be there 12 years from now. Incidentally, Shiller's new book "Irrational Exuberance" (2000) is a must, and should be easy to read for readers of this book.

Most people know that stock markets became indispensible when the mechanization of production brought about a huge increase in the size and make-up of firms. These firms needed financial capital to purchase physical capital (i.e. machines and structures), and the modern joint stock company was the most efficient way to mobilize this money. Thus we had a transformation in the ownership structure from so-called private corporations, with single owners or a narrowly held ownership, to public corporations, which in the US means corporations with a broadly dispersed ownership. (In some countries a public corporation is one that is owned by government.)

As firms expand, new capital is raised by selling more equity, and/or borrowing from banks or issuing bonds. The question then comes up as to what is the optimal financial structure for a firm. Professor Merton H. Miller is probably the leading financial economist in the world today, and his answer to that question is that it does not make any difference what combination of shares and bonds are chosen. On the basis of his early research, he concluded that there was no meaningful relationship between financial structure and firm value: some firms were heavily leveraged, and others were lightly leveraged, but he was unable to determine how the debt-equity ratio affected market value. Professor Miller reaffirmed his position on this subject in the Nobel Prize lecture that he gave at Uppsala University, and apparently he has not changed his mind on the subject.

This is another famous result in economics — the Modigliani-Miller (MM) theorem — that is largely rejected in this book (just as it is rejected by many economists, although most of them prefer not to be identified). If a firm's debt-equity ratio is actually 20–80, then my assumption will be that this makes more sense than if this ratio were arbitrarily set at 80–20. Why is that? One reason is that the ladies and gentlemen in the financial districts are among the smartest in the world when working out the optimality of capital structures. They occasionally make embarassing mistakes, it is true, but dropping a few hundred million or so in the Russian casino is quite a bit different from concluding that a highly leveraged firm has as much chance of surviving a business cycle downturn as one carrying only a modest load of debt, as the officers of many firms became aware at the height of the leveraged buyout frenzy referred to in the first chapter. Of course, on the plane of theory, the MM theorem is an equilibrium result that assumes away such things as uncertainty, which may be the reason that Hal Varian (1993) said that MM was "right in principle, but the details were a little off". I think that it can be added to this evaluation that MM might be suitable in the seminar room, but it definitely is *persona non gratis* in the executive suites of those financial institutions where billion dollar financing decisions are routinely deliberated. It has also been argued by Graham (1999) that real world corporate tax structures are highly relevant to financing decisions, and he insinuates that in the US existing tax incentives favor debt.

In the year 2000, there were about 300 stock exchanges, derivatives exchanges, and electronic trading systems that act like markets, scattered around the world. Just as important, innovations in the form of on-line stock trading, the Internet, and inexpensive telecommunications were making it possible for anyone with a lap-top or access to a phone line to trade in most of these markets. The apparent ideal is one huge global stock market, a global bazaar, trading 24 hours a day. The technology that will make this possible should be available well before the New Year's Eve parties begin on December 31, 2099, but whether regulators and governments will be sympathetic to its utilization remains to be seen. A few of us hope that these regulators will be careful. Someday the Golden Triangle might replace the Chicago Board of Trade (CBOT) as home to the "cowboys of capitalism", and in a completely integrated financial market, it should be a simple matter for drug money from the "Triangle" or the Amazonian panhandle to purchase a large share of the legitimate industries in Scandinavia — assuming, of course, that there are any remaining to buy.

I. Random Walk versus Non-Random Walk

Paul Erdman is a successful novelist and a brilliant observer of the financial scene. Of course, like many of us, he is not always right — but then, who is these days.

In his short book "What's Next" (1987), Erdman states that bull (i.e. rising) markets have their origin in falling interest rates and/or rising profits, or "at least the prospect of rising profits". On the other hand, virtually every day it is possible to hear or read that the great bull market that began early in the 1990s is due to revolutionary technological changes, as manifested in such things as the Internet, "day-trading", and so on. Interest rates and expected profits are conspicuous by their absence, although clearly there is a tacit belief somewhere that this all-conquering technological change also influences profits and interest rates in the right direction, and will continue to do so indefinitely.

As they say on Wall Street, "No one person is bigger than the market," although probably a better saying would be, "The market knows", and one of the things that it knows perfectly is that actual or perhaps even expected interest rate rises, if they are large enough, will break any market upswing, regardless of how "wired up" a community may be.

Erdman offers some investment advice involving price-earnings ratios, book values, etc. that will be considered below in the context of a non-technical discussion; but before going to these subjects, an observation is in order. Most mainstream finance and economics books do not have much to say about stocks (i.e. shares), and so the reader who wants the best available insight into the stock market will turn as soon as possible to the latest edition of Burton Malkiel's "A Random Walk down Wall Street" (1985). This is a book that has everything! A book that may have too much is "A Non-Random Walk down Wall Street", by Andrew Lo and Craig MacKinlay, and so we might as well examine the difference between the approaches of these authors right now.

Malkiel more or less says that the average investor does not have a better chance to outperform most of the unmanaged index funds than a monkey throwing a football at a roster of shares clipped to a bulletin board. Ostensibly, there is some proof of this, but we will not bother with it, because he also says that well over half of all fund managers underperform indexes based on e.g. the "Dow" — i.e. the Dow Jones Industrial Averages based on 30 shares; or the "Footsie" (i.e. the Financial Times Ordinary Index); or the S&P (Standard and Poor's) 500; or any of the others, and even if they do outperform one or more of these indexes this year, it does not mean that they can do so next year. These allegations not only can be easily proved, but it is almost impossible to avoid the copious amount of evidence that such is the case.

Lo and MacKinlay, on the other hand, seem to think that somewhere out there is a model builder who can build a model that will inform Mr. and Ms. stock-picker of the best place to put their money. Admittedly, crunching stock prices, tick-by-tick, with a supercomputer that can can pick up such things as "momentum effects" and "non-chance relationships" might be worth a try, but this kind of attack has nothing to do with "models", as that word is commonly used in science. There is also the matter of the convergence of technologies. If someone were to develop equipment or techniques that could earn above-normal returns, this would be a signal to other persons and/or firms that above-normal returns were possible, and they should mobilize enough money and scientific talent to appropriate at least a part of those returns. Consequently, above-normal trading profits based on new innovations would be a transient phenomenon.

The paramount motif being ventilated here is technology, or better, "proprietary technology" — technology/software that nobody else has — which detects "market inefficiencies" that superstar quants exploit using

e.g. "statistical arbitrage". Whenever arbitrage situations are spotted —
e.g. shares of Volvo selling for $50 in New York, and $50.55 in Stockholm
— you buy in New York and sell in Stockholm, and you do so massively.
Massively in this context might mean utilizing existing lines of credit to
borrow a billion dollars or so overnight. Do such lines of credit exist? If
you have a firm like the New York investment bank D.E. Shaw, which
supposedly indulges in this kind of arbitrage all the time, and in addition
has a gross capital in the hundreds of millions, borrowing a billion dollars
overnight to arbitrage a non-volatile stock like Volvo is as easy as walking
down Park Avenue and cadging enough change to take the next A-train to
Harlem.

What about foreign exchange risk? Ostensibly, some other superstar
is standing by to lay on an optimal hedge using e.g. currency options.
According to Professor Lo, with these resources at your disposal, you might
be able to exploit miniscule market inefficiencies over a large enough
proportion of your wagers to come out ahead in the long run.

Something about this sounds incredibly naive, although it must be
emphasized that Lo and MacKinlay are not trying to run a game on their
audiences. They say straight out that if investors do not have any special
expertise or the time and money to hire or acquire the above mentioned
superstar quants and/or requisite technology, then they should not hesitate
to buy index funds. The position advanced here is that not only do at least
99.99% of all investors lack the necessary wherewithal, but the largest
financial institutions on Wall Street have also come up short in this respect,
and will undoubtedly continue to do so for a while.

There is more to the story. Although Malkiel says that I cannot do better
than an unmanaged index, nor can my financial advisor, he is not saying
that Warren Buffet or John Templeton or John Lynch lack what it takes to
bump heads with any index at any time, and come out on top. The reason
is that those gentleman bring something special to this business, just as Joe
Louis and Rocky Marciano had something special to offer their vocation.
By way of contrast, what the non-random walkers are promulgating is an
abstruse version of a Greater Fool theory such as the one discussed by
Malkiel, only the present rendition is intended to titillate the millions of

investors who are desperate to be put in touch with any radical notion on how to invest, regardless of how many times in the past their lurching after new ideas has had a negative impact on their net worth.

As a future Nobel laureate in finance, Eugene Fama puts it: "I'd compare stock pickers to astrologers, but I don't want to bad-mouth the astrologers". At the same time, however, Fama and his colleagues have shown that one of the reasons why Mr. Buffet has accumulated his billions is his involvement with "value stocks". The logic here is straightforward. Value stocks are e.g. "small company" and" out of favor" stocks. These are stocks with low prices, but a large upside potential. Their prices are low relative to potential gain because otherwise investors would not want to take the risks associated with owning them. The expression "small-cap" often turns up here, and applies to firms that are riskier than larger firms, and have a higher cost of capital — which means that, relatively, they acquire less (physical) capital.

Among the questionable ideas that have popped up in the last two decades, "portfolio insurance" and "day trading" deserve special attention. Anyone interested in the drawbacks of portfolio insurance has only to find out what happened to many insurers during the market crash of 1987. As for day trading, which turns on anticipating the likely move of a stock in the next few minutes or hours, the theory is that if customers have access to the latest technology, they will be able to trade like Wall Street professionals. Unless I am mistaken, however, most Wall Street professionals would hesitate to rush into an activity where the casualty rate is 80% or 90%, and this includes those who are partial to casino gambling. Furthermore, distractions of this nature have caused many investors to overlook promising new concepts like Standard and Poor's Depository Receipts (SPDRs), which is a hybrid of mutual funds and assets that track the S&P 500, and which deserve more attention than the space-age technology that will supposedly turn dilettantes into champion stock pickers. SPDRs have valuable tax advantages, but the real novelty is that they can be sold short. Thus, it is possible to bet on a falling market. (The mechanics of short selling will be taken up in the chapter dealing with futures markets.)

II. A Stock Market Fable

The first thing that will be done in this section is to reiterate that interest rates and profits (and profit expectations) are key items in judging the future of both individual stocks (i.e. shares), and the stock market viewed as an aggregate. Paul Erdman has listed some other rules that he wanted applied to the entire stock market. Remembering that by earnings we mean profits — the excess of sales over costs; while book value is what you would obtain if the enterprise was liquidated, with all assets sold and the money obtained from this sale distributed to owners, these rules are:

1. Buy when the price earnings (P/E) ratio is between 12 and 13.
2. Sell when it reaches 20.
3. Buy when yields on Blue Chip stocks are 4%.
4. Sell when these yields fall under 2%.
5. Buy when stocks sell for 1.25 times book value.
6. Sell when stocks are 2.5 times books value.

It hardly needs to be said, I hope, that the word "about" belongs in those injunctions. The great stock market crashes of 1929 and 1987 in the US took place with the P/E ratio of the market in the low 20s. An observation that applies here is that regardless of any conclusions as to the applicability or lack of applicability of the above rules to individual stocks, as compared with the market as a whole, when a stock market "implosion" begins, or even a sharp market correction, all shares are at risk. As Benjamin Graham noted in his book "The Intelligent Investor", "the market is fond of making mountains out of molehills, and exaggerating ordinary vicissitudes into major setbacks".

This is probably a good time to comment on the popularity of the P/E ratio. It tells how much is being paid for a dollar of the previous period (e.g. last year's) earnings, without regard to the price of the stock, or the size of the firm under consideration. Thus, firms can be compared with each other and with the market. It is often claimed that firms with high P/E ratios are expected to grow much faster than firms with low P/E ratios, ceteris paribus, but it happens to be true that some firms do not deserve a low P/E. These are the stocks to be on the look-out for.

Taking Erdman's rules 1 and 2 together, and applying them to individual stocks, they say that the market does not believe in stocks with a P/E < 12, while those in the 12–13 range are about to take off. Then why get rid of them when they reach 20? The logic here is that when the P/E reaches 20, then it might be true that too much is being paid for an uncertain dollar of future earnings. At the same time we need to understand that while a P/E of 20 is a signal to keep a wary eye on the market, it does not mean a great deal when analyzing firms like Microsoft and Nokia.

As for the price-to-book-value rules (No's 5 and 6), researchers like Eugene Fama and Kenneth French have shown that this ratio has more predictive power than any statistic for forecasting the upside potential of a stock: over the past 35 years, "low" price-to-book-value growth stocks have annually done better, on the average, than other stocks. Now for our fable.

Suppose that the well known Stockholm entrepreneur Sammy "Stagger-Lee" Svensson decides to start a large shoe-shine emporium on Malmskill-nadsgatan in Stockholm, in the heart of the business district. Why a shoe-shine emporium? First of all, Mr. Svensson knows that business persons like to keep their possessions in good trim; but more important, this will be a special kind of shoe-shine establishment. The employees will all be professional economists, and while they buff and spit-shine choice Gucci leather, they will give their banker and civil servant clientele top-drawer economic advice.

Let us also assume that this venture turns out to be a tremendous success. Mr. Svensson has patented his idea, and since he tied up the services of his employees with long-term, unbreakable contracts, he literally has a gold mine on his bejeweled hands. He also has ideas on how to expand his business. His empoyees will be taught to sing. They will sing their advice, and when they have something really good, sing and tap dance.

But Sammy Svensson needs capital for singing and dancing lessons — risk capital — since it is not certain that all his employees possess usable musical and rhythmic talents. He therefore decides to "go public", incorporating his shoe shine emporium as a joint stock company, with himself as as chief executive officer (CEO), and also a member of a distinguished board of directors. He issues 3,000 shares of common stock, and turns 2,500 shares over to an investment bank to price and sell. The investment bank purchases 1,000 themselves at a so-called *par value* of 150 crowns, and sells 1,500 to various investors. To their great delight, the stock is an immediate success. In fact, it is so attractive that the institutional investors that bought the 1,500 shares (at a price of 175) were soon able to obtain 300 crowns for them. Mr. Svensson was almost beside himself with joy as he watched the progress of the stock, which was soon quoted at 500 crowns/share. The 500 shares that Svensson kept for himself are now worth 250,000 crowns.

The position of the investment bank must now be made clear. They could have bought the 2,500 shares themselves at an agreed upon par value, and accepted the price risk that is involved in selling them to investors. This is called underwriting an issue, and the underwriter's fee is the difference between the price paid to the issuer and the price obtained by the investment bank from its customers. Or, as in the case being discussed here, the bank enters into a "best efforts arrangement", and does not buy the entire issue. For instance, they might buy only a fraction, and agree to use their best efforts to sell the remainder at a satisfactory price, for which they receive a fee. For very large deals, syndicates of underwriters are formed, with the lead underwriter "running the book" — i.e. managing the deal.

A digression is also in order on the mechanics of pricing this IPO (Initial Public Offering). The investment bank takes into deep consideration the product being offered, compares its prospects with that of existing and potential competitors, and examines the general market environment, while all the time mulling over the stock price of similar enterprises. It is probably optimal for the investment bank if they can sell a big block of the stock to a pension fund or some other type of institutional investor, and so a prospectus is written, and as part of a "roadshow" a presentation might be made to potential buyers. Quite naturally, this is followed by an expensive dinner, and after the cognac bottle has gone around the table a few times, a price might be floated by the bankers in order to get a reaction.

Suppose that, as noted above, the (*retail*) price at which the shares were launched was 175, and very shortly afterward they were selling for 300. (Remember, the investment bank paid only 150 for 1,000!) Assuming that the bankers held only a few of the shares they obtained, but tried to sell almost the 2,500 shares they came into possession of to pension funds, insurance companies, brokers, etc., how could they have been so wrong about the initial demand for these equities? Isn't this example unrealistic?

It is not unrealistic at all. In the US, and perhaps elsewhere, IPOs are apparently subject to bids from the Internet, and so anything can happen, especially when the IPO involves something that tickles the fancy of a large number of investors. (Dot-Com firms are a good example here.) Also, in our present example, as in real life, investment banks aim to price the stock high enough to obtain the resources that Mr. Svensson requires to obtain the best singing and dancing lessons available, but at the same time low enough so that if their institutional clients take a nice helping, they will experience the thrill of having their shares escalate in price on the first day of trading — which puts them in the mood for buying another big block at a later date. In December 1999, there were more than 50 IPOs, with an average first day gain of nearly 100%. Naturally, ordinary investors will hardly get a crack at a first-day runup without enjoying a snug relationship with a bank or broker.

In some cases, an investment bank might take the initiative in getting a firm to issue securities (or initiate a merger) because of the favorable outlook that they envisage resulting from competitive bidding for these securities by other financial organizations. It sometimes happens that they "presell" the securities to various clients. This is usually called a "bought deal", but the expression "block deal" is useful, since an attempt could be made to get rid of the entire offering at one price. Bought deals usually apply to bonds. IPOs are the most lucrative kind of underwriting and sometimes provide investment banks with as much as 7% of the money raised. The first quarter of 2000 saw the total number of bond and stock offerings in US markets fall to 3,823 from the second quarter high in 1999 of 5,047. Disclosed fees fell to $264 billion from $4.8 billion in the first quarter of 2000. Merrill Lynch was the champion in the second quarter of 2000, followed by Solomon Smith Barney, but Goldman Sachs remained the leading underwriter of IPOs and all issues of common stock.

The good Mr. Sammy Svensson is now a man of substance, and a pillar of Stockholm society. To show his profound gratitude to the citizens who gave him his start, he decides to set up a scholarship fund at the Stockholm

College of Economic Knowledge that is designed to increase the intellectual capital of the unlucky private entrepreneurs on Malmskillnadsgatan who do not enjoy formal training in abstract economic theory. Mr. Svensson is very sensitive on this point, because of the glaring deficiencies in his own economics training; and his situation was not improved when one of the many economics experts at the Stockholm College happened to walk by, and in a belligerent tone of voice, completely without provocation, began to harshly impugn the capital structure of Svensson's firm. According to that gentleman, Mr. Svensson should have issued some preferred stock. These are his unsolicited observations about that kind of security.

Preferred stock is a debt of the company in the same way as bonds, except that the claims of preferred stock holders come after those of bond holders in case the firm must be liquidated. Preferred stock owners also receive, with some certainty, a fixed dividend every year, as compared to the dividends of common stock holders, which is decided on a year-to-year basis by the board of directors. Furthermore, preferred stock is sometimes "convertible", and can be converted to common stock at a fixed "exchange rate". Very often preferred stock is callable, in which case the firm had the option to buy it back should that seem financially advantageous.

Our learned friend moved closer to Sammy Svensson. There was a maniacal light in his eyes as he continued his harangue. First he pointed out that an owner of non-convertible preferred stock is a creditor of a firm, while an owner of convertible preferred stock is generally classified as an owner of the firm. Then he told Herr Svensson that convertible bonds — which in some circumstances could be exchanged for common stock — had become a popular asset in the US. In addition, convertible bonds — like convertible preferred stock — often sold at a premium, since if the common stock of a firm rises rapidly in value, large profits could be made from a conversion. (In the UK, preferred stock = preference shares.)

The scholar paused for a moment to clear his throat, and in those few seconds Sammy Svensson pressed a five-crown coin into the man's hand and disappeared into the crowd that had formed. Director Svensson had suddenly realized that while technology and telecommunications were today's stocks, things like health care (for the elderly), and the knowledge business (for the young and the not so young) were tomorrow's, and he intended to get a bigger piece of the latter starting immediately.

We can now scrutinize some of the financial details of Mr. Svensson's enterprise. The first thing to note is that the forming of a corporation (i.e. a joint stock company) was a natural step. Corporations are the dominant business form in most capitalist industrial countries. The present fable gives one of the reasons for this state of affairs. When Mr. Svensson incorporated his business, he was able to realize a sizable profit on the shares that he had prudently kept in his possession. What happened was that investors recognized the potential worth of the firm, and displayed their faith in its future by bidding up the price of its stock. What they were saying was that over the indefinite future, dividends and capital gains on the shares that they acquired should more than justify the price that they had to pay for the shares.

Note something else here. Those future payments are *discounted* in that even certain future money is (subjectively) regarded as being worth less than money that you have access to with certainty at the present time. This makes sense, of course. A hundred dollars received in one year (with certainty) is worth less than $100 in your possession today, because you may not be in position to enjoy this money in a year's time. You may, for instance, be a guest at Devil's Island. What about when uncertainty enters the picture? Then the discount factor must be larger, because in those circumstances, even the future amount is doubtful, in addition to your capacity to enjoy it. In the first case considered here, you might regard receipt of a certain $110 one year in the future to be adequate compensation for giving up $100 of consumption today. With uncertainty, however, you might reason that you would only give up $100 of consumption today if you believe that there is a decent chance of obtaining $115 in a year.

Put in somewhat more technical terms, the reasoning above turns on most individuals having a positive rate of time preference: they place a higher value (or utility) on income received this year than the same amount received next year, and a higher value on that received next year than that received the year after next, etc.

Now, remembering our discussion in the first chapter of the difference between real and nominal (or money) entities, we can write an expression for the rate of return on a share. This is:

Real rate of return = Nominal rate of return − Inflation rate

The inflation rate will be written $\Delta P/P$: if the inflation is 5%/year, then $\Delta p/p = 5\% = 0.05$. Continuing, we can write for the real rate of return (R_r):

$$R_r = \frac{\text{Dividend} + \text{Capital(gain)}}{\text{Share(purchase) price}} - \frac{\Delta P}{P}$$

An example might be useful here. Suppose that you bought a share for $100, and at the end of the period (e.g. year) its price was $108, while a dividend of $2 was declared. In addition, during that period, inflation was 3%. The real rate of return R_r was thus $[(2 + 8)/100] − 0.03 = 0.10 − 0.03 = 0.07 = 7\%$. Of course, we could work exclusively with percentages. On a base of $100, the dividend was 2%; the capital gain was 8%; and the inflation was 3%. The real return was thus $2 + 8 − 3 = 7\%$. In looking at this number I am reminded that, according to Thomas Easton (1999), the inflation adjusted return on US stocks over most of the 20th century was 7%, with less than half of that resulting from capital gains.

The previous discussion about discounting is important, but its elaboration involves algebra that is best presented later. Something that should be pointed out immediately, however, is that the algebra of discounting is not difficult at all, but the usefulness of discounting techniques has been brought into question. The present US Secretary of the Treasury, Professor Lawrence Summers, once presented some evidence that casts a great deal of doubt on the manner in which conventional discounting methods were being used to determine the viability of capital investment projects. Other scholars have since used Summers' research as a springboard to plump for the use of *real options theory*. This topic is discussed in my energy economics textbook (2000), and does not need to be considered here; however it should be emphasized that the prominence of subjective probabilities in real options theory does not make it the super-efficient tool

ASSETS	LIABILITIES
Current: Cash in bank 125,000	Current: Accounts payable (mostly for shoe polish and tap dancing lessons) 25,000
	Long-term debt: 250,000
	<u>EQUITY</u>
Long-term: Plant and equipment 650,000	Common stock: 450,000:-
	Capital surplus and retained
	Earnings, etc. 50,000

that some scholars believe it to be. There are situations in which it can contribute to our knowledge, and there are others in which it is mostly "window dressing". Now we can examine the balance sheet of Svensson's Shoe-Shine and Economic Prognostications Emporium for 1 January, 2000.

The assets entries in the above balance sheet should be largely self explanatory. For example, plant and equipment consists of the emporium itself, shoe-shine and music stands, etc., and has a current value of 650,000 Swedish crowns. The liabilities also need only a small amount of clarification. Mr. Svensson borrowed 250,000 crowns on his personal I.O.U. to start the business, and he has chosen — for tax and other reasons — not to provide any detailed discussion of this transaction on the balance sheet. In reality, however, he pays approximately 50,000 crowns/year in interest.

The most interesting items for our purposes are under "equity", where as always equity is defined as assets minus liabilities. Total equity is the net (book) value of ownership in the event of liquidation, and in this example is 500,000 crowns. Please note, however, that the stock market value — i.e. the *capitalization* — of the firm is $500 \times 3,000 = 1,500,000$ crowns, and is not only larger than the book value of equity, but also the assets. Capitalization also has an important macroeconomic side that is seldom noticed: the *wealth effect*. In the US, the ratio of stock market capitalization to gross domestic product at the beginning of the 21st century was almost 170%, while in 1997 it was about 100%, and in 1991 it was only about 30%. Consequently, a large move in the stock market can have a huge impact on the real economy, in that it could cause an exceptionally large shift in the consumption function.

When the common stock was issued, it was given a par value of 150 crowns/share. The issued value of the common stock is thus shown as 450,000 crowns, which is a figure of little or no significance, and whose principal function here is merely to serve as a balancing item. Instead, with no preferred stock outstanding, stockholders' equity (i.e. ownership) of 500,000 crowns is the book value or net worth of the firm. The equity per share, which is usually called the book value per share, is 500,000/3,000 = 166.7 crowns/share, but this is clearly of little significance, given that shares are selling for 500 crowns each. This is "supposed" to mean that, right or wrong, shareholders expect each share to realize a stream of net earning with a discounted value of about 500 crowns/share.

The ratio of share price to book value is 500/166.7 = 3.00. Some observers would say that this has no significance, while others would say that it is highly significant. Some of those who feel that it is significant might e.g. say that when the price of a stock is 1.25 times the book value, or thereabout, then it is time to think about buying; and when it is 2.50 times its book value, then it could be time to think about selling. But an important piece of the puzzle is missing, the P/E ratio, and we definitely need to take a look at this before doing anything rash. As mentioned earlier, the prospects for this corporation appear so bright that the price of the stock escalates, and quickly began selling for 25 times earnings. The earnings are not given in the above balance sheet, but they consist of the revenues of the firm, minus all costs — to include taxes and interest; and when these are divided by the outstanding shares of common stock, we get the earnings per share (EPS).

In an unstable or uncertain market, when many observers have started to claim that the market is still in the the bull phase of what has actually become a "bear" market, then the above figures might mean that it is time to dump the still high flying shares in Mr. Svensson's enterprise: to initiate a "flight to quality", where quality usually means the bluest of blue chip shares, or perhaps bonds. However if Svensson is a real winner, then e.g. a P/E of 25 is quite modest. Really successful start-up firms at the cutting edge of new technology, have routinely sold for P/Es that were well over 35. The trick for the investor is to go with the flow, but as a corollary of this logic to remember that timing the right moment to get out of a share is almost as important as choosing the right share to buy. Of course, "timing" might be the wrong word, since it suggests a precision that is seldom if ever encountered in the real world.

A majority of professionals appear convinced that when P/E multiples reach the mid-twenties, or thereabouts, a "correction" is likely. In other words, P/E ratios generally exhibit *mean-reversion*, in that they eventually revert to their long-term average, which for most firms is less than 20. At the same time they have had a problem interpreting the two-tier market that emerged in the US in the 1990s. At the turn of the century technology stocks sold for 37 times earnings, and the rest of the market for 17 times. There was also this matter of technology stocks (plus telecommunications) being 30% of the market, and dominating the indexes.

A number of interviews with the more successful and prominent "market wizards" are presented in an extremely valuable book by Jack D. Schwager (1989). One of these gentlemen, Michael Marcus, suggests that there are three things to look at when contemplating equities: the "charts", showing price movements, but interpreted in a special way; supply and demand (i.e. the fundamentals); and market tone: the tone of the market should be such that it responds vigorously to bullish news, and shrugs off bearish news. The thing to note here is that Marcus does not deny the validity of the EMH, and its (perhaps implicit) assumption that only the emergence of a new piece of information that can be exploited before the rest of the market reacts will enable you to make money, but even so he feels that certain types of movements in past prices might be highly significant.

By the same token, another of Schwager's wizards, the highly successful trader Bruce Kovner, says that technical analysis reflects the vote of the entire marketplace, and thus a new chart pattern can indicate a change in the market's attitude that might be worth studying in detail. Although I consider myself a whole-hearted adherent of the EMH, I think that it might be wise to keep an open mind on this subject, because at some point in the future the computing power available to exceptionally competent chartists might be powerful enough to make at least some of their claims come true.

Many students of the stock market are as interested in earnings per share (EPS) and, more important, EPS growth as they are interested in the P/E ratio. Even more important might be a ranking derived from the EPS growth for a particular stock relative to the EPS growth of other shares selected individually, or in groups, or for that matter those shares that can be considered as "almost" representing the entire market (e.g. the 30 industrials used to calculate the Dow Jones). According to Marcus, a high EPS is not as significant as a growing EPS. Best of all he prefers a share with a high EPS growth, but a low P/E. This indicates that the firm has not yet filled its "niche". This sounds good, but since you would have to be considerably more than a wizard to get an accurate estimate of the growth of the EPS over the next four or five years, some heroic — and perhaps questionable — extrapolation might be necessary.

Stanley Block (1999) has polled a large sample of investment professionals as to what they consider to be the most important factors when valuing a security. A firm's growth potential, and the "quality" of its earnings were given as the most important. (By quality he almost certainly means consistency.) Dividends did not seem to be important at all, which is quite understandable given the shortness of memories, and since in the late 1990s capital gains of 15–20%/year were far from rare; but when investors' returns are viewed over a long time period, dividends were as important as capital gains.

Something else that needs to be emphasized here is that the winners interviewed by Schwager, and for that matter any seasoned market professional, will sell a share as fast as they will buy one, which is something that the rest of us are often reluctant to do. They also know how to get out of one market when the vibrations turn bad, and search for individual stocks or funds in another — perhaps on the other side of the world — where buying power, and the attitude of the international investing community, indicates that a lift-off is imminent.

The P/E ratio, when inverted, gives the *earnings yield*. At the beginning of the 21st century, the Wall Street (real) aggregate earnings yield was

3%; however a perfectly safe (index-linked) government bond would have paid at least 4%. This suggests to some — but not all — observers that equities were over-valued. Not all earnings are distributed, which causes some analysts to prefer *dividend yield*; however undistributed earnings are reinvested, which causes the firm to grow, which in turn increases its value, and thus contributes to a higher share price. The earnings yield, properly analyzed, deserves all the attention it receives.

The average P/E ratio for the S&P 500 for 1950–1999 was 15, which entails an earnings yield of almost 7%, which is about the average yield on US equity over the past 200 years. With this P/E ratio almost 33 in January of 2000, it seemed reasonable to suggest that the US market was overvalued, even though it is true that lower interest rates, faster earnings growth, financial innovations, and higher investor morale (which, among other things, helps to lower risk premiums) "might" justify a higher P/E ratio than warranted by historical trends.

III. The Stock Market in a Larger Perspective

Now let us leave the exciting world of Mr. Sammy Svensson, and turn to what might be called a macroscopic view of the stock market. The stock market is often refered to as "The Market", and is the most widely followed of all financial markets, even though bond markets are usually much larger. According to Julian Walmsley (1991), equity markets go back to at least 1555, and the Muscovy Company, while the earliest known bond was issued by the Bank of Venice in 1157.

Academic macroeconomics has very little to say about the stock market, although plenty to say about bonds, as can be confirmed by examining almost any mainstream textbook. Still, it makes sense to suspect that policies or circumstances that cause investors to demand more bonds — such as an increase in the money supply — would also lead them to desire more stocks, especially when the real interest rate is almost zero. It appears that prior to the stock market collapse in 1987, there was a large decline in monetary growth in the US; while in Japan continued strong monetary growth caused the losses resulting from the crash to be eradicated in a short time.

It also seems possible that investment spending can be influenced by changes in stock prices, although the relationship here is probably far from simple. It has been postulated though that if the value of a firm's shares rises relative to the price of new plant and equipment, then the firm will be tempted to issue more shares in order to finance new investment, especially if only a small increase in outstanding shares will result in obtaining enough cash to buy a large amount of land, capital, and structures. This, in fact, is the basis of Professor James Tobin's "q" theory, where q is defined as:

$$q = \frac{\text{Market value of firm}}{\text{Replacement cost of capital}}$$

If q is high, the theory maintains that firms will have a high demand for capital goods: when the stock market price is high relative to the cost of new capital, the market is supposedly giving a signal that it is time to start increasing the quantity of a firm's physical capital. Sachs and Larraine (1993) offer a more intuitive interpretation: when q is greater than unity, the share price is greater than the cost of physical capital, and thus a firm could issue shares, undertake investment, and still have money left over to distribute to the shareholders. Professor Dale Jorgenson once gave a lecture at Uppsala University in which he pointed out that there were long periods in which Tobin's "q" theory did not function well at all. On the other hand, this theory can probably explain some of the over-investment that took place in Asia prior to the "Asian Crisis" of 1997–1999. The bull stock market of the 1990s undoubtedly made it very tempting to expand investment in consumer goods industries, since not only did high stock prices provide money for investment, but also contributed to the high demand for consumer goods. (In the US, Tobin's q rose by 75% between 1992 and 1998, to reach its highest value since World War II.)

Some readers may be wondering why any attention at all is being paid the "q" theory. One answer is that the market value of a firm's shares is assumed by this theory to be a good estimate of the present (discounted) value of future earnings that can be imputed to the firm's possession of physical capital. This leads to a hypothesis about the role of the stock market in the economy. If there is a fall in stock prices, and little or no change in the replacement cost of capital (which is likely), then q will fall. This fall reflects investors' pessimism about the profitability of capital, which in turn will lead to a decline in the demand for capital (i.e. investment goods), and going one step further, a downturn in the macroeconomy. The conclusion that immediately follows is that fluctuations in the stock market can be associated with fluctuations in output and employment.

This logic did not seem to work particularly well during the large oil price increases of 1974 and 1979, when q fell heavily, but aggregate investment increased in, e.g., the US. One explanation offered here was that these energy price rises greatly reduced the expected earnings on existing, energy intensive capital, but not necessarily on new (less energy intensive) capital.

During the bull markets of the 1990s, the run-up of various stock market indices has been phenomenal. For instance, virtually no serious analyst was prepared to forecast a Dow Jones of 11,000 before the end of the 20th century; but in 1999, with the Dow Jones nudging 11,000, there were serious and highly visible observers who were telling the television audience that a Dow Jones of between 30,000 and 40,000 was not only possible but likely, and soon. The basis for this claim seemed to be an unlimited belief in technology.

The radio and telvision audience has been told this sort of thing before, and inevitably they have believed it. This may not be a bad thing, however, because at least two very nasty prospects await them in the 21st century, although hopefully later rather than sooner: the energy supply situation could suddenly worsen, in that the price of energy could escalate as fossil fuels – and especially oil — are depleted; and the world population should approach, and perhaps exceed the nine or ten billion mark. Since it required less than 40 years for global population to double (from three billion to six billion), the supposition that world population will stabilize before nine billion hardly deserves to be called preposterous. The question that has to be asked here is not the ultimate height of the Dow Jones or the "Dax" or the "Footsie", but what form will financial markets eventually take in the face of these challenges — challenges that many of our political leaders neither understand nor desire to understand. (Note: a *prospect* is an outcome with a probability attached. For instance, an undesirable rate of global warming is an outcome, and according to a majority of the living Nobel Prize laureates in science, there is definitely a non-zero probability that it exists.)

It is now occasionally claimed that the 1929 and 1987 stock market crashes, as well as the Asian Crisis of the late 1990s, will turn out to be no more than "blips" in the macroeconomic history of mankind; but although this is probably true, they resulted in a great deal of excitement while they were taking place, and they undoubtedly changed the lives of hundreds of millions of people — often for the worst. The recent Asian Crisis cannot be commented on at great length in this book, but it might be appropriate at this point to augment the short discussion of stock market history presented in the previous chapter, starting from the end of the first world war, to the denouement of the 1987 meltdown. (The expression "meltdown" comes from (nuclear) reactor physics, and refers to the worst possible nuclear accident.) I would like to recommend that everyone should read this "history", because it is almost certain to be repeated in one form or another, and probably more than once.

IV. Why Monday, October 19, Was Black Instead of Green

London was the financial center of the world prior to 1914, and with the end of the war — in November 1918 — there were high hopes that it could regain its pre-war eminence. In 1919, there were major new share issues covering such key industries as steel, coal mines, textiles, and automobiles, and the general feeling was that four years of a war featuring some revolutionary technological advances had created a situation favoring rapid economic growth and development.

As it happened, however, the international economy ran into trouble right away. The London equity market fell by a third between 1920 and 1921, while in the US the Dow Jones dropped about a half, after reaching its all-time high of 120 in November, 1919. One of the big problems was hyper-inflation in Germany, whose recovery was expected to provide a "motor" for the recovery of the rest of Europe. (This inflation also bankrupted a sizable fraction of the middle class in Germany, which eventually turned out to be a political as well as an economic disaster.)

In 1924, however, Germany had started on the road to economic recovery, and world stock markets were booming. There was a serious recoil in both London and New York due to the General Strike of 1926 in the UK, but when it became clear that the workers were on the losing side, equity markets advanced at a record pace. (The same kind of thing has recently taken place in the US, where the stagnation of real wages can be taken as an important explanatory factor of the bull market of the 1990s.) In addition, in the US and UK the buying of speculative shares on margin (i.e. credit) became a kind of fad. But then, in the UK, a prominent stock market speculator with grandiose ideas — but limited financial resources — became involved in some suspicious activities which were eventually brought to the attention of the police. On September 20, 1929, Mr. Clarence Hatry was arrested, and almost immediately share prices on the nervous London exchange began to slide. On Wall Street — where the Dow Jones had climbed from 90 (in 1924) to 381 (at the beginning of September, 1929) — prices also began to waver, and in a situation in which creditors stopped lending, and wanted to be paid, while debtors switched from aggressive buying to aggressive selling, the market stalled, and then lost all upward momentum. On Tuesday, October 29, panic replaced nervousness, and the market crashed. Contrary to the line in the magnificent song "The Man I Love", Tuesday was nobody's good-news day.

Another catastrophe took place in 1931, when the Austrian bank, Kreditanstalt, was forced to close its doors. Kreditanstalt was not a particularly large bank, but it was a member of the Rothschild "chain", and as a result depositors, creditors, and borrowers all over the world, and particularly in the US, began to wonder about the security of their savings and/or the kind of world they were living in. In the local panics and "runs" that followed, there were thousands of bank failures and other disagreeable events.

The great depression was now a fact. One of the things helping to make it "great", and a depression instead of a recession, was the Hawley-Smoot tariff in the US, which eliminated the possibility of a rapid world economic recovery based on the latent economic power of the American market. (Again we can point to the bull market of the 1990s. This episode was greatly aided by an abnormally high consumption in the US that was accompanied by a record US domestic and international indebtedness.) When the UK left the gold standard in 1931, it completely eroded British confidence in a rapid recovery, and this pessimism took hold in London financial circles. Both the UK Actuaries Index (phased out in 1962), and the Dow Jones index plunged, with the latter bottoming out at a traumatic 41. Although industrial recovery in the US and UK accelerated when it became clear that Hitler meant business, the general unease of that era was reflected by declining stock market indices over the entire world. (The 1929 level of industrial production was regained in 1934 in Britain, 1936 in Germany, and 1937 in the US.)

During and immediately after World War II, the Dow Jones and other indexes climbed slowly until the beginning of the war in Korea. That war initiated the so-called "Korea Boom", which featured high commodity prices and high prosperity in a number of countries, and because of the political climate created by the war, accelerated the industrial reconstruction of Italy, Germany, and Japan. Stock markets climbed rapidly at the beginning of the war, although declining after the war was over; but in a few years the non-communist industrial world was in full expansion, and a powerful upward trend initiated in stock markets that lasted into the 1970s, despite occasional downturns. Several of these downturns were related to balance of payments crises, which often caused governments to raise interest rates in an attempt to maintain the values of their currencies. (By raising interest rates, it increased the demand for their currencies by foreigners who found their bonds and bank accounts more attractive. Ceteris paribus, the increased demand resulted in a stronger exchange rate.) As to be expected, higher interest rates had several bad consequences for share markets. They encouraged a shift to bonds; and since higher interest rates could reduce investment (in plant and equipment), this would eventually impact on competitiveness, and thus profits. Looked at over a somewhat longer time horizon, this could contribute to a very unhealthy climate for the financial market.

The pronounced bear market of 1974 was almost certainly the result of the first oil price shock, and throughout the 1970s the spectre of an out-of-control oil price kept all security markets on edge. The *Financial Times'*

Ordinary Share Index fell from a peak in 1972, to 146 in the first week of January, 1975; while the Dow Jones lost 45% between 1972 and 1974. Real equity and bond yields during this period tended to be low because of the high rate of inflation, although the introduction of monetarism by the Carter government in the US drove interest rates up. Later, with the government of Ronald Reagan administering more of the same medicine to the US economy, and in addition incurring huge budget deficits that pushed up interest rates all over the world, the share markets were often presented as a lost cause — exactly the opposite of the position taken during most of the 1990s. But in September, 1982, the monetarist experiment came to an end; and what happened immediately after left shareholders with little time to dwell on past history. The great bull market of the 80s made its entrance.

Before examining the dramatic end of that event, something needs to be said about the part played by oil in the world macroeconomy. In a valuable short piece in the *Financial Times* (Friday, September 10, 1999), Professor Andrew Oswald points out that it is (a decline in the price of) black gold, and not a golden age, that has been responsible for the macroeconomic upswing of the 1990s, particularly in the US. Furthermore, what he says about employment and unemployment can be immediately applied to the security markets.

"There have been two famous upward oil shocks in the postwar period: in 1973–1974 and at the end of the 1970s. Each move up in energy prices was followed by a slump — and a sharp and then sustained rise in global unemployment". He also says that this applies to the "mystery recession" of 1991. What's next? Oswald says that the rise in oil prices during 1999 from $11 to $25 will be passed on in such a manner as to feed into the prices of goods and services. If this turns out to be the case, then we should expect a rise in interest rates, and a downward pressure on share prices. Of course, the changes in output and employment (and/or output and employment growth) that Oswald predicts could moderate demand, and thus in theory attenuate the aggregate price rise refered to above, but in today's global economy it might not be a good idea to take this for granted.

The crash of 1987 abruptly interrupted the honeymoon that began for many investors, traders, brokers, and investment bankers in the autumn of

1982. In the US, in the nine months between September 1982 and June 1983, the Dow Jones rose by 54%. Over the same period the Tokyo market climbed by 22%, the London market by 30%, and the Stockholm market by 125%. As pointed out by Paul Erdman, in the beginning, every 1% decrease in the interest rate (e.g. from 10% to 9.9%) produced a 50–75 point increase in the Dow Jones. Later on, as interest rates "stabilized" (in the sense that they stopped ratcheting downward), the market kept rising, literally defying the law of gravity. What had happened, as happened in the following decade, was that a large part of the investing public had come to believe in an unending bull market. Most of the professionals knew that this was foolishness, but even so a surprisingly large number of them elected to practice a particularly dangerous variety of brinkmanship — particularly after many of them convinced themselves, and incorrectly as it turned out, that financial assets could be adequately hedged with space age innovations such as "portfolio insurance". When the day of reckoning finally arrived, the Dow Jones had passed 2,700, having started five years earlier at 777. On October 19–20 it lost 508 points, and in one stroke wiped out about $500 billion of investor wealth in the United States.

Although futures and options trading has been accused by the Brady Commission (in the US) of being a major cause of the damage done on Black Monday, the opinion of this teacher of economics and finance is that they were less to blame than the accelerated globalization of world financial markets. For example, equities markets now span the major time zones, which means that local stockbrokers have become multinational traders, with virtually an unlimited capacity to move from one reagional market to another during a 24-hour period. In 1960, Wall Street firms that wanted to trade on overseas markets were blocked by massive paperwork, language problems, and regulations of various kind. Now, however, there is a world market that is largely independent of local regulations and legislation. Accordingly, when New York is hit by a wave of selling, orders can be immediately passed to London, Tokyo, etc where many of the same stocks found on the New York exchange are being traded. This globalization is facilitated by advances in computer technology, which increases both turnover and volatility. In fact, had this technology been available and operating at full efficiency in 1987, then it is likely that President Reagan's intention to keep the New York exchange open could not have been honored. As it was, the Chicago Mercantile Exchange had to suspend trading.

Similarly, with the International Stock Exchange in London, the increased capacity built into the system speeded up selling, and the only thing that slowed it down was the fact that many brokers and traders refused to answer their telephones, and this prevented many investors from selling. However, present developments — involving technology and the Internet — should eventually make both selling and buying automatic after the right buttons are pushed or computer keys are pressed, with trades based on the most favorable price quotations. In certain situations this could bring about market crashes that are much worse than those of 1929 and 1987. In fact, many observers believe that only good luck prevented a complete "wipe-out" in London on October 19.

V. Past the Brink and Heading South

After the next chapter, it will be necessary to reduce the emphasis on recapitulation and its interpretation, and turn to algebra, but even so there are a number of points remaining to be made in our discussion of the 1987 crash that are just as important as this algebra. For example, you need to know more about the EMH, and also to understand certain things about noise trading, fads, and bubbles. The EMH appears at the end of this section, while the other three topics are taken up in the next section.

It might be useful at this point to observe the relationship of stock market prices to the US balance of trade. When trade figures were better than expected, stock prices have shown a tendency to rise; and when they were worse than expected, they have shown a tendency to fall. This pattern was unambiguous throughout the first part of 1987, and what it reflected was a fear of a continued fall in the value of the dollar: should this fear become widespread, it could lead to a retreat of foreign money from US security markets. Put more directly, had the suspicion been aroused in Japan and West Europe that the dollar was going to be allowed to find its equilibrium value, which was a value capable of making a durable reduction in the US trade deficit, it might have prompted an *en masse* sale of US equities. As things turned out, the tension caused by the belief that the dollar would need to fall below the minimum level agreed on by the signatories of the "Louvre Accord" impacted first on the bond markets, where yields began to rise sharply as demand was withdrawn from this market — i.e. bond sellers had to offer higher interest rates in order to sell their securities. (The Louvre Accord was preceded by the "Plaza Agreement" — named after the Plaza Hotel in Washington DC — which was an agreement on currencies made by the finance ministers of the Group of Five (G-5). The point of both of these was to take measures to change the value of the dollar.)

Readers should also discern that movements in the exchange rate can reflect on the price level. If a currency depreciates, then (ceteris paribus) the rise in the price of imports can raise the domestic price level. (For example, if Swedish currency falls in value relative to dollars, then oil — which is priced in dollars — will cost more in term of crowns. The increase in the price of such things as motor fuel and heating oil could then result in a rise of the domestic price level.)

Before taking another look at the EMH, a short summary of the situation in the US is in order. The "crash" began on the morning of the 19th, and by midday of the 20th, the New York stock exchange was within minutes of having to close. The Chicago Mercantile Exchange had stopped trading at 12:15 (Chicago time), and many observers expressed the belief that had the New York exchange closed its doors, the capitalist system would have been shaken to its foundations — which is probably completely wrong. Central banks the world over had long been pondering the effects of a large scale default on Third World debt, and were prepared — on short notice — to provide the liquidity that brokers and banks might need. More important, shortly after they returned from lunch on the 20th, the managers of many institutional funds were hunting bargains in a greatly depressed market where all talk of over-valued equities had ceased, at least temporarily.

But if equities were no longer over-valued, what about certain economic theories? According to a member of the Brady Commission — the presidential "task force" that studied and made a report on the crash — the events of October 19–20 struck a powerful — and perhaps fatal — blow against the "so-called theory of efficient markets". *Business Week* (February 22, 1988) was even more explicit: "Efficient market theory is useless in explaining the biggest stock market calamity in 58 years. What new information jarred investors into slashing their estimate of the value of Corporate America's assets by some 23% in the six and one-half hours the New York Stock Exchange was open"?

There are a number of possibilities here. For instance, on Black Monday, or the days just before, a few players who were aware that the market had been sliding for a week, suddenly discerned the shortcomings of the portfolio insurance concept, and achieved instant wealth by selling heavily into a weak futures market. (This very simple operation will be explained in the next chapter, but it is analogous to the operation carried out by Eddie Murphy and Dan Ackroyd in the film "Trading Places": first you sell futures, and later you buy them back at a lower price.) However, even had many traders discovered this situation, after only a comparatively small number of them began to sell, futures markets prices could have fallen to a point where "balance" was restored, and thus many traders who were waiting in line to sell, changed their minds and decided to become buyers. This is one of the reasons why the EMH makes sense, at least up to now. Regardless of the sophistication of the available technology, most investors will always be too late to take advantage of new information. There in simply no "room" in real world markets for more than a few big winners on these occasions.

This also applied to the market for individual shares. A sharp decline in futures prices at one stage was interpreted by some investors as signalling the forthcoming decline in the price of "actuals", and as a result an aggressive selling of stocks began. That was when very many transactors remembered that P/E ratios were well over 20, and simple observation made it clear that such exotic innovations as portfolio insurance were about as useful as a life preserver made of cast iron. They also remembered what they had heard about the huge debt and budget deficit of the US, unstable exchange rates, and the possibility of a mass flight from the dollar. With insights like this solidifying and buzzing around their frontal lobes, everybody except the hopelessly naïve made a dash for the escape hatch.

Apparently, in both New York and Chicago, a "Custer's last stand" mentality was displayed by a few individuals. For instance, I recall that shortly after the crash there was talk of "stand-up market makers" — where a market-maker is someone who is always ready to make a market in a certain stock, regardless of whether it means buying or selling. These macho men and women kept the flag flying as long as they had ammunition, however like Custer and the troopers of the 7th Cavalry, they did not last long. The same was true of thousands of employees in the financial services industry in e.g. London who were handed their walking papers as a result of worsening business — although it is likely that many of them returned to duty in the 1990s.

The same phenomenon was witnessed after the recent financial crisis in countries like Thailand, Russia, Korea, and Argentina. Emerging markets specialists at many banks saw the the head-count shrink by 20–30% from the 1997 hey-day, although some banks began rehiring as soon as they noted that J.P. Morgan's Emerging Markets Bond Index — considered a barometer of the risk premium investors demand to hold "emerging" debt — was down by 300 basis points in a month and a half. Even so, a continuing skepticism about future developments in Latin America led to J.P. Morgan, Morgan Stanley Dean Witter, Chase Manhattan, Deutsche Bank, and Goldman Sachs underwriting more than 80% of all Latin American debt issues in the last quarter of 1998.

Eighteen months after the 1997 crash in the US, the average P/E ratio of shares on the Tokyo market was about 70. This was possible because "ramping" and "churning" stocks — which means inducing clients to buy or sell when it may not be in their interest to do so, but in order to generate large fees — had become an accepted practice in many Japanese brokerages. On December 29, 1989, the Japanese stock market peaked at a Nikkei (index) of 39,916. Two and a half years later, it had fallen almost 55%. It is still not clear just who took the largest hits in that country, but Japanese brokers estimate that since the late 1980s, more than 75% of individual investors have eliminated the equity component of their portfolios. Twenty years later, most Japanese households still prefer deposit accounts (at the lowest interest rates in the world) to individual stocks or mutual funds of any description (although institutional investors can hardly afford this kind of behavior). It is claimed that this will soon change, however, due to such things as day trading and the Internet, and if it changes, small savers in Japan could be a key factor in initiating the next great bull market.

VI. Noise, Bubbles, and Fads

The late Fisher Black contended that "noise" was essential for active, liquid markets (where his definition of noise was non-informational factors to which speculative prices react). This obviously makes sense: who could imagine a speculative market peopled only by experts. These noise traders — usually eager amateurs who have a misguided judgement of their own capacity — are in the habit of generally getting things wrong, and provide a large part of the money that goes to "information traders", who are pictured as trading on (good) information, and on average making money. This last observation does not ring especially true, because what it means is that any trader or investor who is willing to take the time should be able to upgrade himself or herself to the winner's circle. The circle where highly motivated and knowledgeable men and women consistently outperform the Dow or S&P 500, and make huge salaries and bonuses in the process.

Up to now, the expressions trading and investing have been more or less used synonymously, but it might be wise to distinguish between them. Trading decisions are founded on expectations of a future change in the price of an asset that has nothing to do with that asset's intrinsic value. On the other hand, investment decisions begin with comparing the present price of an asset with (what is believed to be) its intrinsic value in the belief that the market price will eventually converge to its intrinsic value. Long Term Capital Management (LTCM) was supposedly engaged in highly sophisticated arbitrage before its fall. For example, why should there be large differences in the prices of distant long-term bonds issued by the same country? Clearly, there might be serious money that can be made by betting on a convergence.

Competent traders are generally thought to possess a degree of skill and sophistication that "noise traders" lack; but even so noise traders can get lucky. The present US Secretary of the Treasury, Professor Lawrence Summers, has said that in a truly efficient market, noise traders would consistently underperform smart investors, but this is not literally true. After all, one definition of a noise trade is a trade where a transactor has no reason to prefer one asset to another. Mr. Noise can walk into his broker's office, buy stock X because he likes the sound of its name, and occasionally make as big a bundle as Ms. Smart. This happens to be what lotteries are all about! As for buying a share whose name you like, an "experiment" carried out in Germany showed that for the most part, the prices of shares issued by widely recognized enterprises advanced faster than those originating in less known firms, regardless of presumptive intrinsic values.

Noise is in some ways linked to bubbles and fads, in that there is a hint of incurable irrationality associated with these terms. Strictly speaking, a bubble is a price rise that is not justified by fundamentals. Of course, the bubble may be due to the actions of investors who recognize that they have a bubble on their hands, but that it might pay to stick with it for a while and continue to buy the relevant share(s), because it might grow larger. In this situation we speak of a rational speculative bubble, in that although a number of investors get "fried", many of them do well because they leave the market shortly before the bubble bursts.

Some of them do much better than well, at least for a while. Clarence Hatry was mentioned earlier, and the persons who got into the MMM pyramid scam in Russia in 1994, and got out in time, were also privileged to wear the victor's crown. Victor Lustig was a notable administrator of minor bubble schemes. Mr. Lustig sold the Eiffel Tower twice, and conned Al Capone. His lifetime rules were: be a patient listener; never look bored; always agree with the political and religious convictions of the the person to whom you are talking; never be untidy; never be drunk (at least in public); never boast; and do not discuss private lives — unless it pays to do so. Every reader who plans to circulate widely in the financial world should remember this advice. (The MMM arrangement had all the earmarks of a classic *Ponzi Scheme*. Charles Ponzi paid high interest rates by simply borrowing even more money at still higher rates. MMM sold shares, and used the funds from the sale of new shares to pay high returns on old shares.)

As an aside, behavioral economists claim that bubbles are the result of people acting in ways that are contrary to the rational self interest that underlies mainstream economic models. As they put it, investors suffer from "disaster myopia", of which the most important psychological ingredient is the "availability heuristic". This consists of e.g. shareholders basing their view of the likelihood of something happening on how easily they can imagine it, and since many of them have not suffered personally from a previously bursting bubble, or for that matter were even aware of such things as bubbles — by that or another name — they tend to judge fundamental values by recent changes in price. There is an increasing number of observers who insist that the stock-market escalation in the US during the last years of the 20th century was a bona-fide bubble, and among other things indicated the partial demise of investor rationality.

Again we have a proposition that may or may not be true. French individuals only own directly about 11% of the share market capitalization in their country, as compared to 50% in the US; and it is claimed that one reason for this disparity is that French investors will never forget the Eurotunnel and Euro Disney episodes, when commercial banks convinced many of their clients that the shares of these enterprises were a high-quality investment. This turned out to be an exaggeration, and by most accounts the average small investor only managed to recover a small percentage of his or her stake. However it appears that a costly advertising campaign, designed to dispel what Paris Bourse calls "misconceptions" about the market, has given some impressive results. Contrary to much expert opinion, high-powered advertising is often capable of overcoming to some extent the damage visited on net-worths and egos by an earlier *contretemps*. By way of justifying this advertising crusade to possible academic critics, Paris Bourse claims that small investors add stability to the market, because three-fourths of these persons hold shares more than seven years, while institutional investors regularly refashion their portfolios.

Our final departure is the fad. We should already be acquainted with this word. For example, mutton-chop sideburns are a fad that appears now and then. In the stock market, a fad is defined as a deviation of stock prices from their fundamental values, with a suggestion of non-rational behavior somewhere in the picture. An example that can be used here is the proclivity to overvalue the securities of start-up software and electronic firms.

Irrational antics associated with fads, bubbles, and noise trading can have serious consequences for both the stock market and the macroeconomy. For instance, elements of all three of the above were probably behind the 1929 market crashes, which in turn were a main cause of the Great Depression. When more readable literature becomes available, it might be a good idea for all students of finance to expand their familiarity with these concepts.

There has only been a passing reference in the above to irrationality, because many financial economists regard the stock market as a rational place where big-money investors and their high IQ advisors from the top business schools are manifestly on top of the market situation every minute of the day and night. Allan Sloan, *Newsweek's* Wall Street editor, seems to believe that a few questions should be raised about this kind of trust because of some peculiar movements in IBM's stock during 1999: big upswings in April and May, and a 20% drop in a single day in October. Apparently, IBM's stock-market value fell by $39 billion without an appreciable change in fundamentals. IBM's management announced that mainframe sales might be soft for a few months because of concern for problems that "might" arise at the turn of the century, but this is hardly any reason for knowledgeable investors to push the panic button.

VII. Warrants and Convertibles

This is a short section that I would like to exclude, but some persons with a much better knowledge of these matters than myself have assured me that a few remarks on warrants and convertibles are essential.

Equity warrants give investors the right to buy a fixed number of shares in a firm for a fixed period, at a fixed price. This makes them almost identical to options, however options usually expire after a few months, while warrants can have lives of several years.

Perhaps the most widely commented on warrants are those issued in Japan and Switzerland. Japanese firms have borrowed in dollars, and then issued warrants priced in dollars which allowed investors to buy Japanese shares at a fixed yen price. By judiciously choosing the (issuing) value of the warrant, these borrowers have ended up paying considerably less than the prevailing interest rate. The Japanese equity-warrant market (which is a part of the Euromarket), is capitalized in the tens of billions of dollars, and in 1990 Japanese convertibles and bonds with warrants comprised about 20% of the bond market.

In Switzerland, banks have been prone to sell warrants on baskets of shares, and these warrants are often purchased by foreigners who are restricted as to the Swiss companies that they can own. In the late 1980s, when the Tokyo Stock Exchange was breaking all records, investors accepted interest payments on bonds as low as 1% in return for the right to buy warrants on a company's shares at a price that they expected to be under the market price when the warrants were exercised. Japanese firms also thought that warrant bonds were a marvelous invention. They could borrow at very low rates of interest, and when the warrants were exercised (in return for new stock), they obtained money that could be used to service their bond debt.

Just as warrants appear to carry the genes of options and stocks, convertibles are a mixture of stocks and bonds. They start as a bond — or even sometimes a preferred stock — and the investor gets a fixed (bondlike) income while waiting for the underlying common stock to appreciate — at which time the convertible would, presumably, be exchanged for a specified number of shares of common stock. In Japan, the typical warrant gives the right to buy stock at a fixed price for up to five years. Often the warrant is stripped from the bond and traded separately on secondary markets.

Convertible bonds have a "conversion value" that is equal to the product of the common stock price and the number of shares that you would get if you converted. At the same time, the open market price of the convertible is conventionally higher than the conversion value — indicating that normally this asset is purchased when it is believed that the stock price will rise. But even if it does not rise, the holder of a convertible will still obtain a fixed income, which may also be a reason for *not* purchasing the underlying stock: the stock price may fall instead of rise.

Both warrants and convertibles seem to have been good to investors much of the time. During many years the average return for convertibles in the US was below the yields on stocks, but above that for bonds. Similarly, it often happens that if holders of shares can obtain warrants just before a downward movement in share prices, they are favored in that the price of warrants will not fall as fast as share prices, and so the difference between the share price and the warrant price could — in theory at least — be invested in a fixed income security. Note the term "could", because few markets have crashed so spectacularly in recent history as the market for Japanese equity warrants.

That crash caused serious problems for some financial institutions, but the same could be said for the 1987 stock market meltdown, and the bond market implosion of 1994, and various other "corrections". The lesson here is that in these markets, as in show business, something new will always be coming along in the following seasons, and so no matter how bleak the situation may look in the short run, the major players are seldom observed rushing to book space at their local poorhouses.

VIII. Final Remarks

One of the things that has not been done in this chapter is to distinguish between the two main types of exchanges: formal (i.e. organized) auction markets (such as the New York Stock Exchange), and informal over-the-counter (OTC) markets. As compared to organized exchanges, OTC markets have no single location, but consists of large number of dealers and brokers who communicate with each other by telephones and computers. NASDAQ (i.e. The National Association of Securities Dealers Automatic Quotations Systems), which was introduced in 1971, shows bid and asked prices for thousands of securities on video screens that are tied to a central computer system. The securities presented on NASDAQ screens are for both large and small firms, and NASDAQ achieved a much wider recognition during the bull market of the 1990s. The present market capitalization of NASDAQ is about $6,000 billion, as compared to $11,000 billion for the New York exchange. (Tokyo is $4,500 billion and the global capitalization about $37,000 billion.)

Bids and offers for shares that originate from virtually any source can now be entered on terminals linked to the NASDAQ computer, and these are relayed to subscribing brokerage offices throughout the US. A computer search will then make visible the best bids and offers.

Although not widely known, many small stock markets fail. This matter has been carefully examined by Aggarwal and Angel (1999), and they focus on the problem of *adverse selection*. (Adverse selection can arise when people on the informed side of e.g. a market *self-select* in a way that can be harmful to the uninformed side of the market.) What happens in this case is that firms are listed on "start-up" or "small cap" exchanges, and many of those that are successful depart for a listing on a senior establishment. Left behind on the new exchange are a large number of unsuccessful firms, and so that establishment gets a reputation as a haven for losers. To avoid this kind of image problem, NASDAQ e.g. works very consciensciously to keep its listed companies from moving, and up to now has been quite successful. Among other things, Aggarwal and Angel argue that the collapse of the *Emerging Company Marketplace* in the US offers valuable lessons for other countries planning to create similar small cap stock markets.

The shares of many large companies are now listed on exchanges in different countries. The largest stock exchanges are — and will probably continue to be — New York, London, and Tokyo, but as far as opening times are concerned, the opposite sequence, or Tokyo, London, and New York holds. Thus when the market opens in New York, it has already opened in Tokyo. This global nexus means that a selling or buying wave in e.g. Tokyo is soon communicated to London and New York; however as things seem to be developing, trading hours are being extended at all the major exchanges.

Round-the-clock trading in one form or another may be something that eventually every exchange will have to accept, and in the very long run the trading week may also be extended, but there are persons who would argue that this is already happening, and the process will accelerate. In the US, online trading targeted at a mass audience does not stop when the market closes due to MarketXT, a new Internet-based marketplace which offers after-hours trading. It has even been suggested that at some point in the future, MarketXT will become a full-fledged stock exchange, but one free of the layers of intermediaries such as brokers and market makers that are usually associated with these institutions.

The promise and threats of near-comprehensive disintermediation are also never far from the thoughts of the managers of traditional exchanges. Disintermediation apparently offers, in theory at least, much cheaper trading; and it has been suggested that eventually the discount brokers who feed online orders into the exchanges in the traditional way could be dispensed with, since in theory buy and sell orders could be aggregated electronically and fed directly into a stock exchange without being routed through middlemen. Of course, even more extreme, the orders could be aggregated in the computers of an online broker, and in these circumstances the exchange itself could be excluded.

Exercises

1. Discuss book value, Tobin's "q" theory, IPOs, equity warrants, MM!
2. What is earnings yield? What is dividend yield? Discuss the P/E ratio! Why might the failure of Kreditanstalt be the most important bank failure of all time? What is capital gain? The EMH?
3. Discuss the effects, on stock market prices of the announcement of a very high utilization of industrial capacity; a sudden decline in the exchange rate; good or bad political news!
4. The trader William O'Neil says that "The stock market is neither efficient nor random. It is not efficient because there are too many poorly conceived opinions; it is not random because strong investor emotions can create trends". What do you think about this?
5. What does a low P/E signify?
6. Many people who own houses should want the interest rate to fall, even if their interest payments do not fall. Why?
7. What is the approximate logic behind advice calling for the purchase of stocks when they sell for an amount slightly over the book value of a firm, and their sale when they sell for e.g. 2.5 or 3 times the book value?

8. A famous relationship in economics is the valuation formula developed by John B. Williams. Here we have $P_t = D_{t+1}/(r^* - g)$, where P_t is the stock price, D_{t+1} is next year's dividend, r^* is the discount rate, and g is the dividend growth rate. D_{t+1}, of course, should be $E(D_{t+1})$, or the expected dividend for next year; and given D_t, we easily get $E(g)$. The important thing here, however, is r^*. A logical value for this might be $r^* = r + \theta$, where r is the risk free interest rate, and θ is a risk premium: i.e. an investor's perception of risk at a given point in time. The reader should now choose some values for r, D_t, $E(D_{t+1})$, and calculate $E(g)$. Now verify that small changes in θ will cause fairly large changes in P_t.

9. In March 2000, the NASDAQ had a P/E ratio of 186. Comment!

Chapter 4

Introducing Futures and Options

There is no single chapter in any book ever written that can make you an expert on futures or options. For that a fairly thick volume is necessary, and the student of financial derivatives must be prepared to deal with a considerable amount of algebra. However, this algebra tends to be perfectly straightforward. Complicated mathematics and usable derivatives theory do not go together — except for rocket scientists, of course. If you have no plans to become an expert or specialist just now, then this chapter should be very helpful, because it is intended to give you an introduction to derivatives that will make you feel very comfortable in the presence of almost everyone interested in this topic except prima-donna traders and quants with pit-bull personalities. It will also make the specialized literature much easier to read.

Derivatives are used by pension funds, mutual funds, insurance companies, and most of the larger firms in the world; but speculating in derivatives can be done by almost anybody. Paul Erdman (1987) advises against pure futures plays by "small" speculators, but is positive to buying options on futures, with the futures contract of (his) choice being the S&P 500. Anyone reading this chapter should have no difficulty in understanding what this operation involves.

Financial futures were first traded in Chicago in 1972, while the largest financial futures exchange in Europe opened in London in 1982. This is LIFFE (The London International Financial Futures and Options Exchange). Chicago is still the center of financial derivatives in the US because of the Chicago Board of Trade (CBOT), Chicago Board Options Exchange (CBOE), and the Chicago Mercantile Exchange (CME). A 1999 BIS survey of securities markets stated that the notional value of OTC financial derivatives products outstanding was $72 trillion at the end of June 1998, with most of these interest rate instruments. Between March 1995 and June 1998, the

103

increase in the value of financial derivatives outstanding was approximately 130%.

This chapter begins with some remarks on futures, options and swaps. Then there is an important section that is particularly applicable to commodity derivatives — although the terminology is applicable to all derivatives. For a good introduction to financial derivatives, see Keith Pilbeam (1998).

I. Simple Options and Swaps

In a lecture presented to the Fifth Annual Meeting of the German Finance Association, Professor Merton Miller said that if he were starting over and entering the field of finance today, he would specialize in options. He sees options theory as being at the center of gravity of financial economics.

Maybe it is, and maybe it is not; but certain aspects of option theory are extremely important — and not just for finance. Fortunately, I cannot think of any subject in economics whose rudimentary logic is as easily acquired as futures and options. Of course, trying to keep track of the details requires a certain amount of concentration. The basic building blocks that will be covered in this book are futures, options, and to a lesser extent swaps; but things like caps, swaptions, floors, collars, captions, floortions, spreadtions, look-backs, etc. have become an important part of the great world of derivatives, and these are constructed from the basic elements.

Derivatives can be used for speculation or hedging, where hedging refers to "price insurance", and sometimes "risk management". But regardless of what derivatives we are talking about, or where they are used, a widespread opinion outside the financial community is that these are dangerous assets. "The wild cards in international finance", US Congressman James A. Leach labeled them, perhaps remembering that the Brady report on the 1987 stock market crash stated that the enormous sale of stock index futures by portfolio insurers made a large contribution to the 500-point market decline in the Dow that was a memorable feature of that dramatic chain of events. The contention here is that history does not fully support these judgements, although hopefully the 1987 version of portfolio insurance will someday be judged as an idea whose time should never have come.

How do derivatives derive their value? The term derivative indicates that they are derived from some other asset. For instance, if you buy an option on Standard Oil stock, paying the seller of the option (i.e. the writer) the premium (= the option price), then the purchase of that option gives you the right to buy or sell Standard before a specified date (the maturity or expiry date), for a specified price (called the strike or exercise price). As you should be able to verify soon, the writer does not want to see this option exercised, and given the opportunity would set his or her price at such a level that while the option would be bought, the likelihood of its being exercised would be miniscule.

If you have bought the right to buy this stock, then you have purchased a call option; while if you have bought the right to sell this stock, then you have bought a put option. From that point in time until the maturity (i.e. expiry or settlement) date of the option, the value of your option depends on what happens to Standard Oil stock, which is called the *underlying*.

Another example might be applicable here. In 1985, Lufthansa managers ordered almost a billion dollars of US aircraft (Boeings), and since they believed that the dollar would continue to rise against the Deutschemark, bought dollars in the forward market at more than 3 DM/$. By the time payment was due, the dollar was at 2.75 DM/dollar, which meant a loss of several hundred millions of Deutschemarks. What should have been done was to purchase a call (currency) option, which at that time would have meant paying a comparatively small premium for options with an exercise price of 3 DM/$. With the exchange rate at 2.75, the option would have been left unexercised.

Now let us see how the option gets its value. If you purchase a call option on e.g. Standard Oil stock, and the stock price climbs in such a way that it exceeds the exercise price, then you could be in a position to make a lot of money: buy (i.e. call) Standard (from the writer) at the exercise price, and then e.g. sell it in the spot (stock) market at the prevailing (market) price. (The spot market is the market for immediate delivery.) On the other hand, if the stock price does not climb, then you lose the premium, but that is all that you lose.

What about a put option? Here you start out by paying a premium to sell Standard at the exercise price. What you want now is for the price of the stock to collapse. Should that happen you exercise your option: you buy the stock at its bargain-basement price, and sell it (to the writer) at the (higher) exercise price. Once again, as above, if the stock price does not descend below the exercise price, then you simply throw the option into the waste paper basket. You have lost your premium.

Let's sum this discussion up, and add something. (1) A call option gives the right to buy an asset at a specified price, before a certain date. A put option gives the right to sell an asset at a specified price and before a certain date. (2) If the strike (or exercise) price P_E of a call option is equal to the actual market (i.e. spot) price S, then the option is said to be at-the-money. If $S > P_E$ then a call option is in-the-money. If $P_E < S$, then a call option is out-of-the-money. For a put option, the opposite is the case. (3) Often, instead of going through the trouble of exercising an in-the-money option, and becoming involved with the underlying, you can simply sell the option.

Unfortunately, as easy as all this seems — and is — the expression "derivatives disaster" has crept into the language, and apparently it can happen at any time. Metallgesellschaft lost about $1.5 billion on a bad hedging strategy, while in 1992 traders employed by the government of Malaysia were said to have lost something in the vicinity of $4 billion on unsound bets. Some observers have called these enormous losses part of the learning process, but what it comes down to is simple carelessness. UBS also took some heavy hits a few year ago.

Four very undemanding exercises follow. I strongly suggest that they should be done before the reader continues.

Exercises

1. For a call option, if the market price is higher than the exercise price, then the option is in-the-money. Suppose that in the discussion above the premium P is $5, the market price S is $62, and the exercise price is $50. Is this option in the money? Suppose that the option has a maturity of one month, and three weeks have passed. Would you exercise the option?

2. In the above example, suppose that P = 5, S = 58, and E = 55. Would you exercise the option? Discuss!
3. Construct an example for a put option where the option is out-of-the-money (i.e. it does not pay to exercise the option)!
4. What do you think the relationship is between the present price of an asset (e.g. Standard stock), the exercise price, and the premium? What do you think about an option writer who sells an option for $5 when the exercise price for that particular option is $53, and the market price is $60? What do you think would be a reasonable premium for this option?

Now for a few words about swaps. The oil futures and options markets have occasionally been referred to as "the best game in town", but more than one observer of the oil derivatives markets has commented that where long maturities (i.e. settlement dates in the distant future) are concerned, the derivative of choice for items like oil, gas and electricity is swaps. The reason for this is simple, and the reader should keep it in mind when reading the rest of the chapter: there is a shortage of liquidity in the markets for long-dated futures because too many bad things can happen to transactors over a long maturity period for these assets. For example, there can be a radical change in the market background which leads to explosive price "spikes". The same is true of options, and the way the option writers handle this problem is to demand very large premiums.

Roughly, a swap is an agreement by two parties to transfer cash from one to the other over a series of intervals in the future, depending on the relationship of the spot price of an item to some benchmark (price). These transactors are called counterparties. Swaps are sometimes characterized as a series of forward contracts, with every payment regarded as an individual transaction.

At the present time, the monetary value of outstanding swaps can be measured in the trillions. Simple examples of swaps are easy to construct. Suppose that Mr. B wanted to make sure that he always received at least 8 Swedish crowns for every dollar of the 1,200 dollars that he receives from the US every month, while Mr. L is absolutely certain that the dollar will always trade over 8 crowns/dollar.

Accordingly, these two gentlemen are excellent candidates for a swap, with e.g. payments made every month. In the example being constructed here, the swap rate is 8 crowns/$: when the actual exchange rate (P) is under 8 crowns/$, then Mr. B receives 8 − P; and when it is over he pays P − 8; while when it is under Mr. L pays 8 − P, and receives P − 8 when it is over. Suppose, however, that Mr. L will not become involved in this swap for an amount greater than $1,000, and Mr. B accepts this condition. In that case the *notional value* of the swap is $1,000. In other words, the notional value is the amount used as a reference against which the periodic swap amounts are calculated. We also need an index for this calculation. The swap intermediary — often some investment bank — suggests an average of the daily closing exchange rates taken over a month, but Mr. B does not find this satisfactory. He suggests the exchange rate at the end of the month, and Mr. L agrees. Finally, we need a maturity for the swap. Suppose that as a result of negotiations between the two men, supervised by the intermediary, the swap maturity turns out to be three years.

Notice something here! Mr. B and Mr. L could have arranged this swap without the intermediary, but that would mean that they had to worry about the counterparty fulfilling the terms of the swap. As things stand, however, they pay and are paid by the intermediary, and not each other, and if the intermediary is e.g. a bank, this usually eliminates financial risk for the counterparties. That risk has been transferred to the intermediary, who generally has the legal resources to make sure that the counterparties live up to the terms of the arrangement.

Now we are in business! Assume that on the last day of that month the dollar-crown exchange rate turned out to be 8.22 crowns/dollar. When Mr. B cashed his $1,200 check from the US, the crown amount of the notional value ($1,000) was 8,220 crowns, and so 220 crowns of this went to the intermediary, who forwarded it to Mr. L. What about the intermediary's fee? To keep things simple, let us assume that the intermediary takes 50 crowns/ month from each counterparty for three years. Neither of the counterparties is happy about this amount, but they could not get a better offer.

In this example Mr. B used the swap to hedge, while Mr. L is using it to speculate. Note that the swap was "tailor-made" by the intermediary in that there is no standard type of transaction. For instance, instead of the two counterparties negotiating a swap maturity, the intermediary could have negotiated with each, and perhaps things would have worked out so that the maturity was three years with Mr. B, and two years with Mr. L. What about the extra year? The intermediary might find another counterparty to handle that year, or even act as a counterparty itself if they think that the exchange rate will stay above 8 crowns/dollar. In fact, when Mr. B came to the intermediary, and asked if a swap could be arranged, the intermediary might have agreed to write a swap for the entire $1,200, but insisted that the swap rate had to be 7.90 crowns/dollar instead of 8 crowns/dollar. After thinking about it, Mr. B might accept, and the intermediary — probably without telling Mr. B — accepted the role of counterparty. After all, it is none of Mr. B's affair who the counterparty is, since in order to avoid a credit risk, he is dealing with the intermediary. In addition, since the intermediary is an established financial player, if they think that they have made a mistake, they can hedge their commitment later on the futures or options market until they find another counterparty.

It appears that the first documented swap was between the World Bank and IBM, in 1981. The World Bank — which has access to a number of currencies — agreed to finance some of IBM's German mark/Swiss franc debt, in return for IBM financing some of the Bank's dollar exposure. This particular transaction can be explained by the Bank expecting that it will not gain access to enough dollars to fulfill its forthcoming obligations, but would have no trouble acquiring German marks and Swiss francs.

Exercises

1. John, Jack and Jill live in three identical houses. There are identical mortgages on the homes of John and Jack: $100,000 to be paid off in 100 years. One hundred years? Yes, the bank has agreed to take no principal, but just an interest payment equal to whatever the average market rate of interest turns out to be, every year for a century. John is scared out of his wits that the interest rate will go above 10%, while Jack is convinced that the interest rate has peaked. Jill is rich, and does not care what happens to the interest rate, but in order to keep herself

occupied agrees to act as a swap arranger — i.e. intermediary — for the two neighbors. Please continue the story in detail, adding a few calculations!

2. Apple growers like Bill are afraid of low apple prices; applejack producers like Sally are afraid of high apple prices. Can you, as the swap arranger, explain how you might be able to arrange a swap with Sally and Bill as counterparties, so that you can make some money? (Hint: you do not have to introduce these two delightful people to each other!)

The final derivative that will be examined in this introduction is the futures. Once again I would like to remind readers that the materials in this elementary exposition should be taken very seriously because, as Carol Loomis (1994) points out "Like alligators in a swamp, derivatives lurk in the global economy. Even the CEOs of the companies that use them don't understand them". Perhaps you will get a chance to explain derivatives to these ladies and gentlemen some day!

The example that I have chosen to use here is similar to the one employed in the film "Trading Places". In my example, Eddie and Dan set out to make a fortune in the applejack market. Eddie's parrot has been snooping around the Department of Apples and Applejack (in the Pentagon), and finds out that Military Intelligence has comes to the conclusion that that there is going to be a huge apple crop — perhaps the best in history. A few weeks after those apples go on sale, there will be enough applejack in the US to put every applejack lover in the Western Hemisphere into orbit. After selling and/or mortgaging everything they have, and borrowing everything they can borrow, they go down to the Philadelphia Futures and Options Exchange on the day that, at 1200 hours sharp, the Applejack General will inform the exchange, country, and world of the state of the US apple crop.

When trading starts early that morning, the price of applejack futures contracts with a maturity of one month — each of which covers ten barrels (b) of applejack — is $50/b. This will be taken as the price at which you can buy or sell a barrel of applejack on an applejack futures contract. The price of a contract is thus $500. Since the market is extremely liquid at the time, it is possible for a transactor to buy or sell a very large number of contracts without moving the price.

Let's leave Eddie and Dan temporarily, and observe the behavior of another player, a certain Mr. Clean, who opens his position by buying one futures contract — i.e. going long one contract; and shortly after the price of one-month applejack futures suddenly zooms up to $75/b. Then, if he wishes, he can close his position by selling (i.e. going short) one contract, or he might wait and see if the price continues to increase. If he decides to sell — i.e. offset or reverse his opening long position — then his profit on that transaction is $25/b minus a small fee that is paid a broker or dealer for arranging the transaction. The total gain on one contract is thus (almost) $250. (This and the previous paragraph should be read and understood perfectly before continuing!)

In fact, it was unnecessary for Mr. Clean to come down to the exchange to carry out this transaction. He could have done it from his apartment while sitting in front of the TV watching Dallas, by simply calling his broker. Also, he did not need to pay the entire $50/b. Instead he pays margin on the $50/b, which functions as a sort of deposit (but which is actually defined as a "performance bond"). Thus, if the margin was $10/b, and Clean wanted to invest $500 in applejack futures, he could have bought five contracts. If the price increased to $75/contract, his profit would have been $1,250. This arrangement with margin provides players in the futures market with an impressive amount of leverage.

(Note that the five contracts cover 50 barrels of applejack. Why do the contracts cover applejack and not apples. Remember, in "Trading Places" the contracts involved orange juice and not oranges. A better example is the oil futures market. For a long time there was no futures contract for crude oil. Instead, there were contracts for oil products. Now there is a futures contract for crude oil, and it covers 1,000 barrels of crude.)

Continuing, suppose that Mr. Clean had bought one contract for $50/b, paying $10/b margin, and the price had dropped to $45/b. What will happen now is that he will receive a margin call from his broker: he might be asked to bring his margin account up to $100 (for a single contract). As a result of that price fall his contract decreased in value by $5/b, or a total of $50 just as whoever was on the other end of the transaction — the seller of the contract — gained $5/b, or $50 per contract, and in discussing these events it might be convenient to say that his gain is equal to Mr. Clean's loss. Incidentally, this business of keeping track of gains and losses is carried out by the exchange's clearing house. (Almost every exchange has a clearing house, which is a non-profit institution that acts as a seller to buyers of contracts, and a buyer to sellers. In other words, an intermediary who makes all transactions impersonal.) The clearing house deals with brokers.

Every night, after the exchange closes, all open contracts are marked-to-the-market by the clearing house, which means that changes in value are registered. (Definition: revaluing and reporting assets and liabilities at current market prices is called marking-to-market!) If your contract increased in value, then your broker will be so notified, and you will be informed that your account with that good person has increased. If your contract has lost value, your broker will be notified of that sad state of affairs, and might ask you to top up your margin account. If you do not do so after receiving this margin call, she would immediately close your position. Note that in the clearing house's accounting, when someone is registered as losing money, someone else gains. The big problem for clearing houses comes when trans-actors do not eventually offset (i.e. reverse) their contracts. A futures contract is also a forward contract, in that if the contract is held open (i.e. not closed by an offsetting transaction) to the expiry date, then delivery must take place. Managing this delivery — which is made to a specified delivery point, and not to somebody's front yard — requires some extra work on the part of the clearing house, although cash settlement removes this problem.

The above example involved buying a futures contract, but it would have been just as easy to start out by selling a contract. This is what the other Eddie and Dan did in "Trading Places", and it confuses people, because they do not understand how you can sell something that you do not have. However, going back to our previous example, Mr. Clean simply lifts his phone and tells his broker that he wants to sell — go short — X futures contracts (covering 10X barrels of applejack). Then a few hours, or days, or weeks later Mr. Clean lifts the phone again, and closes (offsets or reverses) his position by buying X contracts. Obviously, given the mechanics of this transaction as described here, the location of the applejack is completely irrelevant.

Now suppose that Mr. Clean became so interested in the antics of J.R. and Sue Ellen Ewing that he could not tear himself away from his TV, and forgot to offset his short position. In doing this, he would join the 5% or 10% of transactors who hold their contracts to the expiry date. One of two things could happen now. One of these is that he must find some applejack, and arrange to have it delivered to a specified delivery point. This is probably an operation that he does not want to personally become involved in, because often the delivery points have been chosen so as to discourage delivery. The other arrangement is that the contracts are cash settled at or around the settlement date of the contract, which is no more complicated than arranging for another margin transaction: losers pay winners.

Everything considered, it is possible to contemplate a time when cash settlement will be the rule for most items being traded on futures exchanges, but at the same time flexibility will be added to the extent that if it suits their fancy, transactors will be able to obtain delivery at convenient times, and to convenient locations.

The last point that will be made here is that at the settlement date, the price of "paper" applejack — i.e. the per-barrel price of the applejack on the futures contract — should be almost the same as the market price of the underlying, or the actual applejack. (A heuristic proof of this will be given later in this chapter.) A very usable inference from this is that if the price of "actuals" (or the underlying) rises, then the price of the paper asset should also increase — sooner or later. This is why, when Eddie's parrot brought him word that there was going to be a bumper apple crop, he reasoned that the price of apples would fall by a very large amount, which in turn would mean very inexpensive applejack, *and* a very low price for "paper" applejack.

Finally, let's complete our anecdote about Eddie and Dan. That morning these two gentlemen sold (went short) a very large number of contracts whose price was $50/b. They made $10/b margin payments on each. Then, at exactly 1200 hours, the Applejack General merrily announced that the apple crop was fantastic. He called it an unforgettable triumph of Yankee ingenuity. Upon hearing that, the longs realized what kind of situation they were in, and screamed with rage and frustration. Eddie and Dan were content to stand on the sidelines, congratulating each other and the rest of the "shorts", as they stood and watched the "longs" try to close their positions by selling as fast as they could (i.e. by taking offsetting short positions). Most of the longs took a "bath".

Eddie and Dan eventually moved forward and began reversing their short positions by buying. The price had become stuck at $5/b, and so they were able to realize a profit of $45/b for every barrel they had bought: they opened with a sell at 50, and they close with a buy at 5. Our two heroes are rich men now, and able to indulge in full their taste for wine, watermelon, and wacky behavior.

Exercises

1. Suppose Eddie's parrot had brought word that the apple crop was terrible. Describe in detail what action Eddie and Dan would have taken!
2. Suppose that the producers of apples launch a very expensive advertising campaign to get people to eat more applesauce. Mr. Dirty, the largest manufacturer of applejack in Gotham City, is very unhappy about this. (Why?) He calls his broker, and she tells him that he has every right to be unhappy, but that he can hedge his purchases of apples by buying some of the new futures contracts for apples — one "paper" crate for every crate of apples that he will need to manufacture applejack. Assume that every barrel of applejack requires a crate of apples, and each apple futures contract is for 20 crates. He plans to manufacture a million barrels of applejack, and so how many futures contracts will he need? Now explain why she gave him this advice!
3. In the previous problem, suppose that there was no futures contract for apples. What advice might Mr. Dirty's broker give him now?
4. What is margin? What is a margin call? What is the function of a clearing house? What does it mean to go long? To go short? How do you offset your position? Eddie and Dan became rich by going short in futures. With the information that the parrot brought them, would it have been worth while to use options? If so, what play would they have made?
5. Futures markets are used to both hedge and speculate. Describe how these take place! Now tell why a certain professor once said that he

would be surprised if futures markets continued to be attractive to hedgers who had access to options. How do you feel about this?

When the subject of futures and options comes up in the seminar room, we intermittenly hear references to Arrow-Debreu (A-D) securities. For example, at his Nobel prize lecture, Professor Merton referred to them in such a manner as to suggest that they might soon be joining crude and heating oil futures at the Singapore Monetary Exchange. The idea here is that if there are N states of nature, then for every state i there is an asset that pays \$1 if state i occurs, and zero otherwise. This asset, which is an A-D security, has a present price that can, in theory, be calculated. Obviously, it resembles to some extent an insurance or contingency good. For example, *assuming* that the Chicago Bulls are playing in the NBA finals later in this century, I can pay for a seat in the third row today. If, however, for some reason Michael Jordan decides to play polo instead of basketball that year, and the Bulls finish last, then I get nothing.

I think that even Goldman Sachs would be skeptical about adding A-D securities to their product line. The main reason for paying any attention to them is to be able to claim that even in the presence of uncertainty, a *comprehensive* system of insurance and derivatives markets will permit the realization of the efficient outcomes that bring us so much joy in the basic course in economics. Note the emphasis on "comprehensive".

II. The Next Lesson in Futures

The next lesson in futures and options is similar to the first, but at a slightly higher level of abstraction. In order to make sure that all of the most important basic concepts are covered, the exposition below will be carried out in terms of oil. Why oil? Because oil is generally considered to be a part of the financial market, and the same may eventually become true of electricity and natural gas. Most of the journals that finance professionals read — e.g. *Forbes*, *The Economist*, *Business Week* — generally report the latest developments on the oil, gas, and electricity fronts.

Futures markets operate as follows. Against a background of speculators "betting" on the direction and size of price movements (of both futures and the underlying) by buying and selling futures contracts, an impersonal agency can be created which permits producers and consumers, inventory holders, and various other transactors to reduce (i.e.) hedge price risk. Speculation is often considered a bad word, and so the question should be put whether a futures — or futures type market — could operate without the volume of speculative behavior associated with highly successful futures and options markets.

One answer here is "yes", since in a way a swaps market is a futures market without speculation in the conventional sense. But in a usual futures market of the auction or exchange type, a great deal of speculation should be available in order to ensure adequate liquidity — i.e. the ability to sell or buy futures contracts at or near the last quoted price. When problems arise in the functioning of these exchanges, they are often due to too little rather than too much speculation.

The success of a futures market is dependent on the satisfaction — or near satisfaction — of several well-defined criteria. Perhaps the most important is that the item in question is bought and sold in circumstances that cause its price to fluctuate in a random, or non-systematic pattern. In addition, it should be true that futures contracts can be standardized in such a way that quantity, the expiry or settlement date, delivery location, and to a certain extent quality are unambiguous. It also needs to be made clear that the identity of buyers and sellers is irrelevant, because an impersonal clearing house is interposed between buyer and seller, which acts as seller to all buyers, and buyer to all sellers. The "margin" (or "performance bond") which ensures the security of all transactions goes through brokers to the clearing house. Finally, the reader should understand that futures exchanges are membership organizations, and so the majority of its clients do not deal directly with the exchange. Instead they buy and sell through brokers (who have their employees at the exchange), however it is usually possible for the brokers (or anyone else who has acquired a "seat" on the exchange) to buy and sell on their own account if they so desire.

Readers of the previous section hopefully remember the *modus operandi* (MO) of speculators. If speculators believe that the price of an underlying will rise, they buy futures contracts — i.e. they go long. These contracts are often forward contracts, because delivery conditions are stipulated on them relating to a specified amount of an asset, delivered during a certain period to one or more distinct locations. However it is possible to avoid taking delivery if, at any time before the expiry date of the contract, an offsetting (i.e. reversing) sale is made of a contract for the same amount of the underlying, referred to the same delivery month. When the transactor opens his position by going long, and the price does rise, then he makes a profit when he closes his position with a sale. If he opens by going long, and the price falls, then he suffers a loss.

The usual measure of futures markets liquidity is open interest. This is the total number of open contracts (long or short) in a given market: if a buyer and seller trade one contract, and this is not a reversing trade, the open interest is increased by one contract. (Note: one, not two contracts!) However, even if the open interest in a market was considered adequate, very large transactions often suffice to move the (futures) price.

Now let's go to hedging — or guarding against price risk. Several years ago, Mr. T. Boone Pickens of Mesa Petroleum came to the conclusion that the oil price might fall. He reacted by selling a number of futures contracts equal to the entire production of Mesa Petroleum over some particular period: in other words, he opened his position by going short. In viable futures markets, as we indicated in the previous section, this is no more complicated than going long.

Later, when the price of physical oil fell, he offset his opening (short) position by buying futures contracts for the same amount. The loss on his physical position when the price actually fell was counterbalanced by the gain on the "paper" transaction.

Mr. Pickens deserves our congratulations, however as Carol Loomis notes "hedges may be difficult to put on". She then quotes a Washington lawyer, Eugene Rotberg: "The only perfect hedge is in a Japanese garden". This is not completely true, but as former economics professor Heinz Schimmelbusch — once named manager of the year by *TopBusiness*, a German magazine — found out, the downside risk with futures can be enormous, especially when you adopt a flawed hedging strategy that is put on automatic pilot. He and Metallgesellschaft had to part company.

A transactor whose net position in the cash — i.e. spot or forward market for actuals (or underlyings) — is offset by his position in the futures market, is conventionally labelled a hedger, and if the market functions the way a textbook market is supposed to function, then price risk will be eliminated. But, unfortunately, since any gain in the futures market will be cancelled out by a loss in the actuals market, it follows that any profits due to favorable price movements for the underlying will be eliminated due to a loss in the paper market. Profits or losses in a futures market that accrue to hedgers who are fully hedged are due to shortcomings in the conventional (i.e. textbook) structure of these markets, and it is here that basis risk deserves special attention. (Basis risk will be taken up below.) It is not unheard of, however, that a transactor who is unequivocally a hedger will assume a position that is net long or net short in the overall market: some of the physical product is left "uncovered". A little advanced mathematics will show that there are situations in which this is the optimal strategy for a hedger.

The futures market also enables a transactor to lock in a price. For instance, an oil refiner might be worried about the price of oil in a month. Suppose that the present (spot) price of (physical) oil is 20 dollars/barrel (= $20/b), and the futures price is $20.5/b. It is possible for the refiner to lock-in a price of $20.5/b by going long in futures. (Oil futures contracts are for 1,000 barrels. Thus the hedger in this example would have to pay $20,500 for a contract.)

Assume that one contract was purchased, and that during this month the price of paper oil increased at the rate of one dollar/day. During the month the contract will be marked to the market every day, and so in 30 days its value will increase by $30/b. But as the reader will soon see, at the expiry date of the contract, the futures price and the price of the underlying must be equal (or almost equal). Thus, at the end of the month, the refiner might pay $50.5/b for oil, but has received $30 for the increase in the contract's value. The net price paid for the oil is thus $50.5 - $30 = $20.5/b.

Suppose that instead of increasing, the price of paper oil had decreased, but this time by $0.5 per day. If the hedger starts out by going long, then each decrease reduces the value of the contract by \$0.5, and perhaps a margin call is involved. (Even if a margin call is not involved, the transactor's margin account at his broker is decreased.) However, since the futures and actuals price should converge at the end of the month (as will be shown below), the refiner pays only \$5.50 for the physical oil. The net cost is thus \$5.50 + \$15 = \$20.5.

Exercises

1. Explain what a shortage of liquidity would mean for the stock market.
2. Why would a transactor who is worried about price risk employ a futures contract instead of a forward contract? (In the forward market arrangements are made for the delivery or receipt of an item at an agreed upon price.)
3. Suppose that a hedger told his broker to go long in futures, but the broker misunderstood and went short. What might have happened?

The next two topics are price convergence and convenience yield. This is perhaps the main reason that the discussion in this section does not concentrate on financial assets, since convenience yield is mostly irrelevant for financial assets; but this is an extremely important concept. Together with basis risk, it is one of the (unfortunately many) concepts that you want to know a great deal about if you plan to feel at home in the financial world's corridors and restaurants of power.

The simplest way to talk about price convergence is to bring in the delivery mechanism. Conventionally, when a contract reaches maturity (i.e. the expiry date), the shorts who have not offset their position must deliver the item in the manner designated by the contract, while the longs with open positions must accept and pay for what they have bought. Thus, at the time of delivery, if the spot price (S) of the underlying is greater than the futures price (F), the longs will accept delivery and sell on the spot market. The arbitrage taking place here should work to bring about an equality between S and F — or, in reality, a near equality. Similarly, if $F > S$, the shorts will buy on the spot market and make delivery. Once again, arbitrage will work to equalize prices.

But we can go further. The shorts would not deliver anything that could be sold at a higher price in the spot market, and so, as the delivery date approaches, if S > F they would offset their contracts. This amounts to an increase in the demand for futures contracts that raises their price, and thus drives F closer to S. Similarly, the longs would not want to take delivery of anything that they could buy more cheaply elsewhere. Thus, if F > S as the delivery date approaches, they will offset their contracts. This amounts to an increase in the supply of futures, which tends to depress F, while if there is an increased demand for the underlying, its price will be raised.

As mentioned earlier, there is a growing tendency for cash settlement to replace delivery. This amounts to a great simplification as long as there is a single price that can be used as an index to calculate the gains and losses of transactors — which is sometimes not the case. Pedagogically, however, the presence of cash settlement does not require modifying the exposition in the previous paragraph to any great degree.

Now to the matter of intertemporal arbitrage, which is the second component of the price setting mechanism, and crucial for the understanding of the convenience yield. We can begin by saying something about "equilibrium". A small amount of attention will be paid equilibrium in the next chapter, but this very often used expression will be defined here as a state of rest, which in the context of the forthcoming discussion means that all arbitrage possibilities are exhausted.

We can immediately deduce that if the futures price of a commodity is high compared to the spot price, then transactors will buy spot, store the item, and go short in futures. This simple piece of arbitrage can be concluded by delivering on the contract, which should lead to a profit. Algebraically, we can describe this situation by starting with $F > S(1 + R)$, where R is the total carrying charge: the interest and/or storage cost of holding physical inventories between the initiation of the procedure and the maturity of the futures contract. We should immediately suspect that our equilibrium (or no-arbitrage condition) is $F = S(1 + R)$: there is no profit from following the procedure just described.

At this point it looks like smooth sailing, but if we begin our discussion with the disequilibrium arrangement $S(1 + R) > F$, we run into complications that lead to our having to introduce convenience yield.

Just as $F > S(1 + R)$ resulted in our defining an arbitrage situation (where arbitrage can be described as riskless profit), the opposite arrangement $S(1 + R) > F$ also suggests the possibility of arbitrage. Here it appears that holders of inventories should replace at least some of them by futures contracts on which, in theory, they could take delivery at a later date.

As casual observation makes clear, this is not quite the way things work. The problem is that inventories possess a convenience yield that is derived from their being available when inventory holders need them, and these occasions — or emergencies in some cases — are usually not known in advance. Obviously, the size of the convenience yield depends on the size of inventories: if they are large, then the marginal convenience yield (i.e. the convenience yield of an additional unit of inventories) is small, or even zero; while if inventories are small, the marginal convenience yield could be relatively large. Thus, in this situation, $F = S(1 + R)$ is without interest.

This implies that the no-arbitrage condition that we should be working with instead (which is formally derived in my energy economics textbook) is $F = S(1 + R - Y)$, with Y defined as the *marginal* convenience yield. Accordingly, if transactors have $S(1 + R - Y) > F$, they reduce (sell) inventories and buy futures contracts, and continue until they get $F = S(1 + R - Y)$. Although certain observers make Y a function of inventories, it is more accurate to think of Y as a function of inventories divided by the consumption of the particular commodity — i.e. inventory coverage. In symbols we might have $Y = f(I/Q)$, where I signifies inventories, and Q the consumption of the commodity in units/day. (Defining Q as production might be useful if consumption figures are difficult to obtain.) Thus the units of I/Q would be "days": {inventories/(inventories/day)} = days.

Note also that when I/Q rises, Y falls, and so if we start out with the inequality shown directly above, and there is a fall in inventories (with Q constant), then Y would be increased and, ceteris paribus, this increase might be capable of restoring the equality.

Notice something else here: selling inventories and buying futures contracts does not necessarily mean "using up" these inventories, since they may have been purchased by other inventory holders, and not routed into a current production process. What usually happens is that the price of these inventories will be driven down to a level that will make transactors willing to hold them. Thus, when inventories are placed on the market, S falls. This contributes to decreasing the left-hand-side (LHS) of our inequality. Moreover, as additional futures contracts are demanded, F rises, and considered in the aggregate, the redistribution of inventories could raise Y.

A slight problem arises here because logically the discussion of inventory behavior should turn on the behavior of individual transactors: convenience yield is almost certainly a subjective variable. However as long as we stick to theory it seems quite appropriate to think of inventory holders in the aggregate. Consider oil again. When too much oil is produced, it invariably happens that many — though not all — inventory holders immediately elect to reduce their inventories by selling them to others or using them in current production activities, before the over-supply depresses the price. Besides, if they decide to rebuild their inventories, it can be done later at a lower price. Those who make this decision early enough might be happy with the outcome, but many end up holding inventories whose value will have to be written down by a considerable amount.

Now we come to a topic that anyone who thinks that they might work with or take an interest in commodity futures markets should pay particular attention to. Common sense tells us that in the relationship between S and F, F should be larger than S. In other words, in the usual textbook situation involving commodity markets, we would define our equilibrium as $F = S(1 + R)$; but due to the presence of inventories we can — and do — have something quite different a large part of the time. The equilibrium relationship that we have examined is $F = S(1 + R - Y)$, and immediately we see that if Y is large enough, we can have $F < S$. This is the condition called *backwardation*, and interestingly enough, there are commodity markets — like oil — which are in backwardation more often, percentage-wise, than they are in *contango*, with $F > S$.

The general explanation here is that when consumption jumps, or is expected to jump, the spot price (S) must rise in order for producers to raise production by the amount necessary to boost inventories. Take the Gulf Crisis as an interesting example. Transactors expected that the availability of oil would decline relative to consumption, and in the light of the trouble ahead, existing inventories were probably inadequate. In bidding up the price of existing inventories, they bid up the spot price of oil. This led to a sharp backwardation.

Put another way, the rise in the spot price, along with the rise in the demand for near-term futures contracts (relative to distant-term contracts) resulted in a declining term structure of oil prices: a term structure with a prominent negative slope that meant the spot price higher than futures prices, and near-term futures higher than distant-term futures.

We now turn to the final topic in this section, and one of the most important in this book: basis risk.

Suppose that you have a portfolio of 15 US shares, and you are worried that the price of these securities is about to fall. Your investment advisor might then suggest that you sell a stock index futures contract based on, e.g. the S&P 100 index. The idea here, of course, is that if the price of your shares fell, the index futures should also fall, and what you lose on your portfolio, you should gain on your futures position. This is so since in the offsetting transaction, you close your position with a "buy" that is lower than the sell price at which you opened your position. This, incidentally, was what the mechanics of portfolio insurance was all about.

Obviously, things might not work out the way you planned. Your particular portfolio and the index futures contract are two entirely different animals. You could lose on your portfolio, and also lose on your futures position, because the price of the index-futures appreciated instead of fell. In that case, the offsetting transaction takes place at a higher price than the short transaction with which you opened your position. This is clearly possible, since the S&P 100 contains many shares that are not included in your portfolio. What we have here is a simple and unambiguous example of basis risk. If, however, there was an S&P 15 futures contract comprising the same shares as in your portfolio, then there could hardly be any basis risk in the present transaction.

Some elementary algebra should illuminate this issue, and also help serve as a "soft" transition to the more technical presentations in the following three chapters. To begin, let me point out that I will once again be using something below called an expectations operator, which will be designated E. For instance, in thinking about the price of oil on 1 January of 2005, I might write $E(P)$ or $E(P_{2005})$; while in thinking about the price of the same commodity on January of last year, I would simply write P. It is also useful to think of $E(P)$ as the ex-ante (i.e. expected) price, and P as the ex-post (i.e. realized) price.

The basis is usually defined as $(S - F)$, where again S is the spot price, while F is the futures price. I will also take S_0 as the spot price at time "0", which can be taken as the time at which a transaction is initiated, and S_1 as the spot price at the time at which the transaction is terminated. The same notation holds for the futures price, with F replacing S.

Now let us take an algebraic look at a long hedging example. Hedging might take place because we have $E(S_1) > S_0$: Expectations are that the spot price at time "1" could be larger than the spot price at time "0", and as a result a loss would be forthcoming. (For instance, the transactor plans to purchase some asset at time "1".) The key assumption is, however, that this possible loss could be compensated for by a rising futures price: $E(F_1) > F_0$. We can thus write as our expectation of a profit $[E(V_1)]$ from a long hedged position the ex-ante relationship:

$$E(V_1) = [S_0 - E(S_1)] + [E(F_1) - F_0]$$

What this long hedge basically involves is a decision as to whether to buy the item now (at time "0"), or later (at time "1"). If the transactor decides to wait before making a purchase, then the (ex-ante) profit (or loss) is $S_0 - E(S_1)$. If a pure long futures transaction were entered into, then the expected (ex-ante) profit would be $E(F_1) - F_0$ (due to the appreciation of the contract). With both transactions taking place as a result of the long hedging scenario posed above, we get the above expression, and this can be rewritten to yield:

$$E(V_1) = [S_0 - F_0] - [E(S_1) - E(F_1)] = B_0 - E(B_1)$$

B is the basis, which we defined earlier as $(S - F)$. Now, let us turn from an ex-ante to an ex-post scrutiny of this operation, with $E(B_1)$ replaced by B_1, and $E(V_1)$ replaced by V_1. That gives us $V_1 = B_0 - B_1$, which immediately raises three possibilities: B_1 is equal to, greater than, or less than B_0. (In words, the terminal basis is equal to, greater than, or less than the starting basis.) Taking the first of these, $V_1 = B_0 - B_1 = 0$. This implies that S and F moved in the same direction by the same amount. How do we know this? Write $V_1 = (S_0 - F_0) - (S_1 - F_1) = 0$, and so $S_1 - F_1 = S_0 - F_0$, or $B_0 = B_1$. This arrangement is sometimes called a perfect hedge, but without the emphasis on perfect.

But if the basis moves in the wrong direction, it could result in a negative profit, or $V_1 < 0$, which is what basis risk is all about. How did we get this? Well, obviously, the basis increased (i.e. $B_1 > B_0$), which means that S increased relative to F, or F decreased relative to S (and so we have an increase in backwardation, or a decline in contango). Good news thus consists of a decline in backwardation, or an increase in contango.

If we had started out with a short instead of a long hedge, then the bad news would have consisted of a fall in backwardation, or an increase in contango. With a short hedge the reader is afraid of a price fall, or $E(S_1) < S_0$. The reader will be referred to this case in the exercises.

In an ideal textbook situation, price convergence will take place, and so $S_1 = F_1$: there is no basis risk. Unfortunately, in some futures markets (e.g. electricity) basis risk is occasionally enormous. For that reason, in these markets the derivative of choice will inevitably be swaps.

Exercises

1. What is arbitrage? If arbitrage is possible, why do futures and spot prices converge at the terminal date of a contract? What is the difference between total convenience yield and marginal convenience yield?
2. Algebraically, what is the basis? What is basis risk? Suppose that there was no futures contract for crude oil, and you decided to hedge your purchases of crude oil with futures for heating oil. Why might this work, and why might it not work?
3. What does the clearing house do? What is marking-to-market? What is a margin call? Assume that the demand for cocoa is stagnant, and you own huge inventories of cocoa. Say something about the convenience yield of your cocoa inventories; and say something about the marginal convenience yield of your inventories.

4. Just above the exercises there is a simple algebraic discussion of what could happen if you hedge long, and basis risk is possible. Complete that discussion by explaining what happened to make $V_1 > 0$!
5. Now take the case of short hedging, and repeat the discussion referred to in the previous exercise, taking up all three possible outcomes for V_1.

III. The Next Lesson in Options

It is a fairly common belief that options are much more difficult to understand than futures. This is not true up to a certain point, and it behooves everyone with even a slight interest in the subject to attempt to master the basic operations associated with this particular derivative. To me, the word "master" implies repetition, and so I do not hesitate to repeat some earlier materials.

An option provides the buyer of the option the right to buy or sell a given amount of an underlying asset at a fixed price, called the exercise or strike price, within a given period that is called the expiry or maturity period. As noted earlier, the physical or financial asset in question is often called the "underlying", or the "actual". The end of the period is called the expiry or maturity or settlement date. If the transactor buys an option to purchase the underlying, he has bought a call option; while if he buys an option to sell the underlying, he has bought a put option.

But remember, an option does not have to be exercised. It can be discarded if the purchaser so desires; and so as compared to futures, no reversing transaction is necessary. In fact the seller of the option, the writer, wants nothing more than to see the option go unexercised.

When the initial transaction takes place, the buyer of a put or call option pays a premium to the option writer. This premium is the option price, and ideally it would be formed in an auction type market (such as a stock or futures exchange) by the interaction of supply and demand. Supply and demand undoubtedly plays a part in option pricing, but for the most part these assets are sold on an over-the-counter (OTC) basis by financial institutions. OTC products do not have to be standardized, and can be tailored to the needs of the buyer. On the other hand, exchange traded assets are often easily sold back to the exchange. Even when this is possible for OTC products, a liquidity shortage could make the price uncertain.

An American-type option can be exercised at any time before the expiry date, while a European-type option can only be exercised at expiry. Most options are American-type assets, and this is true in all parts of the world.

Once a position is opened on a futures market, it stays open until the expiry date of the contract or, in the usual case, the contract is closed by a reversing transaction. During the time a futures position is open, its owner must face the possibility of margin calls if the price of the contract moves in the "wrong" direction — as well, of course, as margin windfalls if the price moves in the right direction. ("Right" means up in the case of a long position, and down if the buyer is short.)

As for the option buyer, once the premium is paid, the downside is fully accounted for. On the other hand, with a call option, if the market price of the underlying rises and sails past the exercise price, the option buyer still has the right to purchase the underlying at the exercise price. Similarly, if the market price falls beneath the exercise price of a put option, the underlying can still be sold at the exercise price. Put another way, the option writer has the obligation to deliver the commodity if a call option is exercised, and the obligation to take delivery (at the exercise price) if a put option is exercised. Obviously, a cash settlement can replace delivery, and often does.

Clearly, some categories of option sellers could be in an uncomfortable situation if the options that they have written are exercised — so much so that the question must be raised as to why anyone would write options. The answer is that the options writer intends to sell an option at a price which, she thinks, will provide a comparatively small profit with a very large probability, although it means accepting a small probability of a large loss. This loss, large or small, is the (absolute) difference between the market price of the underlying and the exercise price of the option.

On the other side of the transaction, the buyer of a put or call option is accepting a high probability of a comparatively small loss in return for a small probability of a large gain. When put this way, we are clearly thinking about speculators. Hedgers, of course, are in the position of insurance buyers: we do not think of ourselves as losers if our house does not burn down, and as a result we do not gain access to the amount for which it has been insured. In fact, when looked at from this point of view, it suggests that speculators as a group make money in the options market for performing this insurance or risk-bearing function.

Next, let us introduce two important concepts. Calling the exercise price P_E, and the market (spot) price of the underlying S, the intrinsic value I_P of a put option is $I_P = P_E - S$. If $P_E > S$, then $I_P > 0$, and the option is said to be in-the-money. By way of contrast, if $S > P_E$, a put option is out-of-the-money. (In addition, trivially, if $S = P_E$, then the option is at-the-money). Conventionally, the intrinsic value of an out-of-the-money option is set equal to zero, and so $I_P = Max(P_E - S, 0)$. Similarly, for a call option we can write, $I_c = Max(S - P_E, 0)$.

Once we have added these simple concepts to our vocabulary, we can proceed to a short discussion of price formation for an option. The factors that are most important in explaining this price are the exercise price of the underlying in relation to the market price of that asset; the time to expiration of the option; the interest rate; and most important of all, the volatility of the underlying.

If there is a very large difference between the exercise price and the market price, then (ceteris paribus) the price of the option will be low. The reason is obvious: it is unlikely that the option will move into the money and be exercised. Thus writers will be generous in specifying their premiums.

If there is a very short time before expiry, then (ceteris paribus) the option price will be low. An option can have time value as well as intrinsic value, and the shorter the time to expiry, the lower the probability that the option will move into the money and be exercised. An out-of-the-money option has no intrinsic value, but it does have time value; however this time value is very small for an option that only has a few days to "run".

The lower the volatility, the lower the price. A low volatility means less likelihood of the option jumping into the money. Obviously, with everything else the same, an American-type option has a higher price than a European-type option, since the American-type option can be exercised at any time during the maturity period. Volatility is considered the most important factor in determining the option price.

The interest rate must also be taken into account. This is because instead of buying an option, a potential option buyer can e.g. purchase a bond. Thus the option price is inversely related to the interest rate: the higher the interest rate, the lower the option price must be (ceteris paribus) to attract buyers.

These conditions furnish a starting point for obtaining the price of an option employing the famous Black–Scholes formula — or as it is sometimes called, the Black–Scholes–Merton formula, since Robert Merton solved an important mathematical puzzle that had stalled Fisher Black and Myron Scholes. The original formula was for a European option referred to a non-dividend paying share, and it has presumably been modified by various well paid "quants" to take into consideration other underlyings. However when he received the Nobel Prize in economics, Myron Scholes made it quite clear that the formula is a starting point, and it works better with certain underlyings than with others. He also made it clear — at least to me — that even the most elegant rocket scientist in the world should have access to a substantial line of credit before he or she decides to use the Black–Scholes formula in real-world options markets.

At the beginning of the 21st century, irrational buying pushed some shares to incomprehensible valuations. A few fund managers openly longed for a way to establish big short positions specifically for these shares. Unfortunately, this was not possible. Instead, some of them bought out-of-the-money put options on the *Stoxx 50* with settlement dates fairly far in the future. (The Dow Jones Stoxx 50 is an index of the 50 largest stocks in Europe.) These puts appeared to be comparatively cheap — e.g. Adrian Holmes, Merrill Lynch's European equities manager mentions 1%. With the value of the fund that Holmes is managing steadily increasing, the implied volatility of the shares in this fund has decreased. Volatility is the most important factor in determining an option's price, and thus if options can be purchased on a bundle of shares similar to those in his fund, their premiums would be low. (See the next section.) Clearly, Mr. Holmes' fondest wish was that if the market fell, the profits on his options would more than compensate him for any losses on his portfolio, as well as previous options losses. Mr. Holmes obviously realizes that finance is not just about yields, but yields, liquidity, and risk.

IV. Conclusion: The Black–Scholes Equation

People who really and sincerely want to know about the world of finance, need to go beyond the world of textbooks. After completing this book, I strongly recommend Bernstein (1992), Goldstone (1988), Leeson (1998), Lewis (1988), and Valdez (1997). The next step in your education is a textbook like Bodie and Merton (2000), and after that turn to the finance section of the largest library within range.

   One of the things that we find out in the first four books named above is that real-world finance is a great deal different from that sometimes taught in academia. An article in *The Economist* once cited a well known finance scholar as saying that the Black–Scholes (B–S) option pricing formula is "the most successful theory not only in finance but in all economics". *This is precisely what it is not*, and anyone using it in that spirit in the real-world is heading for real trouble. The original B–S paper deals with a non-dividend bearing European call option instead of the almost universally traded American options, and the many costly attempts that have been made — and are being made — to generalize it to more prevalent instruments have not been particularly successful. As a concept, however, it is well worth mastering, which is why the book by Zvi Bodie and Robert Merton is an important pedagogical contribution.

   According to Peter Bernstein, a great deal of work went into deriving the B–S equation, but it is simple enough for you to remember. Using the notation given earlier in the chapter, where P_E was the exercise price, S the spot price, and P the premium (i.e. the option price), we can write $P = SN(d_1) - P_E e^{-rT} N(d_2)$. In addition to the variables already mentioned, σ is the instantaneous standard deviation — a surrogate for volatility; T is the time to expiry in fractions of a year ($0 < T < 1$); r is the riskless rate of interest; $d_1 = [Ln(S/P_E) + (r + 0.5\sigma^2)T]/\sigma T^{1/2}$, and $N(d_1)$ = cumulative probability distribution for the standard normal variate, from $-\infty$ to d_1. $N(d_2)$ is the same for d_2, where $d_2 = d_1 - \sigma T^{1/2}$. Bodie and Merton give an interesting linear approximation for the above equation. This is for $T < 1$ year, and is $P = \sigma S (T/2\pi)^{1/2}$.

In engineering and gunnery, we learn not to use formulae indiscriminately. Amazingly enough, this is usually how the B–S formula is used in the classroom, and is why many persons with a background in the "hard sciences" regard it as a prime specimen of analytical gobbledygook. This is definitely not the case.

Amram and Kulatilaka (1999) provide an interpretation for the B–S formula in their short book on real options theory. The first expression on the right hand side (RHS) is the expected value of S if $S > P_E$ at the expiry date. (They note that expectations are taken using risk neutral probabilities.) The second term on the RHS is the present value of the cost of investment. The importance of volatility was mentioned earlier, and the absence of volatility in some well known approximations to the original B–S equation probably vitiates their applicability to real markets.

A couple of questions always appear when students initially confront the above analysis. The first concerns the absence in this equation of the *probability* of the asset price rising or falling: this absence is highly counterintuitive. The answer here turns on the asymmetric nature of an option: the downside is limited to the premium, while the potential profit depends on how far the price might move on the "upside", and the volatility — where the volatility is in the B–S equation. As for the presence of the risk-free interest rate, this says something about the attractiveness — or lack thereof — of investing in an option instead of an asset such as a short term government bond that is essentially risk free.

And how, *in theory*, is the B–S relationship used? One answer is that P is calculated, and then compared to the existing (market) P. If they are not the same, then arbitrage is *theoretically* possible. Note the emphasis on *in theory* and *theoretically*! In his Nobel Prize lecture at Uppsala University, Professor Scholes made it clear that carrying out this kind of "arbitrage" is far from riskless, and whoever is involved with it should have a good relationship with his or her banking "support".

Something that was not mentioned earlier is that option writers are asked for initial margin, and if their position loses value then *variation margin* can be requested. Some of us would hesitate to write options, but the writing of short dated options is done by very many experienced speculators.

A book recommended earlier was Schwager's "Market Wizards" (1989). Three terms that are often used in that book are "tick size", "limit-up", and "limit-down". A tick is the smallest allowable price movement for a contract. For example, on a LIFFE 3-month Eurodeutschmark contract, where the unit of trading is one million DM, a tick mark is 1 basis point (= 0.01% = 0.0001).

As for limit-up or limit-down, this is the maximum daily movement that is allowable up and down on a contract. This concept is very unpopular in some quarters because it keeps the market from clearing, but regardless of supposed or real shortcomings, it keeps prices from exploding up or down.

The London International Financial Futures Exchange (LIFFE) is now closing down its trading pits, and some of the self-employed "locals" who traded on their own accounts are going into screen-based trading boutiques, where traders are provided with computers and telephone access to markets.

According to Sathnam Sanghera of the *Financial Times*, a quick brain and unbridled self-confidence will no longer be enough to succeed in the new computer-driven LIFFE, and presumably in the smaller boutiques. I certainly hope that nobody reading this believes that supposition. Regardless of your luck in the genetic draw, rest assured that both a quick brain and unlimited self-confidence can be acquired by patience, concentration, and meticulous attention to details; and these qualities are useful everywhere.

And, incidentally, it is *never* too late to begin.

V. Appendix: More Options Theory

It may not be a good idea to overload beginning students with algebra, but it seems likely that some readers will be interested to know a little more about some of the rudimentary algebraic concepts that are associated with options. For financial derivatives, readers should turn immediately to Keith Pilbeam (1998) and Frederic Mishkin (1998).

The profit of buyers of put options can be written as as follows: $V_{Bp} = \text{Max}\{(P_E - S - P_p), -P_p\}$. Sellers' profit is $V_{Sp} = \text{Min}\{(P_p + S - P_E), P_p\}$. If, for example the option is exercised, then the profit is $(P_E - S - P_p)$. Otherwise it goes into the waste paper basket and the buyer loses P_p, which happens to be the gain to the writer. Suppose that we take a situation where $S = 15$, $P_E = 30$, and $P_p = 5$. The buyers profit is then $\text{Max}\{(30 - 15 - 5), -5\} = 10$. The seller's profit is -10. If S were 50, then $V_{Bp} = -5$, and $V_{Sp} = 5$. You should verify this result.

In an earlier discussion, the B–S formula was written out and briefly discussed, but Professor William Sharpe — another Nobel Prize winner — has developed a simple version designed to illustrate some of the basic logic.

Suppose that we have an "underlying" with a price S, that could move to either U (up) or D (down) at the end of one year. Suppose also that the interest rate is r, and it is possible to buy a call option where $P_E = S$. What is the "competitive" price P of the option.

To begin, if the underlying falls to D, then the option is worthless: the gain $G_D = 0$. If it rises to U, then the option is worth $U - P_E$. Suppose that an investor creats a synthetic option by buying one unit of the underlying for S, and borrowing L. At the end of the year, the investor must repay the loan with $L(1 + r)$. Now, if we make it so that if the underlying falls in value, but the loan can be repaid, then we must have $L(1 + r) = D$: the gain is thus "zero" on both the synthetic and the actual option for a price fall.

However, if the underlying rises to U, then the investor receives a gain of $G_U = U - L(1 + r)$ because of the loan. In order for the synthetic option to replicate the actual option when U rises, then a number of calls equal to $N = [U - L(1 + r)]/(U - P_E)$ must be bought, where $N > 0$. Where do we get this from? The *total* gain from a move up must be the same for option and loan, and it is unlikely that this will be the case for *precisely* one option.

As for the price of this option, since the synthetic option required an outlay of $S - L$, then the price of a single option is $P = (S - L)/N$.

Note what we have done here! In order to make the synthetic option equivalent to the actual option, then the gains G must match. Essentially this was done by choosing the right values of L and N.

Exercises

1. When we have a call option, the profits of buyers and sellers are, respectively, $V_{Bc} = Max\{(S - E - P_c), - P_c\}$ and $V_{Sc} = Min\{(P_c + E - S), P_c\}$. Use numbers similar to those in the beginning of this appendix to discuss situations where call options buyers and writers gain. What are the maximum gains?

2. Suppose that the price of the underlying, S, is 17 (and is equal to P_E), while U = 23, D = 11, and r = 10%. What is P? Discuss!

3. "Buying an option gives you the right to buy or sell ..." Buy or sell what; and if you buy, haven't you paid twice for the option?

4. My monthly income is uncertain, and so is yours! Could a swap be arranged?

5. Why did Mr. T. Boone Pickens use futures instead of options?

6. What happens to the convenience yield when (I/Q) increases? The marginal convenience yield? Draw a couple of diagrams!

7. Volatility is important when considering both futures and options. Explain!

8. Oil futures and not orange juice futures are often referred to as the "best game in town". Instead of being like Eddie and Dan and choosing orange juice, wouldn't it have been better to take a crack at oil?

9. What is "contango"? Backwardation? At the beginning of the Gulf War, there was an enormous backwardation in the oil market. Why?

10. What is the meaning of "limit up" and "limit down"? What is intrinsic value? What do you think happens to the time value of an option as the expiry (or settlement) date approaches? Why?

11. I have memorized the original Black–Scholes formula because I never know when I might need it. How does that sound?

Chapter 5

An Introduction to Exchange Rates

Algebraic notation has entered this book earlier, though perhaps not to such an extent as to be noticeable to many readers. What will be done now is to make an unequivocal move from words to words *and* music — i.e. words and elementary algebra.

The chapter begins with a few important definitions, and then proceeds to a discussion of exchange rates employing supply and demand curves. Needless to say, many of the calculations carried out in this chapter are done in the real world by simply depressing a few computer keys, however it was impossible for me to convince myself that these algebraic and graphical materials should be excluded. They are not difficult; they provide an excellent application of supply and demand curves — a much better application in fact than most of those that you have seen or will see in the textbooks employed in the introductory courses in economics; and they will help readers to take another step toward acquiring the kind of attitude and presentation skills that are traditionally associated with successful residents of the financial and/or scientific world.

Hopefully, readers will feel comfortable with this simple exposition. But if they decide that they would rather wait before singing along, then it might be best to reread the first four chapters, while at the same time initiating an all-out attack on the opening chapters of any elementary general economics textbook. After a few pleasant hours of drawing supply and demand curves, you should have more than enough background to deal with the modest graphical analyses that you encounter in this and subsequent chapters.

I. Some Elementary Definitions

If doing activity X means not being able to do activity Y, where Y is the most highly valued alternative to X, then Y is the opportunity cost of doing X. If the activity involves consumption, then the price (i.e. cost) of consuming a certain good or service — e.g. a weekend in Paris — is the bundle of goods and services that you could have enjoyed if you had refrained from taking that trip, and instead used the time and money for something else.

Going to production, the opportunity cost of an extra unit of a good is the most valuable bundle of those goods not produced using the same resources: the opportunity that is sacrificed. The same logic can be applied to a resource or an input. For example, the wage rate or salary is the opportunity cost of leisure in those situations where the employee prefers leisure to work, but has the opportunity to work. This can be turned around: a great many hours of well deserved leisure is the opportunity cost of my having to write this book. Presumably, the satisfaction that I will get from completing this mission will outweigh the cost. Similarly, the opportunity cost of using an additional unit of an input is the loss of the goods that could otherwise have been produced if that input had been used in another production process. Often it is appropriate to measure inputs and outputs in money.

Every shareholder/stockholder has the opportunity of selling her shares and putting her money in bonds, adding the stipulation that if she is thinking about portfolio investments, she considers the bond investment the best alternative use of her money. Of course, if her thoughts are elsewhere, we could also say that she could sell her securities and head for the ski resort of Åre in Northern Sweden to do some serious skiing and partying, assuming that when she thinks about getting rid of her Volvo and Microsoft shares, she almost simultaneously starts thinking about mountains and snow.

When the subject is financial capital, the opportunity cost is usually taken to be the (monetary) return that could be earned elsewhere if this money was not put into the asset under evaluation. Normally we would not say that it was the (non-monetary) satisfaction experienced by Ms. Skier as she raced down a ski trail on still another Åre mountainside. Often, when uncertainty enters the picture, the opportunity cost is often taken as the "best" certain financial return — e.g. the interest rate on government securities. Furthermore, the best certain interest rate often functions as an opportunity cost for physical investments: why build an applejack factory whose sales are uncertain, when you can buy treasury bills (T-bills), and retire to Cayenne or Guadacanal and clip coupons?

Book value appears often in finance, but book value is not the opportunity cost of an asset, as is sometimes implied. If the intention is to replace near-obsolete physical capital with new equipment, then opportunity cost turns on the market value of the capital, which is the only cost that is relevant for making decisions involving these machines and/or structures. This is why market-value based accounting has become so important.

The term equilibrium has already appeared several times in previous chapters. Strictly speaking, in economics equilibrium means correct expectations: a consistency between beliefs and occurances. Unfortunately, this is not a very useful definition for the work that we are doing in this book. A better definition is the one sometimes used in physics — a state of rest, because it ties in with the law of one price: in a competitive market, if two assets provide an equivalent yield, they will tend to have one price (per dollar of return), and this will be brought about by arbitrage. Rewording that definition somewhat, we can say that in equilibrium there are no opportunities for arbitrage or, as it is usually expressed in financial economics, the no-arbitrage condition prevails.

There are more definitions in this book, although the use of the word equivalent brings to mind (Albert) Einstein's equivalence principle, which applies just about everywhere: if two phenomena produce equivalent effects, they must be manifestations of the same fundamental law.

II. Introduction to Exchange Rates

Foreign exchange markets feature the trading of one country's currency for that of another, where the exchange rate is the price of one currency in terms of another. At the present time, one American dollar is quoted at 8.83 Swedish crowns (kronor). This is the sell (or *offer*) rate — the rate at which a Swedish bank will sell you a dollar; the buying rate — the *bid* rate — is lower. Thus we can write 8.83 cr/$ as the exchange rate for the dollar in terms of crowns, and $P_{cr} = 8.83 \, (cr/\$) \, P_\$$. The difference between the offer and bid rate is the *spread*.

The foreign exchange market roughly comprises a number of large commercial banks in the main financial centers of the world. Note the term "large". What it means is that while most banks are in a position to supply tourists and business persons with foreign banknotes, etc., the banks referred to here have trading rooms that are linked to each other by highly sophisticated equipment, where bank deposits worth millions of dollars, denominated in most of the leading currencies, are bought and sold during virtually every minute of the working day. The amount traded daily in the currency markets in January 2000 was very close to $2 trillion (versus $0.6 trillion for bonds, and $0.1 trillion for equities), and thus is the largest financial market. The people who do the trading are very well rewarded, although those who "underperform" (i.e. do not do what is expected of them) are quickly told to think about finding another line of work.

Exchange rates are basically determined by the supply of and demand for various currencies. Those rates that will be considered below are both the spot exchange rate (P) and the forward exchange rate (F), where the latter is the price of currency that will be delivered at some point in the future: usually one to three months, even though forward contracts have been written with a maturity of two years. For example, the quoted price of one pound that will be delivered in three months was 13.25 Swedish crowns when I wrote these lines ($F_{3M} = 13.25 \, cr/\pounds$). Thus, someone needing 1,000 pounds in three months could sign a contract specifying that they will pay 13,250 crowns in three months. In Sweden, persons often purchase forward exchange from the bank in which they hold deposits, which reduces credit risk for the bank.

In both the spot and forward markets, we have supply and demand curves for dollars that might look like those in Fig. 5.1: what we get from our daily paper is P, and not the shape of the curves. But regardless of how these curves look, the dollar has had a dominant place in foreign exchange markets since the Second World War. It has functioned as the *numeraire* —

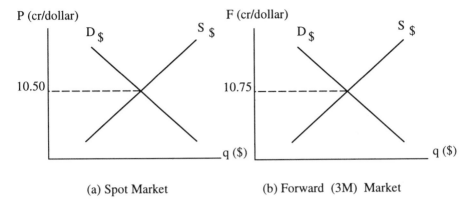

Fig. 5.1. Supply/Demand Curves for Dollars in terms of Crowns

i.e. the (benchmark) asset whose units are employed when measuring the value of other assets — and it still does to a considerable extent.

Pay very close attention to the units. As an exercise, you might try explaining why they must be the way they are. Then try inverting the exchange rate, making it dollars/crown, and redrawing the diagrams!

Notice the units: when we have supply and demand curves for dollars (and not crowns) the unit on the horizontal axis is dollars, and the exchange rate (P) is measured in crowns/dollar. Had this situation been reversed, and we had supply and demand curves for crowns, then the unit on the vertical axis would have been dollars/crown, and the unit on the horizontal axis crowns. As is usually the case for any good, when the price (i.e. exchange rate) increases, more dollars are supplied — the supply curve (S) goes up to the right — and the demand curve for dollars (D) goes down to the right. Before reading further, the reader should make sure that he or she understands why this makes sense.

Now let us discuss some reasons for a shift in these curves. In the case of the spot market, if e.g. wages or the money supply rose rapidly in Sweden relative to the US, then it seems likely that this would lead to a relative increase in the demand for US currency in order to buy US goods: the relative increase in wages might be interpreted as a prelude to a rise in the Swedish price level. This would shift the demand curve for dollars to

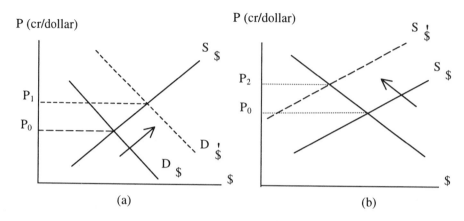

Fig. 5.2. Supply and Demand Curves for Dollars

the right, as in Fig. 5.2(a), depreciating the crown relative to the dollar. (That is, causing the price of the pound to rise from P_0 to P_1.) Similarly, if there was a recession in the US, then demand would fall in that country, to include the demand for foreign (i.e. Swedish) goods and services. This situation would be represented by a shift in the $S_\$$ curve to the left, which also causes the crown to depreciate relative to the dollar (or the dollar to appreciate relative to the crown); and as shown in Fig. 5.2(b) results in a rise in the price of the (crown) price of the dollar from P_0 to P_2.

A useful observation is that the supply of dollars is the demand for crowns, while the demand for dollars is the supply of crowns.

The same kind of reasoning employed above applies to both the spot and forward markets; but as a useful exercise, let us consider one of the ways that speculation can influence the demand for forward crowns. Suppose that a certain speculator believes that the price of the US dollar will be 8 crowns in one month: $E(P_{1M}) = E(P_{t+1}) = 8$ crowns/dollar, where E is the expectations operator, and in order to give readers some practice in using subscripts, I am taking the price in one month as P_{1M} or P_{t+1}. This being the case, let us consider the actions of this person in the light of several possible values of the forward exchange rate — being careful to keep in mind that, to begin with, we are considering the behavior of a single market actor.

Expected Value of Spot Rate in One Month $E(P_{t+1}) = E(P_{1M})$	$F_{t,t+1}$: Forward Rate at Z "t" for "t + 1"	Speculator's Behavior
8 crowns/dollar	7.5 crowns/dollar	Buy forward dollars (sell forward crowns
8 crowns/dollar	8 crowns/dollar	No action
8 crowns/dollar	8.5 crowns/ dollar	Sell forward dollars (buy forward crowns)

The logic of the behavior of Mr. or Ms. Speculator should be readily apparent: if the expected value today of the spot rate in one month is 8 crowns/dollar [$E(P_{t+1}) = 8$], and it is possible today to buy a dollar for delivery in one month for 7.5 crowns/dollar ($F_{t,t+1} = 7.5$), then if the one-month dollar is bought on the forward market, and the spot rate turns out to be 8 crowns/dollar, a 0.5 crown profit will be made on the transaction. Notice, however, that this is not arbitrage, which is defined as a riskless profit opportunity. There is a risk that the spot rate will be 6 or 7 crowns/dollar in a month, in which case the purchase at the given exchange rate would result in a loss. Before continuing, it might be wise to generalize the preceding discussion. If the reader has any problem in following this discussion, then it might be a good idea to insert some of the above numbers into the equations.

Suppose that we have a situation where the expected value of a spot rate at time $t + 1$ is greater than the forward rate for the same point in time. Then we have $E(P_{t+1}) > F_{t,t+1}$. This can be put in crown-dollar "units", which immediately suggests the following "action":

$$\left(\frac{cr}{\$}\right)_{t+1} > \left(\frac{cr}{\$}\right)_t \text{ (and so) crown}_t \longrightarrow (\mathbf{F_{t,t+1}}) \longrightarrow \$_{t+1} \longrightarrow (\mathbf{P_{t+1}}) \rightarrow \text{crowns}_{t+1}$$

Notice how this functions: crowns at time t are transformed to dollars at time $t + 1$ by the forward exchange rate (at time t), and these dollars are then turned back into crowns by the spot rate prevailing at $t + 1$. If this operation was successful, then the speculator has more crowns at t + 1 than she had at t. Do not forget, however, that P_{t+1} is unknown at time t: this is not authentic arbitrage! Suppose now that we have $E(P_{t+1}) < F_{t,t+1}$. This means that we have:

$$\left(\frac{cr}{\$}\right)_{t+1} < \left(\frac{cr}{\$}\right)_t \quad (or) \quad \left(\frac{\$}{cr}\right)_{t+1} > \left(\frac{\$}{cr}\right)_t$$

We therefore get the following scheme:

$$\$_t - (F_{t,t+1}) \longrightarrow crowns_{t+1} - (P_{t+1}) \longrightarrow \$_{t+1}$$

The above behavior concerned a single market actor — a speculator. Next, using the same numbers that we have above (in order to keep things simple), let us examine the speculators' market supply-demand curve for one month forward dollars. The first step is to draw an aggregate (i.e. market) supply-demand curve. This is shown in Fig. 5.3(a), and it is for all persons and/or institutions speculating in foreign exchange; but it should be remembered that the market for foreign money also consists of tourists,

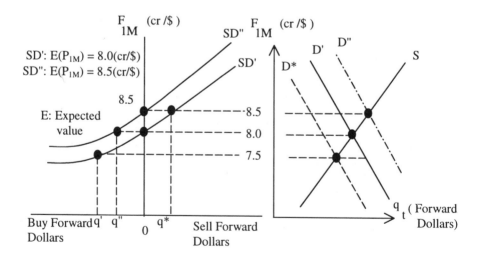

Fig. 5.3.   Speculators' Supply-Demand Curve for Forward Dollars; and Aggregate (Market) Supply and Demand Curves for One Month Forward Dollars

exporters, importers, etc. Even if these other transactors do not interest us, they influence the price of foreign exchange. Thus, the no-action point in Fig. 5.3(a) is where the same amount of dollars is being bought by speculators (as a group) as are being sold by them. In addition, remember that they are buying from each other, as well as anyone else in the market at that time. The total market is shown in Fig. 5.3(b), with initially $D = D'$.

To begin, assume an equilibrium (i.e. the no-action situation), with a forward rate of 8 crowns/$. Now, with expectations by speculators unchanged, suppose that another large group of transactors — e.g. the oil importers — increase their demand for forward dollars, because they expect that the price of oil will be adjusted up. In Fig. 5.3(b), the price of one month forward dollars is shown moving from 8 crowns/$ to 8.5 crowns/$.

If expectations are unchanged, speculators as a group move from the no-action position ($q = 0$) to q^*, where they are selling forward dollars. Why are they doing this? Because if they expect a dollar to be worth 8 crowns in a month, and they can obtain 8.5 crowns for a dollar in the forward market, then in a month these crowns can be exchanged for $8.5/8 = \$1.0625$

A question that might be asked now is how does this sequence of events influence expectations, and thus the actions of speculators. A possible assumption might be that after speculators have substantially increased their access to forward crowns, their expectations about the future price relationship changes. Accordingly, their demand (for forward crowns) might decrease, and their supply might increase. If this happens, the supply-demand curve might shift up to SD". How long will all this take? Not very long as compared to the speed at which things move in many markets. Traders employed by financial institutions are hyper-active, while many market actors encountered in economics are passive. Also recognize that when $SD' \to SD''$, D" moves to the left, and/or S moves left!

Note something else. The suggestion made above about the movement of the SD curve is merely a suggestion — an unproved theory at best. Moreover, as the good people on CNN like to claim, prices on the world's financial markets never stop moving, and often they move too fast for it to be worth while brooding over whether a given theory is or was applicable. It is always time for the next move, and if a player is unable to analyze previous misconceptions in intervals measured in seconds, then it is only a matter of time before he or she will be watching the action from the sidelines.

Academic economics may mix fact with fantasy, but reality is different. Nick Leeson became a highly successful trader without having cause to think about stochastic calculus. In fact, if he had been the type who confuses algebra with action, he would not have gotten in the door at Barings, despite the genteel image that house attempts to project. The money he lost was annoying, but the gentlemen who hired him know that there is plenty more where that came from, and people like Nick Leeson will get it for them. As part of their training, a group of US Marine Corps infantry officers were taken to the Chicago Board of Trade where, against a background of non-stop screaming and shouting, they were given some advanced instruction in high-velocity decision making. According to a trader at that noble establishment, "If you have an ego, then there's no point in spending time on the trading floor unless you're super aggressive".

There are supply and demand curves for every forward market, and we often speak of a *term structure* of forward exchange rates. For example, consider the following hypothetical trajectory of crown-pound exchange rates for June 1, 2000 shown in Fig. 5.4. (What the reader should comprehend here is that, on the dates shown, the only thing we see are the prevailing prices — although quantities can be determined.) Another point worth noting is that although quantitative economists sometimes claim that advanced statistical techniques have turned economics into a genuine science, they are unable to estimate supply and demand curves. It is often possible to obtain estimates of *elasticities*, where these are defined as the percentage change in quantity divided by the percentage change in price [$= (\Delta q/q)/(\Delta p/p)$], but unfortunately these estimates show a tendency to vary from economist to economist. On the other hand, as Professor Karl Vind once pointed out, in economics empirical work can never take the place of theory. What he meant by that was complicated or sophisticated empirical work. This is particularly true in finance, where the separation of advanced statistical techniques and the trading desks or executive suites is almost total.

Notice the units in these diagrams — cr/£. This means that P is an exchange rate. (Of course, any price can be viewed as an exchange rate.)

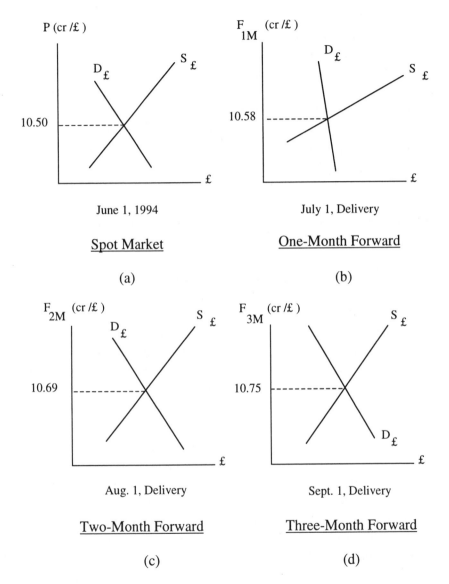

Fig. 5.4. A Spot and Four Forward Exchange Rates for Pounds

Occasionally, however, we hear of a *real exchange rate* (P_r). In Sweden this is usually written $P_r = PP_F / P_D$, where P is the money exchange rate, P_F a price index of foreign goods, and P_D a price index of domestic (Swedish) goods. Some theorists feel that while money exchange rates may change, real exchange rates tend to remain constant as a result of price changes initiated by the change in money exchange rates. This contention is interesting, but definitely unproved.

At this point, the reader should make sure that he or she understands that the forward prices shown in Fig. 5.4 are prices that prevail at a certain time on June 1, 2000, and there is no reason to believe that the forward prices existing a day (or for that matter a minute) later will be the same as those registered above. And remember that the spot price for e.g. July 1, 2000 need not be anywhere in the vicinity of the 10.58 crowns/£ forward price. The spot price for July 1 will be determined by supply-demand conditions in the spot market on July 1. At the same time, it can be observed that many economists regard the forward price as the best estimate of the spot price on a particular day. In other words, had these economists been compelled to estimate (or "guess") on June 1, 2000, the spot price of the pound sterling on July 1, 2000, the value they probably would have chosen was 10.58 crowns/£. In choosing this value they would have been assuming that no single individual could do a better job of estimating the future value of a currency than The Market, which makes a great deal of sense.

In the case of auction markets — where bids and offers are openly displayed, and prices fluctuate day-by-day or even minute-by-minute — this kind of reasoning (which is an offshoot of the Efficient Markets Hypothesis) — has a great deal to offer. A remark on terminology is also important here. The price patterns shown in Fig. 5.4 has the forward pound at a *premium*, while the forward crown is at a *discount*. Had the price trend been such that forward pounds were less expensive than spot pounds, then the forward pound would have been at a discount, and the forward crown at a premium.

Where interbank dealing is concerned, foreign exchange transactions often take the form of swap arrangements. These will be taken up in a later chapter, but roughly they combine a spot and a forward transaction. For example, suppose that Bingham-Manhattan Bank needs Swedish crowns.

They might find it possible to borrow crowns from Stockholm Handelsbank, while lending dollars to that bank. In e.g. three months the arrangement is reversed, with Bingham-Manhattan sending crowns to Stockholm's Handelsbank, and Stockholm's Handelsbank sending dollars to Bingham-Manhattan. The swap rates could be determined by discounts or premiums in the forward exchange market.

III. Forward Rates: A Technical Note*

It is customary in banking to quote forward rates by referring to spot rates. To begin, the spot rate is given in the form P_B/P_A, where P_B is the spot rate bid, P_A is the spot rate asked, and we always have $P_A > P_B$, since a trader dealing in a currency will always sell at a higher price than she will buy.

For instance, we might have 6.5712/6.5788 for the spot rate of the dollar in terms of Swedish crowns — or, sometimes, just 6.5712/88, with the understanding that the "88" is preceded by 6.57. As already noted, if the value of a foreign currency (in terms of the domestic currency) is greater forward than it is spot, then it is at a premium to the spot rate; otherwise it is at a discount; and the amount of the premium or discount is often written X/Y, where X is added *or* subtracted to P_B in order to get the forward bid rate, F_B, and Y is added *or* subtracted to P_A in order to get the forward asked rate F_A. It is not obvious whether X and Y should be added or subtracted, and this matter will be clarified below with the help of some elementary algebra; while it should be understood that if X and Y involve two figures, then they should be added or subtracted to the last two figures of the spot rates.

An example might help us before we get started with the algebra. Suppose we assume that we have forward crowns at a discount (and thus forward dollars at a premium), with the ratio X/Y = 20/30. Since forward crowns are at a discount we know that X and Y must be added to the spot

---

*All discussions marked with an asterisk (*) can be skipped if the reader desires.

quotations. This gives us $F_B = P_B + X = 6.5712 + 0.0020 = 6.5730$ crowns/$\$$, and $F_A = P_A + Y = 6.5788 + 0.0030 = 6.5818$ crowns/$\$$. Notice how we have added X and Y!

Something that should be noticed right away is that the spread — or the difference between asked and bid — has increased for the forward quotation. Calling the spot spread θ', we have $P_A - P_B = 6.5788 - 6.5712 = 0.0076$, while the forward spread $\theta'' = F_A - F_B = 6.5818 - 6.5730 = 0.0088$. Conventionally, the forward spread is larger than the spot spread, since uncertainty increases the farther into the future we go. (Note also that forward kronor might be quoted F_B/F_A, or 6.5730/6.5818, or even 6.5730/818).

These observations are crucial for the algebraic analysis, and so we can duplicate some of them:

$$\theta' = P_A - P_B \tag{5.1}$$

and

$$\theta'' = F_A - F_B \tag{5.2}$$

Remembering that we have our premium or discount written in the form X/Y, we can write θ'' as:

$$\theta'' = F_A - F_B = (P_A \pm Y) - (P_B \pm X) = (P_B + \theta' \pm Y) - (P_B \pm X)$$

This can be simplified to give:

$$\theta'' = \theta' \pm Y - (\pm X) = \theta' \pm (Y - X) \tag{5.3}$$

If the spread increases as we move forward, then we must have:

$$\theta'' > \theta' \Rightarrow \pm (Y - X) > 0 \tag{5.4}$$

The implication here is clear:

(1) If $Y > X$, then $(\pm) \Rightarrow (+)$ $\qquad\qquad\qquad\qquad$ (5.5)

(2) If $X > Y$, then $(\pm) \Rightarrow (-)$ $\qquad\qquad\qquad\qquad$ (5.6)

In the numerical example earlier in this section, X/Y = 20/30, and since here Y > X, we add X and Y to the spot quotations to get the forward quotations (as shown in the example). Adding, of course, meant that the currency of interest — which in the example was Swedish crowns — was at a discount (to the dollar). By way of contrast, had forward crowns been at a premium, we would have had X > Y, and X and Y would have been subtracted from P_A and P_B. Put even simpler, when X/Y is in the form {(large number)/(small number)}, subtraction should take place, otherwise addition.

While these rules may appear complex to outsiders like myself, they are second nature to a trader. They have to be, because foreign exchange trading sometimes accounts for half the profits of the major commercial banks, where it appears that up to 90% of the trading of convertible currencies takes place with respect to the US dollar. They are presented here only to show readers how these materials should be approached, and to provide some practice in elementary algebra.

IV. Elementary Arbitrage

The term arbitrage is perhaps one of the most used in economics. What it is supposed to involve is riskless profit making. Buying "cheap" in one market, and selling "dear" in another, is the sort of thing that most people think of, but there are less accurate examples. A former classmate of mine at the International Graduate School of Stockholm University became a well known "arbitrageur" who functioned more or less as follows. He would find a firm that was doing fairly well but which, in his opinion, could do better. He and his associates would then buy the firm, and get rid of a fairly large number of its employees. Assuming that production and revenues did not fall as far as costs, the firm was now a ripe candidate for a profitable sale. In case the reader is interested, Professor Michael Jensen of Harvard once called "arbs" like my former classmate "heroes of capitalism", because they put the boot to tired and inefficient management, and injected new ideas, enthusiasm, and management into corporations that were supposedly

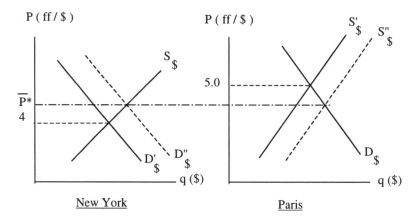

Fig. 5.5. The Supply and Demand Curves for Dollars in New York and Paris

giving their stockholders a bad deal. Some ramifications of this kind of confused thinking are brilliantly illustrated in the film "Wall Street".

We can now consider a simple, even trivial example of arbitrage in the currency markets. Suppose that it is possible to buy a dollar for four French francs in New York, and five francs in Paris, as shown in the following diagram.

In the circumstances shown in Fig. 5.5, there will be an increased demand for dollars in New York — where in terms of francs they are inexpensive — in order to supply them in Paris, where dollars fetch a higher price. As indicated in the diagram, this two-point arbitrage eliminates the price difference, bringing about a common price, $\overline{P}^*$, in the two cities. Now let us turn to a three-point arbitrage situation, beginning with the following exchange rates in London, New York, and Frankfurt:

LONDON (L)   £1 = \$1.90   (or) \$/£ = 1.90   (and) £/\$ = 0.5263

NEW YORK (NY) \$0.45 = DM 1.0 (or) \$/DM = 0.45 (and) DM/\$ = 2.22

FRANKFURT (F) £0.20 = DM 1.0 (or) £/DM = 0.20 (and) DM/£ = 5.00

As one possibility, let us consider the London–Frankfurt, \$/DM rate. This can be obtained immediately by doing the indicated cancelling as:

$$\left(\frac{\$}{\text{pound}}\right)\left(\frac{\text{pound}}{\text{DM}}\right) = 1.90 \times 0.20 = 0.38\,\frac{\$}{\text{DM}} \quad \text{(or)} \quad 2.63\,\frac{\text{DM}}{\$}$$

We have thus effectively reduced this problem to one of two-point arbitrage, where in terms of the dollar, the deutschemark is cheaper in London–Frankfurt than it is in New York. Therefore we can suggest the following transaction:

$$\$ \longrightarrow (\text{L}) \longrightarrow £ \longrightarrow (\text{F}) \longrightarrow \text{DM} \longrightarrow (\text{NY}) \longrightarrow \$$$

In terms of the numbers employed above, we have:

$$\$1 \longrightarrow (\text{L}) \longrightarrow £0.526 \longrightarrow (\text{F}) \longrightarrow \text{DM } 2.63 \longrightarrow (\text{NY}) \longrightarrow \$1.18$$

Arbitrageurs exist to pursue information that is not wholly public in the economic sense of being fully reflected in the price. Arbitrage seems like an easy way to make a fortune, but the reader should be warned that in the real world arbitrage margins are much smaller than those featured in the example above. The opportunity to turn a dollar into 1.18 dollars does not come too many times in a lifetime, and anyone faced with it should beg, borrow, and mortgage to the absolute limit of their ability. Furthermore, given the efficiency of the computers and communications equipment used in exchange markets, should such an opportunity arise, it will only exist for a very short time.

Before going to some exercises, it might be a good idea to remember what a price ratio is all about. If we write $p_x = 2p_y$, it means that $1x$ is exchanged for $2y$. In general, if $p_x = kp_y$, then one unit of x trades for k units of y. For example, if $p_x = kp_y$, then $1x \longrightarrow (1/3)y$. Now suppose that in Canada, $1x$ trades for $2y$, while in the US, $1x$ can be exchanged for $3y$, and then the barbed wire at the border was taken away, and unrestricted free trade instituted. We have:

US: $p_x/p_y = 3$, and so $1x \longrightarrow 3y$, or $1y \longrightarrow (1/3)x$

CANADA: $p_x/p_y = 2$, and so $1x \longrightarrow 2y$, or $1y \longrightarrow (1/2)x$

With this price scheme to begin with, Canadians would take x to the US, where they got $3/2$ as much y as in Canada. Similarly, Americans would take y to Canada, since to begin with 1y in the US trades for (1/3)x, while in Canada a unit of y trades for (1/2)x. This, we might remember, is what Ricardo's law of compative advantage is all about: as long as price ratios are different in two countries, then trade can take place due to "comparative" as opposed to "absolute" advantage.

The work of David Ricardo was followed — in terms of importance — by that of Eli Hecksher, and then (Bertil) Ohlin and Hecksher. The pure theory of international trade seems to have fallen into disrepair laterly, and for a very good reason: technology has not been introduced into the pure theory in a meaningful way, and of course we all are aware of what role technology is playing, and the role that it will have to play in the 21st century, and later. Similarly, population movement has not appeared in the pure theory in an entirely convincing way. At the same time we should recognize the brilliance of many of the pure trade theorists. Here I am thinking in particular of John Chipman, Murray Kemp, and Ron Jones, although there are at least a half dozen scholars among the younger theorists who deserve to be recognized.

Exercises

1. In the arbitrage exercise above, work out the dollar–pound rate for NY– Frankfurt! Now compare it with London! Can arbitrage take place? If so, how might this arbitrage work?
2. Suppose that we have the following price ratios for x and y in the UK and Germany: $(p_x/p_y)_{UK} = 1/3$ and $(p_x/p_y)_G = 2/5$. Will trade take place, and if so, who will trade for what?

V. Trade Weighted Exchange Rates and Purchasing Power Parity

This section is more-or-less optional. The topics taken up here are often found in books on international finance, and so in order to make sure that readers do not feel themselves at a disadvantage if they encounter influential or important persons who have read these other books, a brief presentation seems in order.

At the same time it must be admitted that there are many stimulating and perhaps important topics that should be included in the present book, but which were omitted. The simple fact of the matter is that this book contains things that I believe to be essential both for the beginning course in international financial economics, and as a quick refresher. For example, if you were on a plane from Stockholm to Sydney, which means a trip of about 30 hours, and you needed to impress someone in Sydney with your knowledge of global finance, then it might be better for you to spend the greater part of your trip reading this book, than watching the in-flight movies. This is especially true if that someone you needed to impress was considering you for a highly paid job in or near Sydney's Eastern Suburbs.

Let us begin by considering a country that trades with only one other country, and has an exchange rate on January 1, 2000, of 8 crowns = 1 dollar. This exchange rate will now be given an index value, P_{00}, of 100. The country, incidentally, is Sweden.

Next, let us move forward to January 1, 2001, and suppose that on this date the exchange rate is 8.5 crowns/dollar. In other words, the crown has depreciated. In index form, this will be taken as $P_{01} = (8.5/8) \times 100 = 106.25$ on January 1, 2001.

Now let us go to a situation where Sweden trades with two countries, say the United States (US) and the United Kingdom (UK). In order to get a base index of 100, we must "weigh" the indexes of the two countries, and customarily the weights would be assigned on the basis of the proportion of foreign trade that Sweden has with the two countries. For the purpose of this example, let us assume that 60% of Sweden's foreign trade was with the US, and 40% was with the UK. The weights would thus be $W_{US} = 0.60$ and $W_{UK} = 0.40$: they always sum to unity. Now let us look at the exchange rates on January 1, 2000. Assuming that $P_{US,00} = 8$ crowns/dollar, $P_{UK,00} = 12$ crowns/pound, and $P_{US,00} = P_{UK,00} = 100$, our index $P_{00} = W_{US}P_{US,00} + W_{UK}P_{UK,00} = 0.6 \times 100 + 0.4 \times 100 = 100$. This is a trivial but necessary observation.

Moving ahead to January 1, 2001, let us assume that $P_{US,01} = 8.5$ crowns/dollar, while $P_{UK,01} = 11.4$ crowns/pound: the crown has depreciated with respect to the dollar, but appreciated with respect to the pound. Now let us calculate P_{01}:

$$P_{01} = (8.5/8) \times 100 \times 0.6 + (11.4/12) \times 100 \times 0.4$$
$$= 63.75 + 38.00 = 101.75$$

In the convention employed here, the trade weighted exchange rate shows a depreciation. In general, employing 2000 as the base year, and with N countries, the index for 1989 would be:

$$P_{01} = \left(\frac{P_{US,01}}{P_{US,00}}\right) \times 100 \times W_{US} + \left(\frac{P_{UK,01}}{P_{UK,00}}\right) \times 100 \times W_{UK} + \dots \qquad (5.7)$$

Introducing for the first time in the book the Sigma notation (e.g. $\Sigma a_i = a_1 + a_2 + \dots + a_i + \dots$) we can write Eq. (5.7) as:

$$P_{01} = \sum_{i=1}^{N} \left(\frac{P_{i,01}}{P_{i,00}}\right) \times 100 \times W_i \qquad (5.8)$$

If, however, we wanted P to fall when there was a depreciation, which is a practice in some countries, then we would have:

$$P_{01} = \sum_{i=1}^{N} \left(\frac{P_{i,00}}{P_{i,01}}\right) \times 100 \times W_i \qquad (5.9)$$

The main advantage with trade weighted exchange rates is that, to some extent, they permit the exchange rate situation to be summarized in a single parameter. It is also the practice in Sweden and other countries to maintain P within certain limits by selectively buying and selling foreign currencies. Traders and the analysts they work with need to know this. In addition, the weights are changed from time to time.

Exercises

1. Start with Eq. (5.8), and write out the situation for a four-country world!
2. It is stated above that it is the practice to maintain the trade weighted exchange rate within certain limits by selectively buying and selling foreign currencies. Assuming that Sweden only traded with two other countries, construct a simple numerical example to illustrate this concept. (Hint: use the example above where Swedish currency has depreciated to 101.75, but it is desired to keep it within the bounds $0.99 \leq P \leq 101$!)
3. Foreign exchange dealers (and sometimes the banks that they work for) are referred to as market-makers. What does this mean? How do these market-makers make a profit?
4. Write out four terms of the following: $\Sigma(\Phi_i m^i + t)$!

The purchasing power parity hypothesis is implicit in the writings of most of the classical international economists (e.g. David Hume and David Ricardo), but is particularly associated with the work of the Swedish economist Gustav Cassell. The absolute version is based on the familiar "Law of One Price". For example, if sill chutney costs 10 crowns/kilo in a store a few meters on the Swedish side of the Swedish–Norwegian border, then the same kind of chutney must cost the same thing in a Norwegian store a few meters on the Norwegian side of the border. Otherwise, assuming no physical barriers or heavy transactional costs involved in crossing the border, one of these sill stores will go out of business.

But how can they be the same price? They are incontestably in two different countries, where one country uses Swedish crowns, and the other Norwegian crowns? The answer is that they must be the same price, taking into consideration the exchange rate. For example, if sill chutney costs 8 Norwegian crowns/kilo, then the exchange rate P (Scr/Ncr) must be $P_S/P_N = 10/8 = 1.25$ Scr/Ncr. Any other exchange rate will mean that sill chutney will have different prices in the two countries, and the store with the highest price will no longer be able to sell this delicacy.

Obviously, a theory or hypothesis of this nature is not going to be of much help in determining the Swedish–Norwegian exchange rate. First of all, the example above referred to a single good, sill chutney, but the exchange rates that we see on the financial pages of our local newspaper are concerned with hundreds — or perhaps even thousands — of goods. Put another way, we are not just comparing Swedish sill chutney with Norwegian sill chutney, but a bundle of Swedish goods and services with what can be a very dissimilar bundle of Norwegian goods and services. Furthermore, where the prices of these two bundles are concerned, let us remember that not all of these goods are traded internationally, and thus when the price — or better, the price index — of the non-traded goods in the Norwegian bundle changed, it would change the price index of the entire Norwegian bundle. There is also the matter of freight charges, tariffs and preferences that can be influenced by such things as packaging and advertising. For instance, in the example above, the sill chutney in Norway might be chemically and genetically identical to that in Sweden, but consumers preferred the Swedish product because their favorite television celebrities convinced them that it came from happy fish.

The Economist has often voiced the opinion that under certain circumstances absolute PPP can be useful. For example, in April of 1994, when the Swiss price of a Big Mac was 5.70 Swiss Francs (SFr), and the average price of a Big Mac in four American cities (including sales tax) was \$2.30, the exchange rate between these two countries should have been 5.70/2.30 = 2.48 SFr/\$. The actual rate was 1.44 SFr/\$, which means (ceteris paribus) that the Swiss Franc is overvalued against the dollar, which in turn suggests that the SFr/\$ rate should rise. In the real world, however, burgernomics must face the fact that the dollar failed to adjust to the Big Mac index over a very long period — so long, in fact, that it raises serious doubts about the suitability of the Big Mac index as a forecasting tool.

A somewhat more satisfactory version of the PPP hypothesis involves rates of change, rather than absolute values. To get the so-called relative version we start from the general form of the exchange rate expression, $P = P_S/P_N$, where S refers to Sweden, and N, Norway. Now write this simple relationship in the form $P_S = PP_N$, from which we immediately get $\Delta P_S = P\Delta P_N + P_N\Delta P$. Now we divide both sides by P_S — which means dividing the right hand side by PP_N — and obtain after rearranging:

$$g_P = \frac{\Delta P}{P} = \frac{\Delta P_S}{P_S} - \frac{\Delta P_N}{P_N} = g_S - g_N = \overline{P} \qquad (5.10)$$

If there was no change in the price levels of both countries, then $g_S = g_N = 0$, and according to this version of PPP, then there should be no change in the exchange rate: g_P (or $\overline{P}$) = 0. Similarly, if prices increase more rapidly in Sweden then in Norway ($g_S > g_N$), then g_P would increase, which is tantamount to a depreciation of the Swedish crown: Scr/Ncr increased.

Some readers are probably aware that instead of using g in the above, E(g) might be a more interesting selection for financial economics, especially if it turns out that the version employing g was verified by the data. In these circumstances, if the *ex-ante* g — that is E(g) — was on target, then some profitable speculation might be possible.

As things have worked out, however, the above version of PPP is not always reliable. For Canada and the US between 1973 and 1982, the Canadian dollar depreciated with respect to the US dollar by an amount which almost corresponded to the difference in inflation rates between the two countries. But it would not be easy to find other periods in which reality corresponded to the theory.

Similarly, in the period 1973–1979, the rate of inflation in the US averaged 7.5%/year, as compared to 3.6%/year for Switzerland; but Swiss currency appreciated at a rate of 11.3%/year (on the average), instead of 7.5% − 3.6% = 3.9%/year. One of the reasons for this was the high rate of capital inflow into Switzerland during a period which was characterized by a great deal of uncertainty because of the manner in which the war in Vietnam concluded, as well as increases in the price of oil. With major political and economic changes taking place in the world, many persons came to the conclusion that Switzerland was a nice place to park their money until the smoke cleared. Of course, something to remember here is that a large rise in the price of oil (ceteris paribus) should increase the value of the dollar, since oil is purchased for dollars. This was one of the main (ceteris paribus) reasons for the continued strength of the dollar in the last half of 1999.

Just as we have these two PPP hypotheses, we can also speak of the something called the real interest-rate parity. The hypothesis that follows from this expression is that the expected interest rate on risk free loans is the same all over the world. Given two countries, with $r = r_r + E(g)$ for one country — where r_r is the real interest rate, and $E(g)$ the expected rate of inflation — and similarly $r' = r_r' + E(g')$ for the other country, then if we have $r_r = r_r' = r^*$, we get $r = r^* + E(g)$, and $r' = r^* + E(g')$. Suppose that we have $r^* = 3\%$, $E(g) = 2\%$, and $E(g') = 3\%$. The nominal interest rates that are implied by the real interest-rate parity hypothesis are thus $r = 3\% + 2\% = 5\%$, and $r' = 3\% + 3\% = 6\%$. If these interest rates have some other value, and this hypothesis is applicable, then some profitable "arbitrage" might be possible.

VI. Final Comment

By this time readers should be getting the feel — or the rhythm — of international financial economics. Something that should be kept in mind here is that unlike many branches of academic economics, some of these materials are of immediate value. Furthermore, if you manage to read this book, then you will have taken the first step in understanding many real-world financial processes.

It is also appropriate for readers to begin thinking about expanding their horizons by examining the financial pages of their local newspaper, and by becoming better acquainted with the international financial press. Although it is not commonly realized, newspapers like the *Wall Street Journal* and the *Financial Times* are among the most informative in the world, and not just on financial matters.

Exercises

1. Suppose that we have $A = BD$. From one of the first lessons in calculus we know that $\Delta A = B\Delta D + D\Delta B$ when the changes (Δ) are small. Start by taking $B = 100$ and $D = 200$, with $\Delta B = 1$ and $\Delta D = 2$. Using these numbers, calculate ΔA directly beginning with $B = 101$ and $D = 202$.

Now use the right hand side of the expression to get ΔA. Next, get the growth rate of A, which is $\Delta A/A$, in terms of the growth rates of B and D.

2. Give a general explanation of how we turned three-point arbitrage into two point arbitrage!

3. Suppose that a huge pool of oil is discovered on the outskirts of Paris. Using supply and demand curves for francs, discuss changes in the franc/dollar exchange rate!

4. "The supply of francs is equal to the demand for dollars". Starting with a supply curve for francs, show how we construct the demand curve for dollars.

5. Suppose that you believed completely in *The Economist's* "Big Mac" application of absolute PPP. How would you use it to make some money?

6. How might the credibility of a country's central bank influence future values of its currency?

7. Solve in 30 seconds the following cross-rate arbitrage: Stockholm 10 crowns/pound; London, 0.25 dollars/crown; New York 2 dollars/pound! I cannot do it, but maybe you can.

8. Special drawing rights, which are liabilities of the IMF, were once called "paper gold". Is this a good name?

9. When the free market price of gold went from \$32/ounce to more than \$800/ounce, the US government was not very happy, although there was a lot of gold in official hands in the US. Explain! About the same time this was happening, it was decided to establish a "two-tier" gold market. What do you think that this means?

10. What is securitization? Market capitalization? A "repo"? Random walk?

11. Value in economics means exchange value: the value of any commodity is the maximum amount of some other good that an individual will give up in order to gain an extra unit of the good in question. Is "value" the same as opportunity cost?

Chapter 6

Interest Rates, Yields, and Bonds

A long chapter on bonds in a beginners' textbook? Perhaps a few readers will recall a famous question asked by millions of US soldiers during the 20th century: is this trip really necessary? Well, the present trip is necessary because it contains some very important financial economics, as well as some extremely useful algebra. Among the former are the term structure of the interest rate, and among the latter a derivation of the annuity formula. This is a chapter where concentration and patience on the part of the reader will pay considerable dividends.

Something that you might remember before you commence your work is that Keynes labeled the interest rate the most important of all economic variables; while yield — defined for our purposes as the return to an investor expressed as an annual percentage — is arguably the most important term in financial markets. (Liquidity and risk come next.)

As for bonds, in 1981, new public issues of bonds and notes in the US (excluding Treasury securities) came to almost $100 billion. In 1993, this figure was about 1.27 trillion, and 1.5 trillion seems a reasonable — but probably low — estimate for the first year of the new millennium. Thus, when a market of this size goes from bull to bear, enormous losses are possible. For example, 1994 was a year that featured the worst bond market losses in history for the holders of US bonds: a decrease in value of somewhere in the neighborhood of a trillion dollars, as compared to the 500–600 billion lost during the stock market implosion of 1987. As the late Sidney Homer once remarked, "Almost every generation is eventually shocked by the behavior of interest rates", and given the rate at which the bond market is growing, the next shock may go right off the Richter scale.

The shock of 1994 was greatly enhanced by the rise in 30-year Treasury bond rates from 6.2% at the start of the year to 7.75% at the end of the 3rd quarter. This reduced the value of outstanding bonds by at least 600 billion dollars, since when interest rates on official "paper" goes up by that amount, it pulls up all rates. Moreover, what that episode showed was that even bond funds can provide some bad surprises, in that experienced fund managers might be too late in adjusting the maturity and composition of their portfolios when that little voice somewhere in the back of their heads begins to tell them that the time has come for interest rates to escalate. Why is this? The answer is that if they e.g. go to cash or less volatile short term securities, and rates do not rise, then they increase the risk of underperforming the market, and that is definitely not the way to find yourself on one of the journal *Institutional Investor's* all-star teams of superstar analysts. (*Institutional Investor* is a publication that everyone interested in financial markets should make themselves acquainted with.) Readers of this book might be interested in knowing that there are *analysts* in the US who are now being paid more than a million dollars annually.

A famous concept in academic economics is the so-called principal-agent problem. This is a moral hazard problem that occurs when the managers in control of some operation, the agents, act in their own interest rather than that of the owner (the principal) of the resources that they are managing because of a different structure of incentives. If we consider mutual funds and fund investors, then investors want funds to maximize fund returns, while fund managers are more concerned with taking steps to maximize the attractiveness of their firms or their own personalities in order to increase the amount of money under management.

This may be an insoluble dilemma in real life. For example, a fund manager could frequently find that the best investment policy is to continue to hold her present portfolio — i.e. to do nothing. The principal will then have to determine whether the agent is "actively" doing nothing, or "simply" doing nothing. If I were the principal, one possible approach to this quandary would be for me — a university teacher who purchases funds — to manage my own money, which immediately leads me to think of something that they say in the legal profession: the person who acts as his own lawyer has a fool as a client. Occasionally this sort of departure works out, but all too often it has an unhappy ending.

I. Interest Rates and Annuities

Probably the simplest way to describe an interest rate is to say that it is the payment, expressed in percentage points per year, that a borrower makes to a lender in exchange for the use of the lender's money. We can also say that the opportunity cost of holding currency is the amount of interest income that is given up. For example, if your bank pays 5% on a deposit — or you can get the same amount on a (presumably safe) government bond — then the opportunity cost of holding currency is "about" 5%. Why about? Because if you held all your financial assets in deposits or securities, there would be a cost in time and energy in constantly going to the bank or an ATM to obtain the cash that is necessary to pay for certain kinds of goods and services. It is often claimed, however, that well before the end of the 21st century, the "cashless" society will be a fact in much of the world.

That leads immediately to our trying to get a better understanding of the rate of interest than we achieved in earlier chapters. We already know the difference between real and money rates of interest. If r is the money (or nominal) rate of interest, r_r is the real rate of interest, and g (= $\Delta p/p$) is the rate of inflation, then we have $r_r = r - g$. This is an ex-post relationship, but we noted that we also had use for its ex-ante counterpart: $r_r = r - E(g)$, where E is the expectations operator. The movements of short-term interest rates should also be observed. In looking at the periods 1981–1989, 1990–1995, and 1998, average short terms rates for the US (in %) were (8.5, 4.9, 4.8), for Japan (6.0, 4.3, 0.7), for the present EU countries (10.5, 9.0, 3.9), and for Mexico (61.1, 24.9, 26.1).

Next, let us consider four vehicles through which debt is contracted: simple loans, fixed payment loans, coupon bonds, and discount bonds. Most of our attention will be directed toward the last two, but in examining the first two we can refresh our knowledge of several key concepts.

A simple loan provides a borrower with a sum of money (the principal) which must be paid back, together with the interest, at the maturity or due date of the loan. Let us take two simple examples: 1,000 dollars borrowed for one year at 10%, and the same amount of money borrowed for two years at the same rate of interest. In the first case, the amount to be paid back is $1,000(1 + r) = 1,000(1 + 0.10) = 1,000(1.1) = 1,100$ — remembering that 10% must be written 0.10 in this kind of exercise. In the second case the amount is $1{,}000(1 + 0.10)(1 + 0.10) = 1{,}000(1.1)^2 = 1{,}210$. The principal in both cases is 1,000 dollars, while the interest payments are $100 paid at the end of one year in the first case, together with the principal; while it is $100 paid at the end of the first and second years in the second case, or — what amounts to the same thing algebraically — $210 paid at the end of two years in the second case. The principal is repaid at the end of the second year.

Note also how this exercise could have been turned around. If M_0 is the amount loaned for T years, then the amount to be paid back is $M_T = M_0(1 + r)^T$, but we can also say that the present value of M_T is $M_T/(1 + r)^T = M_0$. For example, in our numerical example, the present value of 1,210 dollars, received two years from now, is $1{,}210/(1 + 0.1)^2 = 1{,}000$ dollars. This point should be understood perfectly before the reader continues, because it provides another insight into why the present value of a bond declines if interest rates go up: the price now for all future payments goes down, and so the sum of these payments (which is the bond price) will be less!

In the matter of fixed payment loans, a certain amount (M) is borrowed, and then repaid by making the same payment every year (or fraction of a year) for a given number of years. Mortgages are a very good example of this kind of loan. Fortunately, it is a simple matter to obtain the amount of the periodic payment, A, from the well known annuity formula (that will be derived later), which is one of the most important expressions in economics and finance, and should be memorized immediately.

$$A = \frac{r(1 + r)^T}{(1 + r)^T - 1} M \tag{6.1}$$

For example, if we borrow 1,000 dollars for two years, and the interest rate is 10%, then payments at the end of each year (= amortization + interest) will be:

$$A = \frac{0.1(1.1)^2}{(1.1)^2 - 1}(1{,}000) = 576\$/\text{year}$$

Something that should be noticed here is that the present value of these two payments is equal to the amount borrowed (= loaned): $A/(1+r) + A/(1+r)^2 = 576/(1.1) + 576/(1.1)^2 = 1,000$. Let me emphasize again: present value is an extremely important concept in both economics and finance, and you would be doing yourself a very great favor if you make a special effort to understand it now!

As will be made clear later, another important expression is the "yield to maturity". This is the interest rate, r, that equates the present value of an asset (e.g. a debt instrument) to the stream of payments received from that asset. For instance, if we take the first example given above we have $1,000 = 1,210/(1+r)^2$, and the yield to maturity (or r) in this case is 0.10 (= 10%). Perhaps a recasting of this example is in order: the yield to maturity is the value of r which sets the present value (e.g. the cost of the asset) equal to the discounted value of 1,210, which might be the net income generated by the asset. "Net" in this context means the after-tax income.

Similarly, in the example where we employed a two-year fixed payment loan with annual payments of 576 dollars, we would have:

$$1,000 = \frac{576}{(1+r)} + \frac{576}{(1+r)^2}$$

Or, in terms of the expression for an annuity:

$$576 = \frac{r(1+r)^2}{(1+r)^2 - 1}(1,000)$$

What we need in either of these expressions is the value of r that will equate the left hand side (LHS) to the right hand side (RHS). We can obtain this r employing the same trial-and-error methods that are used to adjust field artillery or mortar fire: a value of r is chosen, and we observe the relationship of the LHS of these expressions to the RHS. If LHS > RHS, then we raise r, possibly with the intention of getting an "over", and therefore "bracketing" the true value of r. Or, on the other hand, we might prefer to creep up on the correct value. In any event, where this example is concerned, the correct value of r is 0.10 (= 10%).

Before continuing, it should be pointed out that the previous discussion, which appears to be completely straightforward, may contain the basis for some confusion. If the market rate of interest — which can be thought of as a kind of average interest rate on high quality bonds and bank accounts — is (unrealistically just now) 10.5%, and you pay 905 dollars for a one year discount bond — to be explained below — with a face value of 1,000 dollars, you have obtained a yield (or rate of return) of exactly $(1{,}000 - 905)/905 = 0.105 = 10.5\%$. In this example, the yield (= return) and the interest rate are numerically the same. But suppose you could buy this bond for 900 dollars. With this the case, the yield is 11.1%, although the rate of interest remains 10.5%. Accordingly, yield and the rate of interest are not necessarily the same thing.

It might be useful to know something about the interior mechanics of paying for an asset (e.g. a house or machine) whose annual payment A can be determined by Eq. (6.1). In A, we have both amortization (i.e. capital) and interest payments. Taking the example that we had earlier, with $M = 1{,}000$ and $r = 10\%$, payments are 576 dollars/year for two years, and the following table is relevant:

Year	Balance	A	Interest	Capital	Balance (End of Year)
1	1,000	576	100	476.0	524 (= 1000 − 476)
2	524	576	52.4	523.6	0

Notice that the capital payment (i.e. amortization) for the second year is $576 - 52.4 = 523.6$. There are some small rounding errors in the above.

As an aside, where the annuity formula is concerned, there is a simple relationship for the number of years (T) before the money in an annuity (M) runs out. This is:

$$T = \frac{\text{Ln}\left(\dfrac{A}{A - rM}\right)}{\text{Ln}(1 + r)}$$

In this expression, Ln is the "natural logarithm". Remember that the logarithm is defined as the exponent to which the base is raised. For example, 2 is the logarithm to the base 10 of 100 because $10^2 = 100$. The base of the natural logarithm system is "e" (≈ 2.71828).

A few definitions might be useful before you try some exercises. The expression *embedded option* is quite common. This is an option attached to a bond that could apply to either the bondholder or the issuer. The issuer might have a call provision that grants the right to retire the debt, partially or fully, before the maturity date. On the other hand, an issue with a put provision gives the investor the right to sell the issue back to the issuer at par value on designated dates. The *par value* is just another name for maturity value, redemption value, or face value.

It has been emphasized in this book that a palpable increase in the money supply will usually raise expectations of a price increase, which in turn will lead to a rise in interest rates; but for those who are familiar with mainstream macroeconomics, an increase in the money supply also has a liquidity effect which, ceteris paribus, leads to an increase in the demand for bonds, and thus a fall in interest rates. Timing is important here, but of late the price-expectations effect seems to be the strongest.

Finally, nothing is said in this book about taxes, but this does not mean that the tax rate on investor income is not important. It would not have been useful to include them however because they vary from country to country.

Exercises

1. With the same value of M and r as in the above exercises, construct a table like the one above for three periods.
2. In the first exercise, suppose that you decide to pay off this loan at the end of the first year. How much would you have to pay? (Hint: think about present values!)
3. Taking values of M, A, and r from the above exercises, calculate from Eq. (6.1) the value of T. Does the value that you get make sense in terms of the discussion held earlier?

II. Coupon and Discount Bonds

A coupon bond is a bond with a given face value; a given time to maturity — which is expressed in terms of the date of redemption of the bond, at which time the bond purchaser receives the face value (or principal); and a periodic payment to the owner of the bond which is specified on a "coupon" associated with the bond. In theory, the owner of the bond clips a coupon from his bond once or twice a year, puts it in the mail, and then returns to the beach to await the arrival of his payment. However in reality most of this — excluding the beach — can take place via computers.

An important point here is to distinguish between the price of the bond and its face value. The price is what is actually paid for the asset. It may be the face value, and for the original owner this is often the situation; but if the bond is traded in secondary markets, then its price is very likely to be lower or higher than the face value. To get some idea of the topics that we encounter in bond pricing, let us begin with a simple numerical example where we have a two-year coupon bond with a face value of 1,000 dollars, and coupons of 100 dollars. This might be described as a 10% coupon-rate bond maturing in two years, with a face value (or par value) of 1,000 dollars. If this bond sold for 1,000 dollars, then its yield to maturity is equal to its coupon rate. But suppose that it only sold for 966 dollars. In these circumstances we would have to calculate its yield to maturity from the following expression:

$$966 = \frac{100}{(1+r)} + \frac{100}{(1+r)^2} + \frac{1,000}{(1+r)^2} = \frac{100}{(1+r)} + \frac{1,100}{(1+r)^2}$$

In other words, we pay 966 dollars to obtain 100 dollars after one year, and 1,100 (face value + interest) after two years. By trial and error methods, or with the right kind of pocket calculator, it is easy to obtain $r = 12\%$, which can be interpreted as the yield to maturity, and redefined as r_m.

Taking V as face value, C as coupon payments, P_b as the bond price, and T as maturity (in years), a very useful approximation for yield to maturity (r_m) is:

$$r_m = \frac{C + \left(\dfrac{V - P_b}{T}\right)}{(V + 2P_b)/3}$$

Some further elaboration on the above might be useful here. Suppose that the bonds were printed on Monday, when the interest rate was 10%, and sold from pushcarts on Tuesday when the interest rate was 12%. On Monday, when the bonds were issued, the firm issuing the bonds (i.e. the borrowers) estimated that they would have to pay 10% for money, and therefore issued liabilities with a 10% coupon. But when these bonds hit the street the next morning, the market rate of interest was 12%. Accordingly, nobody in their right mind would have been anxious to pay 1,000 dollars for a bond that only provided a 10% yield. Instead, in order to get people to purchase these bonds, they must be given a discount. If the bond we are talking about now was a one year bond, providing a 100 dollar coupon and the 1,000 dollar face value (principal) after one year, a purchaser might be willing to pay 982 dollars for it, which would mean that they were obtaining a 12% yield.

This is an important example, and the reader should take particular care to make sure that he or she understands it. If, for example, you are the owner of 10% coupon bonds, each of which has a face value of 1,000 dollars, then if the rate of interest falls, you can sell these bonds for more than 1,000. Falling rates of interest have greatly improved the financial health of many bond buyers over the last five years of the 1990s! Similarly, if you wake up some fine morning with the intention of increasing your inventory of long-term bonds, but a know-it-all voice from the TV insists that the interest rate will go up soon, then it might be best to delay your purchase. This is also a reason why strong expectations of interest rate rises lead to the selling of bonds.

Discount bonds function in much the same way as coupon bonds where the reaction to interest rate changes is concerned, however otherwise there are important differences. Discount bonds tend to have shorter maturities, and usually they are sold by governments and municipalities. Their most important characteristic, however, is that they do not explicitly yield interest, but sell at a discount. For this reason discount bonds are often called zero coupon bonds. For instance, a one year US treasury bill with a face value of 1,000 dollars might sell at 935 dollars. (It is also common practice to auction off these treasury bills.) It is a simple matter to obtain the yield to maturity on this particular bond. We have merely to solve the following simple relationship for r_m: $935 = 1,000/(1 + r_m)$. This gives $r_m = 0.0695 = 6.95\%$.

If we ask why the price of the bond was 935 dollars, a sensible answer would probably include some comments about the present market rate of interest (which would most likely be in the vicinity of 7% for a security of the same quality), and notice would also be taken of interest rate expectations for the one year life of the bond. Referring to the previous discussion, if interest rates were expected to rise in the year after the bond was sold, and there was a large and dynamic secondary market for these securities, then the price would probably be slightly lower.

An expression that one sees only rarely is the present value (M) for an annuity with A for the initial payment, that grows at a constant rate g. Assuming that $r > g$ we have:

$$M = A \frac{\left(1 - \left(\frac{1+g}{1+r}\right)^T\right)}{r - g}$$

Suppose, for example, that you could lease an asset for ten years for an initial payment of 50,000 dollars, and your payment increases by 10%/year (i.e. $g = 10\%$). With $r = 15\%$, and payments made every year at the end of the year, the above relationship gives $M = \$358,860$. Note also that we can use these annuity relationships for semi-annual, quarterly, etc. payments. (Exercises: calculate r_m using the approximate formula for $V = P_b$; and in the above calculate M when $g = 0$.)

It should be appreciated that Treasury bills are basically a short-term security with a maturity of from three to six months. In the US, large numbrs of T-bills are owned by private persons, many of whom are wealthy. The former presidential candidate of the Reform Party, billionaire Ross Perot, apparently likes to keep some of his ample fortune in T-bills. Interestingly enough, in 1999, there was a shortage of treasury securities in the UK due to the lack of borrowing by the government, whose accounts apparently showed a surplus, and the same was true in the US. These government securities are important for several reasons. They make markets more liquid, in that they can almost always be traded in the vicinity of existing prices, which at least in theory facilitates shorting large numbers of them in order to cover risky long exposure (i.e. to balance long positions with short positions).

In addition, pension funds are heavily dependent on high quality bonds to provide the fixed annuity payments they have guaranteed their policy holders. These funds have been squeezed by the prevailing low inflation, which has contributed to the exceptionally low yields on long bonds.

As was pointed out in the first chapter of this book, knowledgeable bond purchasers are very sensitive to inflationary pressures. They know that macroeconomic price rises tend to lead to interest rate rises, because bond purchasers demand compensation (in the form of higher yields) for the loss in purchasing power caused by inflation. (Remember that inflation reduces the real interest rate.) As a result, many bond analysts believe that wage increases — which are often a prelude to price increases — and high rates of growth of the money supply, are deadly enemies of the bond markets. If we consider the UK, it has even been claimed that what bond owners lose through inflation, they never regain — although this would be difficult to prove. For these bond analysts, as well as their employers and clients, the disinflationary trend of the 1990s that stretched across the turn of the century was regarded as wish fulfillment. And, as to be expected, some of them genuinely thought that it would last forever.

Of course, in the 15-year period after 1964, interest rates on long-term government bonds in the US moved from 4% to more than 15%. This rise should have been bad news for physical investment, and therefore economic growth, but such was not the case. (The Vietnam war was probably an important factor here.) During that period average after-tax corporate profits as a percent of gross national product remained at least as high as during the following 15 years, although the stock market was depressed. Warren Buffet would say that this depression was due to "the gravitational pull of interest rates", but apparently high profits kept the bottom on the market.

Thus, even though many financial players have approached the new century with smiles on their faces and steel in their strides, they know in their bones that inflationary panics can occasionally sweep across the bond market, causing bond yields to "spike" to irrational levels. In the UK there are more than a few nagging doubts about the inadequate supply of government "paper"; and the "comeback" of junk bonds – especially in Europe – has caused some anxiety. (This topic will be treated in the next section of this chapter.) In the background, there are e.g. suspicions that the collapse of the Japanese bond market in September, 1987 — barely a month before the stock market crash in the US — triggered various economic instabilities in the world economy that caused the crash, and the same type of occurrence could be repeated.

The causality chain here was fairly simple to detect, with the key link being the dependence of the government bond market in the US on Japanese purchasers. The sale of US securities by the Japanese because of some bad economic vibrations in Japan or the US, while at the same time the US economy was losing some of its robustness, meant that financial markets in the US, and elsewhere, were suddenly vulnerable to any number of potential problems. Events such as the sudden depreciation of an important currency, or even the wrong kind of speech by a head of government or central bank director, could make things a great deal worse in a hurry.

Exercises

1. In Eq. (6.1), prove or show that if we have LHS >RHS, then we raise r.
2. The face value of a bond is 1,000 dollars; the time to maturity is four years; the yearly coupon payments are 100 dollars; and its price is 939 dollars. What is the approximate yield to maturity?
3. "Officials are hoping that the private sector will take advantage of low long-term gilt yields and issue a flood of 30-year bonds. This would provide pension funds with an alternative, and higher yielding type of

asset". (*Financial Times*, December 4, 1999.) "Gilts", of course, are UK government securities. Discuss this statement in full!

We have broached the concept of long bonds vis-à-vis short bonds, but we have not said anything about bonds that never mature. This kind of bond is called a consol or perpetuity: it is a bond with no maturity date and no repayment of principal, but which (in theory) makes coupon payments C forever. (For readers who are familiar with "The Forsythe Saga", Soames Forsythe's advice was "Never sell consols". What the good Soames did not say, however, was that often these assets were "called in", and replaced by consols with a smaller coupon.) By taking the limit of Eq. (6.1) above as T approaches infinity, we get as the price of these bonds $P_b = C/r$, where P_b is used for the present value (= price) instead of M, and the annual payment is C instead of A. In addition, if we merely have a long bond (20 or 30 years) instead of a consol, then C/P_b — which is called the current yield — is a good approximation of the yield as calculated from e.g. (6.1). It is not, however, a good approximation for a short bond.

Continuing, let us look at the very important situation where an amount P_b is invested for n years at a rate r, and is compounded m times per year. The terminal value of the investment is:

$$V = P_b \left(1 + \frac{r}{m}\right)^{mn} \tag{6.2}$$

Now let us apply this to a situation where a transactor can buy a one-year discount bond for 900 dollars, that pays 1,000 dollars at the end of the year. We can get the yield on this from $900 = 1,000/(1+r)$, and thus $r = 11.1\%$.

Next, suppose that our transactor wants to buy a three-month bond with the same yield. We go to the above equation and make the following substitutions: $1,000 = 900[1 + (r/4)]^{4 \times 1}$. This can be easily solved for $1 + (r/4)$, and here we get $[1 + (r/4)] = (1,000/900)^{1/4}$. From this expression we get $r/4 = 0.0267 = 2.67\%$, and so $r = 0.1068 = 10.68\%$.

An obvious question is "what happened to the 11.1%"? One way of answering this is to note that interest is an annual concept, and so if you are offered an annual interest rate of 10.68%, but it is compounded four times a year, then you are actually obtaining an annual yield of 11.1%. Of course, it works in the other direction too. If you borrow money for 10.68% a year, but must repay your debt four times a year, you are actually paying 11.1%. The 11.1% would then be called the effective interest rate, where the 10.68% is sometimes designated the nominal interest rate.

This can be put another way. If you save $900 for three months, and after the three months this money is increased by 2.67%, then you have $924; and if you save this $924 for three months, and it is also increased by 2.67%, then after six months you have $949. Doing this twice more will give you $1,000. As we earlier confirmed, if $900 become $1,000 in one year, then the (annual) interest rate is 11.1%. What we also have here is $900(1 + 0.0267)^4 = 1,000$. Once again I must suggest that you work with these numbers until you understand perfectly what is going on. It will be well worth your while.

For continuous compounding we get $V = P_b e^{nr}$ [or $V = P_b \exp(nr)$], where continuous compounding means in Eq. (6.2) that $m \to \infty$: compounding takes place every fraction of a fraction of a second for n years. In this expression, "e" is the base of the natural logarithm system, and is equal to 2.71828. Suppose that we see what continuous compounding means if we have $r = 10\%$. Now we have for one year $V = 900e^{0.10 \times 1} = 994.6538$. In terms of an annual interest rate, we have $900(1 + r) = 994.6538$, and so $r = 10.52\%$ (instead of 10.0%). Exercise: what is V with continuous compounding and $r = 10.68\%$?

Ideally, purchasers and potential purchasers of bonds (and other assets) would always have reliable yield forecasts at their disposal, but in truth these forecasts are extremely difficult to obtain, since forecasters would have to predict and interpret the strength of the local and world economy, the profitability of alternative investment opportunities (such as real estate), future inflation rates, the size of government budget deficits, etc. Clearly this is asking a great deal from mortal men and women, and as a result even the most esteemed and best paid forecasters are prone to make large errors.

In the US, it became fashionable to refer to bond rating by Moody's and Standard and Poor's (S&P). In fact, these organizations have gone on

Moody	S&P	Comment
Aaa	AAA	Top grade
Aa	AA	Very good
A	A	Acceptable investment grade
Baa	BBB	Medium grade
Ba	BB	Lower medium grade
B	B	Speculative Grade
Caa	CCC-CC	High default risk
Ca	C	Junk
C	D	Sub-junk

to rate international issues, and of late the heavily indebted Swedish government has become greatly concerned about its ratings, since a change in the rating of a particular bond is often reflected by a change in the yield that must be offered on new bond issues.

There is clearly something grotesque about this phenomenon. For example the proposed merger of Swedish and Norwegian telecoms resulted in a downgrading of Swedish Telecom, although clearly the purpose of the merger was to enable a firm that was doing extremely well to do better. The same thing may have have happened in Norway although, objectively, the Norwegians have little reason to complain: taking everything into consideration, they are probably the richest country in the world.

The middle of the quality range — or the low end of the investment grade range — for corporate bonds in the US is the BBB rating by Standard and Poor's. In April 1999, this quality of paper was being issued for a spread of 127 basis points (= 1.27%) over the Treasury benchmark. Five months later, this spread had widened to 170 basis points. This widening of spreads was reflected right up to the top-grade paper, and it has been estimated that the rise in spreads on just the high-grade corporate bonds issued in the US in the first nine months of 1999 cost issuers more than

$10 billion dollars over the life of the bonds. According to the head of portfolio research for J.P. Morgan, Peter Rappoport, what this is all about is "a flight to liquidity rather than a flight to quality". This statement would make a good exam question, because what it means is that it is not good enough to buy higher quality corporate bonds, where long-term yields were relatively attractive; but that demand has increased in the market for (highly liquid) government bonds.

Regardless of the rating, bond (and share) purchasers are never quite sure of what they are getting. Even the highest quality bonds might fail to meet expectations. For instance, a Japanese buyer purchasing bonds in the US would, on the average, have gained an annual yield of 10% during the period 1979–1988, but would have lost 4.5%/year on the depreciation of the dollar relative to the yen. This can be compared to the 7.7% yield that was available on domestic Japanese bonds during the same time span. (These yields include capital gains.)

Another interesting case was an offering of $1 billion of five-year notes by Norway in 1992. These notes carried a coupon of 7.25%, and were initially priced in such a way as to yield 25 basis points (= 0.25%) more than comparably dated US government notes (which, at that time, served as the "benchmark" or "datum" for many government issues). Apparently, this was the price at which the Norwegian government "sold" the issue to a syndicate or consortium of European banks, with Deutsche Bank as the most important lead manager. This 25 basis points represented what the syndicate thought was the maximum spread necessary to market the offering.

How did they come to this conclusion? Norway's previous dollar issue was offered at a spread of 28 basis points over the (US bond) benchmark, and was selling at a 12-point spread. By itself, this indicated to the lead managers that the spread on the new issue did not have to be more than 12–15 points over the benchmark. Assuming that this was the case, then there was an expected minimum profit (per bond) of 25 minus 15 basis points, assuming that the bonds could be sold to yield a 15 basis points spread. This would be split between the syndicate, other banks (categorized underwriters and sellers) who buy from the syndicate, and the dealers and brokers who sell to the final investors. But as bad luck would have it, US bond markets suddenly changed character, and brokerages reported that their clients were losing interest in highly liquid, but low yielding sovereign (i.e. government) paper, and had become more interested in less liquid but higher yielding corporate issues. Instead of 25 basis points, the market clearing price had to fall in such a way as to provide the final investors with 28 basis points (over the benchmark). Thus, instead of a profit, there was a loss of 28 minus 25 basis points for someone — probably the underwriters — to absorb. The underwriters had bid for these deals, and the understanding generally is that they must accept any losses, however since many governments and large corporations are permanent borrowers, they cannot do without the services of underwriters, and so it can happen that during the occasional bad run of luck, losses will be shared by everybody, to include the issuers.

We can end this section with an important definition. The term of interest is *securitization*, which is the process of transforming conventionally illiquid financial instruments into marketable financial assets. For example, such things as loans and residual mortgages have been bundled into assets on which interest and principal payments can be collected at regular intervals, and then this assortment sold as a distinct security. (It was the US government that initiated this ploy.) Another example that is relevant here is collateralized mortgage payments (CMOs), which are bonds that "pass through" the payments from a portfolio of mortgages. Many financial institutions devote considerable gusto to expanding off-balance sheet activities that fall outside regulatory frameworks. Some securitized assets have functioned in this capacity together with e.g. financial derivatives and letters of credit.

III. Bonds Limited and Unlimited

According to William Gross (quoted in *Fortune*, September 27, 1999), a managing director of PIMCO, the huge California bond investment firm, bond spreads "won't narrow anytime soon. Liquidity is down because there is a lack of market making, but the big story is the credit-quality problem that is unfolding behind the scenes". He then went on to cite the default rate on junk bonds, which apparently increased considerably during 1999.

Such is the great world of the bond markets, because while all this was going on in the US, in Europe the junk bond market was moving into high gear. This came as a very great surprise to me, because I can remember giving a series of lectures in which I unwisely claimed that junk's day was essentially over in the US, and it might never come in Europe — even though at the same time I was aware that the very knowledgeable Peter Nadosy at Morgan Stanley Asset Management confessed that while he made a practice of avoiding bonds with maturities of longer than ten years, he did not avoid what he called "higher quality junk bonds".

The next step will probably be a revival of the once popular term mezzanine financing. A "mezzanine" is often a low ceilinged floor between two others, and in the present context often means loans not secured against assets (i.e. subordinated loans), but which pay unusually high (junk level) interest rates, and sometimes include access to a small stake in a firm's equity via a convertibility option. Having been so wrong before about the future of junk, I hardly see any point in making any predictions on that subject in this book; however even though there are logical reasons for the reappearance of junk based debt, as well as sound pedagogical reasons for discussing this topic, I think it useful to remember a remark made by the well read and innovative Meyer Lansky, when he was installing and supervising dice tables and roulette wheels from Las Vegas to Havana: "The winners are those who control the game, the professionals who know what they are doing; all the rest are losers".

Thanks to the continuing globalization of capital markets, both bad and good habits from one part of the world are rapidly transferred to another. European investors were once reluctant to buy anything except top-quality securities, but they have come to love the very high yields that junk typically pays. According to the latest calculations, there could be almost $300 billion in outstanding high-yield bonds credited to European firms by 2005, unless there is an inflationary blowout that incites a flight to quality. This is still behind the present $600 billion US market, but the thing to remember here is that it is still early days for Europe. With the eastward expansion of the EU, the demand for both physical and financial capital is going to be enormous.

Ostensibly, one of the main reasons for the sudden appetite for junk was the attraction of borrowing via junk as compared to borrowing from banks, although this appetite tends to change from time to time. Typically, European banks like to limit the maturities of loans in the half-billion and up bracket to less than five years, and they sometimes insist that 20% of the loan be repaid each year. Borrowers do not like this arrangement, because since the loans are often for investments in capital intensive ("large-cap") new facilities, they need time for these investments to pay off. On the other hand, bond maturities tend to be much longer. Still, having to pay 11% or 12% for money should cause some company treasurers to think twice before issuing a billion dollars worth of junk, especially when the prime rate — the rate to the best borrowers — may in some cases be as low as 5% to 6%.

In the *Fortune* article that was cited above, it was pointed out that Kirch Group, a German media firm, was unable to float a $1.1 junk issue "because investors wanted higher yields than the 12.75% to 15% that the company was ready to pay". Fifteen percent sounds like the going rate on sub-junk, and even if investors feel that they need "yield and diversification", sub-junk is the wrong way to obtain it. With all due respects, since investment banks are earning 1.5% to 3% underwriting fees, or even more in some cases, it seems clear that some issues being promoted by these establishments should never have seen the light of day.

According to a recent tribute to junk, "European markets are at last getting what they have long lacked: choice and flexibility — and some real competition". There is another way of looking at this, however. Donald Tsang, Hong Kong's Financial Secretary, recently said that "Globalization of the world's financial institutions means that, irrespective of where a major financial problem began, it will spread almost immediately to the rest of the world". Considered in this light, the "choice and flexibility" associated with a too rapid expansion of sub-junk poses a threat to the entire world economy.

The driving force behind world bond markets is the huge amounts of money pouring into such establishments from e.g. pension funds and commercial banks virtually every single day of every year, regardless of the state of the international macroeconomy. Almost as important is the risk aversion of the great majority of humanity. Bonds are needed in many portfolios because most investors regard them as safe; although (because of comparatively low bond yields at the present time) there is a growing belief that pension and trust funds should pay more attention to yield, and less to risk. This, incidentally, is a wonderful example of how widely advertised speculative success rather than basic logic causes unwary persons to gamble with their future by developing a crush on financial and other assets that are plainly overvalued.

This happened on the US bond market in 1994–1995. At the beginning of this period, some very prestigious funds had taken severe hits on their inventories of long-term bonds, while some money market funds that were buying mostly short-term bonds turned out to be big winners. The reason for this is undoubtedly that holders of short bonds collected their face value, and then bought new short bonds with higher rates of interest; while higher rates of interest merely pressed down the price of long bonds. (These long bonds often had several decades to go before the principal could be collected.) In addition, although it is not sufficiently appreciated, the purchase by US investors of foreign bonds reached a frenzy. To a certain extent, this spiraling demand could be attributed to the insistence by these investors on higher yields, which at that point in time meant a diversification into the securities of "emerging" markets. (Thus we have an analogy with the diversification into "junk".)

It has been claimed that other factors were equally as important for the bond market bloodbath that eventually took place. One of these was the response by US investors to falling inflation — and, concomitantly, falling interest rates. Unanticipated inflation had been very bad news to the holders of long bonds during the 1970s, while the disinflation of the early 1990s was penalizing the holders of short bonds and banks accounts. (If you wanted to continue to hold short bonds, you had to roll them over at falling yields.) Many short bond holders and depositors then transferred their affections to bond and equity mutual funds — or as they are called in the UK unit trusts — which often promised superior yields because of their professed expertise in emerging markets.

In addition, commercial banks all over the world increased their demand for higher yield (and higher risk) securities. Of course, when the officers of these institutions were asked about this kind of activity, their lips inevitably said no, but to the initiated, their eyes said yes. In the US, for instance, the Federal Reserve kept short-term interest rates extremely low, which was instrumental in keeping deposit rates low. As a result, commercial banks generally found it impossible to resist borrowing short and lending long, which made good business sense as long as the Fed continued this practice.

What happened was that the Fed unexpectedly changed its policy after February 1994, and the rest of the world found itself facing a kind of "margin call" on variable interest rate loans. This included US banks requesting more collateral on new debts as a backing for investments whose market values were threatened due to rising interest rates. What should be noticed here is the similarity with the Savings and Loan debacle in the US in the 1980s. The S&Ls typically borrowed short — which is what taking deposits is all about — and loaned long; but when interest rates (and deposit rates at other banks) increased, they experienced a massive loss of funds. Some of these S&Ls were relegated to the "zombie" class — i.e. the living dead — and proceeded to take colossal risks, hoping to make the score that would move them out or away from insolvency.

In 1981 alone, withdrawals from S&Ls and similar institutions exceeded new deposits by $40 billion, and a government bailout was essential to safeguard housing loans. The estimated cost of that rescue operation was $150 billion and by 1990 over 1,000 S&Ls had failed. No mass bailout was possible for the commercial banking system in 1994, and so an adjustment in the form of higher long-term rates (a "massacre") was inevitable.

The damage that might have been inflicted on the international macro-economy was moderated by rising share prices, a gradual reversal of the higher long-term rates, and robust economic growth in Asia and elsewhere. Even so, a few governments congratulated themselves on their luck a bit too soon. As the effects of the bond market implosion were being dissipated, the Mexican peso "unexpectedly" collapsed, which showed once again that regardless of the enthusiasm often expressed for the prospects of certain developing countries where a quarter of the population — at most — enjoys a Southern European type of lifestyle and outlook, the judgement of wide-open global capital markets hangs over almost everybody like a Sword of Damocles. Specifically, Mexico allowed the enthusiasm of traders and money managers in New York and London for Mexican financial assets to inflate the value of the peso well over its fundamentals.

The US government then mobilized an international rescue package of $50 billion. The logic behind this bailout was that a Mexican default might cause a stampede of foreign capital out of other emerging nations, trigger various instabilities that could lead to a string of defaults, and undermine economic growth in a number of politically sensitive regions.

This kind of phenomenon needs to be given careful consideration. When Russia defaulted in 1998, it resulted in a global liquidity squeeze. Foreign investors lost interest in Argentina (and several other countries that appeared to be doing well economically), and as a result interest rates on Argentine bonds escalated. With foreign financing almost prohibitively expensive, domestic investment fell drastically, and unemployment increased by a large amount. Similarly, the Mexican "peso crisis" had a global impact. For instance, the Brazilian stockmarket immediately dropped by 30%, and even the Italian lira was caught in the fallout.

Robert Solomon, who was formerly a distinguished member of the US Federal Reserve Board, says that this kind of thing does not make sense. Actually, in a globalized economy, it makes all the sense in the world. When the alarm bells started to ring in Russia, the young men and women in the trading rooms in London and New York, and their employers, suddenly recalled some gossip that had come their way in the recent past, and began shouting into telephones. The result was that almost immediately several large countries in South America found themselves in deep trouble.

Similarly, when the Thai baht crashed, then it was time to start asking pointed questions about balance sheets, balances of payments, excess industrial capacity, consumer confidence and so on in the rest of the countries in

Asia. Some of the answers to these questions were shockingly wrong, but in that kind of situation it hardly made any difference. Why stay when the party might be over? Besides, garbled talk about a "flight-to-quality" had started to make the rounds, and it was not long before certain individuals came to the conclusion that it would not be a good career move if they got on that flight after all the first class seats were taken.

A few definitions might be useful before we go to the next section. The asset pledged by a borrower as a guarantee that a loan will be repaid is called collateral. Similarly, the collateralization of loans means giving the lender the right to seize specific assets in the event of a default. When we discuss repurchase agreements, or "repos", the expression collateral is sometimes used. "Repos" are usually defined as the sale of an asset with a commitment to buy the asset back at a specific date and at a specific price. The asset in question functions as the collateral, and the presence of the collateral helps to hold down the rate of interest (i.e. the repo rate). The repo market is extremely important, and at least once a year the *Financial Times* publishes a long survey on the topic.

Caculating the cost of a loan is a simple matter. Algebraically we have Interest = Principal × Repo Rate × (T/360), where T is the maturity of the loan in days. (In some countries, a year is taken to be 360 days instead of 365.) The last time I looked, the repo rate in the US was 5.53%, and so if the amount was $10,000,000, then the interest cost of an overnight loan would be $10,000,000 \times 0.0553 \times (1/365) = \$1472.2$. Not a great deal perhaps, but as they say in the banking world, it helps to pay somebody's salary.

Exercises

1. The S&Ls were borrowing short and lending long, but when the interest rates jumped up, they found themselves in deep trouble. Why?
2. Holders of very short bonds gained when interest rates increased, while holders of long bonds lost. Explain this very important point!
3. What is the usual relationship between yield and risk? Show this in a diagram! What are some of the problems associated with buying the securities of "emerging countries"? In the text it states that most investors

are risk averse, but even so a very large percentage of the population in any county play "Lotto". Is there a contradiction here?

IV. Some Important Calculations

The ensuing numerical calculations are important but simple. The algebra is also straightforward, and in fact you have seen much of it earlier.

The main thing to remember here is that interest rates, unless otherwise specified, are *annual* interest rates. Suppose that we have a 60-day rate of 8%. This does not mean 8% over the given period, but instead it applies to a year (of e.g. 360 days). Thus, for a one-dollar investment, at the end of 60 days the investor will receive $[1 + 0.08\ (60/360)] = 1.0133$ dollars.

For a 30-day deposit and the same interest rate, this would have been 1.0067. Now, let us work a few more simple examples which, at this stage, should require no explanation. For example, find the price of a $100,000, 180-day security, issued at 10%, so that it will yield 15%. The year is 360 days, and the security has 90 days to maturity.

$$\text{Maturity value} = 100,000[1 + 0.10 \times (180/360)] = \$105,000$$

$$\text{Price} = \frac{\$105,000}{1 + 0.15(90/360)} = \frac{105,000}{1.0375} = \$101,205$$

As a very valuable exercise, the reader should attempt to generalize the above example — i.e. replace the numbers by symbols. Next we can consider a situation where we have a deposit with a maturity of 180 days, and a maturity value of 108,000 dollars. What rate of return is earned on the deposit if the year is taken as 365 days (as in e.g. the UK and Belgium), and the deposit is 100,000 dollars? The (180-day) "interest income" is $8,000, which means that the yield — or annual rate of return — is $100\% \times (365/180) \times (8,000/100,000) = 16.23\%$.

Another example will be given here, while a similar and important calculation associated with yield curves will be presented in the next section. Here we will assume a bill with a face value of 100,000 dollars, and 90 days to maturity, is purchased to yield 15%. After 45 days, it is sold for a yield of 14.5%. What is the amount of interest earned, assuming a 360 days year?

$$\text{Purchase amount} = \frac{100,000}{1 + 0.15(90/360)} = \$96,385 = P_{bb}$$

$$\text{Sale amount} = \frac{100,000}{1 + 0.145(45/360)} = \$98,219 = P_{bs}$$

$$\text{Interest earned (over 45 days)} = 98,219 - 96,385 = \$1,834$$

Now that we have the interest earned, we calculate the yield as above: Yield (over the holding period) $= 100\% \times (360/45) \times (1,834/96,385) = 15.22\%$. The thing to notice here is that the 1,834 dollars is earned in 45 days, and not one year. Notice also that the base for calculating the yield is the amount paid for the asset.

Some algebra is now in order. We can commence by deriving the expression for the price of a consol. It should be pointed out first that the relation between price changes and interest changes function in the same manner for all types of bonds, regardless of maturity. If we have P_b as the price of this consol, while C is the annual coupon payment (received at the end of the period), we can write:

$$P_b = \frac{C}{(1 + r)} + \frac{C}{(1 + r)^2} + \frac{C}{(1 + r)^3} + \cdots + \frac{C}{(1 + r)^i} + \cdots \tag{6.3}$$

We can now write $1/(1 + r)$ as h, giving us:

$$P_b = Ch + Ch^2 + Ch^3 + \cdots + Ch^i + \cdots \tag{6.4}$$

Multiplying both sides of this expression by h, and then subtracting from (6.4) will give us $P_b - P_b h = Ch$, or $P_b = Ch/(1 - h)$. Now, replacing h by $1/(1 + r)$ gives us the familiar result $P_b = C/r$.

Suppose that we do not have a consol, but a bond with a maturity of T periods. The price of this bond in an ideal market is the discounted value of the coupon yields on this asset plus the discounted value of the principal, F.

$$P_b = \frac{C}{(1+r)} + \frac{C}{(1+r)^2} + \frac{C}{(1+r)^3} + \cdots + \frac{C}{(1+r)^T} + \frac{F}{(1+r)^T} \quad (6.5)$$

Once again we can let $h = 1/(1+r)$, but to begin we consider only the first T terms, and obtain $\overline{P}_b = Ch + Ch^2 + \cdots + Ch^T$. We can multiply (6.5) by h, and then subtract from the original expression to obtain as our result $\overline{P}_b(1-h) = Ch - Ch^{T+1}$, or $\overline{P}_b = C[h - h^{T+1}]/(1-h)$. Finally, we can substitute $1/(1+r)$ for h to obtain:

$$\overline{P}_b = \frac{(1+r)^T - 1}{r(1+r)^T} C \quad (6.6)$$

If we compare this with the expression for an annuity given in (6.1), we see that they are the same thing. We can thus add (6.6) to the discounted face value to obtain $P_b = \overline{P}_b + \text{(present value of F)}$, and this is equal to:

$$P_b = \left(\frac{(1+r)^T - 1}{r(1+r)^T} \right) C + \frac{F}{(1+r)^T} \quad (6.7)$$

The reader should immediately see that as T approaches infinity, P_b approaches C/r. Next, let us solve a simple problem where we have a 10% coupon bond which was issued at 10%, but which has a yield to maturity of 11.75%. If the bond has a face value of 1,000 dollars, then $C = 1,000 \times 0.10 = 100$ dollars. Employing expression (6.7) we get:

$$P_b = \frac{(1.1175)^{10} - 1}{0.1175(1.1175)^{10}} 100 + \frac{1,000}{(1.1175)^{10}} = 900$$

A few comments seem appropriate here. This bond was probably issued with the intention of selling it for 1,000 dollars, which meant that the issuers would pay 10% for money. (This can be checked by putting $r = 0.10$ in (6.7).) But apparently buyers wanted 11.75% — which very likely was the market rate when selling actually began. To get that rate, the bond had to sell for $900.

The penultimate topic in this section is the so-called coupon effect, which states that bonds with low existing coupons will be more price volatile than those with high coupons. An analytic proof of this should not be too difficult to assemble, but readers have had enough algebra for the time being, and so a numerical example will be presented. Let us consider two consols having a face value of 1,000 dollars. One has a coupon rate of 4%, and the other a coupon rate of 6%. Assuming a 1% rise in the interest rate, we can observe the price changes.

For the first consol, the coupon must be $40, given a price of $1,000 and r = 4%. The reader can check this. If r increases to 5%, then with an unchanged coupon — and the coupon on consols remains constant — the price must fall to $800. The percentage change in price is thus $\Delta P/P = -200/1,000 = -20\%$. As for the second consol, the coupon must be $60 with the given price and interest rate (which you can check), and when the interest rate rises from 6% to 7%, the price moves down to $857. The percentage change in this case is $\Delta P/P = -143/1,000 = -14.3\%$.

Finally, suppose that we have a consol and a one-period coupon bond, each costing 1,000 dollars, with coupons of 100 dollars, and issued on January 2, 2000. Accordingly, the coupon yield is 10% for each. Now suppose that the market rate of interest goes to 12% the following day. The price of the one-period bond then becomes (almost) $1,100/1.12 = 982$ dollars, while the price of the consol goes to $100/0.12 = 833.33$ dollars. Obviously, this (unexpected) "spike" in the interest rate was an unpleasant surprise for the owners of these bonds, and especially for the owner of the long bond (i.e. the consol).

V. Yield Curves and the Term Structure of the Interest Rate

John Y. Campbell (1995) begins his important survey of the yield curve by pointing out that many people are happy to ignore this construction until they are involved with such things as saving for retirement or buying a house. "At such times the term structure of interest rates may become unexpectedly fascinating".

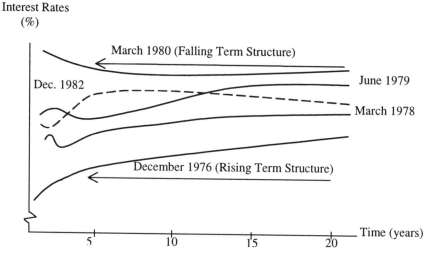

Fig. 6.1. Some Yield Curves for the United States 1976–1980

The key word here is "may", because I happen to be unaware of a great deal of interest being expressed in the term structure by anyone at any time except the large staff of economists who advise the United States Federal Reserve Board. A few years ago, these persons became convinced that the yield curve, which is a graph showing the interest rate on securities of the same type, but with varying maturities, imparts a great deal of valuable information about the future of the macroeconomy.

As shown in Fig. 6.1, if interest rates rise with increasing maturities, then we say that we have a rising term structure; while if they fall we say that the term structure is falling. If interest rates are approximately the same regardless of the maturity date, then the term structure is called flat. In late 1987, yields on 30-year US Treasury bonds fell from 10% to 9%, while the yield on 3-month bills climbed from 6% to more than 8%, narrowing the gap between these assets from 400 basis points to about 70 basis points — which was the flattest yield curve in the US for seven years; and by the end of 1988, short-term rates were higher than long-term rates. A few observers began to suggest that a recession was on the way, and by the middle of 1989, the US economy began to slow down. By the spring of 1991, the US was experiencing the downturn that caused President George Bush to lose the 1992 election. Some of this story can be detected in Fig. 6.1.

Before looking at the algebra, we can ask why a number of economists and market analysts in the US find something special about these curves — even going so far as to claim that their steepness is an indicator of future inflation, interest rates, and even the level of macroeconomic activity.

Customarily, we have a rising term structure because investors demand higher interest rates for long bonds as compared to short bonds in order to protect themselves against interest rate risks; but if the belief is that inflation will be low, then only a modest premium will be required. On the other hand, if the curve slopes downward (i.e. is inverted), it is supposed to mean that investors (on the average) fear a downturn, and have taken steps to lock in the yields on long bonds, and therefore interest rates on these bonds have declined in response to the increased demand. In addition, investors fear the reinvestment (or "rolling over") risk associated with short bonds. According to Professor Frederic Mishkin, the yield curve in the US has been the best predictor of downturns since the end of World War II: every time it inverted (with the exception of 1966) a recession followed a year or so later.

The curves in the above figure were constructed from US government securities, although corporate bonds would almost certainly have the same configuration, but with higher interest rates because of the greater risk. There are three competing hypotheses of the term structure of interest rates, and various details having to do with two of these hyportheses will be examined below, but first a short summary of each seems in order.

1. The Expectations Hypothesis: Long-term rates are an average — geometric or simple — of short-term rates. If, for instance, investors feel that short-term rates, on average, will be higher than long-term rates, then on average they would borrow long and lend short. This would tend to bring long-term yields into line with a succession of expected short-term yields. This hypothesis presumes complete substitutability between long and short bonds, with expected return determining the composition of portfolios.

2. The Segmented Markets Hypothesis: According to this approach, the market is segmented by maturities. On the average, the transactors operating in one market will not operate in another, and thus there is no substitutability — or only very limited substitutability — between long-term and short-term bonds.

3. The Liquidity Premium or Preferred Habitat Hypothesis: Investors as a rule tend to be risk averse, and prefer to lend short; while many (risk averse) borrowers prefer to borrow long, rather than starting a project and then being forced to borrow at unknown interest rates. Lenders thus demand a risk premium which borrowers are inclined to pay. The premium generally increases with the time to maturity, and thus is instrumental in causing interest rates to rise as the maturity of the bond increases. There is substitution between long- and short-term bonds, but not as much as under the expectations hypothesis.

Now let us employ a little algebra in our examination of these hypotheses, and also attempt to identify the hypothesis that is generally considered to be the best representation of reality. If we let R_i represent the interest rate on a bond having a maturity of "i" periods (where "i" is greater than unity), while r_i is the known interest rate on a one period bond, and r_i^e is the expected interest rate on a one period bond in period i, then with an N-period situation our equilibrium condition for the expectations hypothesis is:

$$(1 + R_N)^N = (1 + r_1)(1 + r_2^e)(1 + r_3^e) \cdots (1 + r_N^e)$$

As mentioned earlier, a very basic disequilibrium situation might be $(1 + R_N)^N > (1 + r_1)(1 + r_2^e) \cdots (1 + r_N^e)$. The appropriate behavior in this situation would be to lend long while borrowing short.

Suppose for example that $R_2 = 8\%$, $r_1 = 10\%$, and $r_2^e = 3\%$. Then we have $(1 + 0.08)^2 = 1.1664 > (1.1)(1.03) = 1.133$. The investor could, for example, borrow \$1,000, and use it to buy the two-year bond. The money borrowed would require a repayment of 1,100 after one year, but the intention is to borrow the 1,100 at the expected rate of interest ($r_2^e = 3\%$), and thus at the end of the second year repay \$1,133 dollars. Assuming that all goes as planned, the investor's profit at the end of two years is 1,166.4 − 1,133 = 33.4 dollars.

Something that should be observed here is that the bond we are discussing above is a discount type bond, in that the bond is bought for $1,000, and held for two years, after which time the owner obtains the $1,166.4 face value. This is not a very elegant or realistic way to discuss long-term bonds, since discount bonds for very long maturities may not exist in most countries. But by the same token it would be unusual to form expectations for short bonds over very long periods: can there really be anyone who thinks that he or she can forecast interest rates on one-year bonds 20 years in the future, or for that matter two or three years in the future?

It can be easily shown however that had this been a coupon bond, essentially the same result would have prevailed for these particular interest rates. For example, purchase a two-year coupon bond for $1,000, and if it is an 8% bond it yields $80/year. If the $80 received at the end of the first year is invested at $r_2^e = 3\%$, it becomes $80(1 + 0.03) = 82.4$ a year later. At that time the bond matures, and so the owner receives the principal of $1,000, as well as another coupon payment of 80 dollars. Thus at the end of two years she will have $82.4 + 1,000 + 80 = \$1,162.2$, which can be compared with the successive purchases of the two one-year bonds in our example.

The business of borrowing short and then buying long looks like a sure winner at times, but like most things in global finance, some unpleasant surprises are always possible. In 1993, some US hedge funds were buying European long bonds with borrowed money that involved margins of only one or two percent: securities dealers and banks provided the remainder, and were glad to do so. Some firms showed total returns of more than 50%; but in 1994, when interest rates suddenly turned up, a hedge fund like that of Steinhart Partners, with a 30-billion-dollar position in Eurobonds, suddenly found itself losing $4 million on their position for every basis point (0.01%) rise in European interest rates. Another result of this turnaround in interest rates was that some borrowers found themselves facing devastating margin calls as bond prices fell.

Now for a simple algebraic exercise involving the expectations hypothesis, whose outcome suggests that a rising term structure means that, on the average, short-term interest rates are expected to rise. A nice examination question might ask what a speculator should do if he or she saw a yield curve suddenly become steeper, and the expectations hypothesis was valid? The answer is to buy long bonds, and then sell them when players who were afraid of reinvestment risk switched from short to long bonds. Unfortunately, however, the expectations hypothesis leaves a great deal to be desired, although there are financial economists who claim that it deserves to be taken seriously.

Our next step in the algebraic analysis is to show that when the rate of interest is small, a geometric average can be approximated by an arithmetic average. For instance, considering the two period case above, our equlibrium condition is $(1 + R_2)^2 = (1 + r_1)(1 + r_2^e)$. Multiplying this out we get $1 + 2R_2 + R_2^2 = 1 + r_1 + r_2^e + r_1 r_2^e$. But R_2^2 and $r_1 r_2^e$ are close to zero for small values of R and r, and so $R_2 = (r_1 + r_2^e)/2$. For three periods the equilibrium relationship is $R_3 = (r_1 + r_2^e + r_3^e)/3$, and for k periods it is easy to extend these results to obtain: $R_k = (r_1 + r_2^e + \cdots + r_k^e)/k$.

We can now examine the conditions for a rising yield curve: $R_k > R_{k-1}$ for any "k". To begin, we can try $R_3 > R_2$. Using the information above we can write:

$$R_3 > R_2 \Rightarrow \frac{r_1 + r_2^e + r_3^e}{3} > R_2 \quad \text{(or)} \quad (r_1 + r_2^e + r_3^e) > 3R_2 = 3\left(\frac{r_1 + r_2^e}{2}\right)$$

Simplifying, we obtain $r_3^e > (r_1 + r_2^e)/2$. In words, the expected value of the short-term rate in the third period is larger than the average of short-term rates in the previous periods. This means that short-term rates, on the average, are expected to rise. What does on the average mean here? It means, for example, that we can get $R_3 > R_2$ even if $r_3^e < r_2^e$.

Using the same approach as in the three period case, we can generalize this result to:

$$r_k^e > \frac{r_1 + r_2^e + \cdots + r_{k-1}^e}{k - 1} \tag{6.8}$$

Put simply, with the yield curve rising ($R_k > R_{k-1}$ for any k), the expected short-term rate at time k is larger than the average of the previous short-term rates. Put slightly different, a rising yield curve signifies that, *on the average*, short-term rates are expected to rise. Something else that might be relevant here is that a sharply rising yield curve might indicate that the inflation rate is expected to rise, since rising inflation rates and rising interest rates usually go together.

Unfortunately, the real world provides a counter-example that probably vitiates the expectations hypothesis. With long-term rates related to expected future short-term rates as in the expectations hypothesis, a rise in short-term rates will raise long-term rates, and thus cause long- and short-term rates to move together. Similarly, a fall should lower long-term rates.

Real world yield curves are usually upward sloping, implying that short-term rates are expected to rise in the future. But in reality, short-term rates are as likely to fall as rise. Falling short-term rates do not, however, invariably alter the shape of actual yield curves (i.e. cause them to turn down). This is patently inconsistent with the expectations hypothesis.

Now let us consider the market segmentation hypothesis. This says that there are separate markets for bonds of different maturities. Accordingly, bonds of different maturities are not substitutes for each other, and bond prices (and therefore interest rates) are formed in different markets. If the yield curve normally slopes upward, this is because the demand for short-term bonds is relatively higher than for long-term bonds (which seems to be true), and means that short-term bonds have a higher price and lower yield. Put simply, investors — on the average — prefer to hold short bonds rather than long bonds.

The problem here is that if bond markets are completely segmented, then there is no reason for a rise in the interest rate for one maturity of bond to influence the interest rate on another maturity. Therefore the segmented market hypothesis cannot explain why the interest rates on bonds of different maturities tend to move together most of the time.

That brings us to the liquidity premium or preferred habitat hypothesis, which is the hypothesis that is generally regarded as the most satisfactory. To begin, it argues that there are good reasons for many investors to avoid long bonds. Interest rate changes, for example, cause much larger changes in the price of long-term bonds than of short bonds, as has been thoroughly discussed earlier. Of course, 20 years ago even the interest rates on the best quality long bonds were high, and as a result pension funds were able to lock in impressive yields. Unfortunately, however, this matter of obtaining satisfactory yields is one that must be faced by e.g. pension funds every day, and more and more the argument is being heard that the optimal way to do this is to buy fewer bonds and accept more risk in the form of equities.

The liquidity premium hypothesis is consistent with the basic empirical observation that, on the average, interest rates on different maturity bonds tend to move together: a rise in short-term rates often means that long-term rates will also rise. It should also be expected from previous discussions that upward sloping yield curves are to be expected if risk premiums are positive, since investors must be paid to accept risk. Suprisingly, as the following algebra will show, even a flat yield curve signifies a moderate expected fall in short-term rates. The thing to be noticed below is that an "ivory tower" (i.e. completely unequivocal) equilibrium condition of the type obtained in connection with the expectations hypothesis is no longer encountered. In fact, where the liquidity premium hypothesis is concerned, shifts and changes in the slope of the yield curve are probably more significant than the mere shape of the curve, although an exhaustive discussion of this phenomenon would require a mathematical apparatus that is considerably more sophisticated than the one that will be used to secure the results to which we have just been referred.

We start our algebraic analysis by investigating the way in which the risk premia $\{U_i, \overline{U}_i\}$ are to enter our calculations. The first simple possibility is:

$$(1 + R_N)^N = (1 + r_1)(1 + r_2^e + U_2)(1 + r_3^e + U_3) \cdots (1 + r_N^e + U_N) \quad (6.9)$$

And for the other possibility we can take:

$$(1 + R_N)^N = (1 + r_1)(1 + r_2^e)(1 + r_3^e) \cdots (1 + r_N^e) + \overline{U}_N \quad (6.10)$$

These geometrical averages will be approximated by turning them into arithmetical averages. Thus, instead of (6.9) we get:

$$R_N = (r_1 + r_2^e + \cdots + r_N^e)/N + [(U_2 + U_3 + \cdots + U_N)/N] \quad (6.11)$$

As above, this is obtained by simply multiplying out (6.9), and discarding the very small terms (e.g. $r_1 r^3$, R_N^3, etc).

If we had N = 3, the above would give

$$R_3 = (r_1 + r_2^e + r_3^e)/3 + [(U_2 + U_3)/3]$$

Next, corresponding to (6.10) we get

$$R_N = [(r_1 + r_2^e + r_3^e + \cdots + r_N^e)/N] + U_N^*$$

where we write $U_N^* = \overline{U}_N/N$. For N = 3, we have

$$R_3 = [(r_1 + r_2^e + r_3^e)/3] + U_3^*$$

In (6.9) and (6.11) we expect to have $U_N > U_{N-1} > \cdots > U_1$, since the risk premium should increase as the maturity of the bond increases. We could also argue that although, conceptually, these two treatments of the risk premium are different, U_N^* might be a suitable proxy for $(U_2 + \cdots + U_N)/N$ in theoretical work, particularly since it is virtually impossible to estimate numerical values for the Us.

Now let us investigate the situation with a *flat* yield curve, employing a model with three periods. To begin we have $R_3 = [(r_1 + r_2^e + r_3^e)/3] + U_3^*$. With a flat curve we have $r_1 = R_1 = R_2 = R_3$, and so $3R_3 = 3r_1 = r_1 + r_2^e + r_3^e + 3U_3^*$. Thus we can write:

$$r_1 = \frac{r_2^e + r_3^e + 3U_3^*}{2} = \frac{r_2^e + r_3^e}{2} + \frac{3}{2}U_3^*$$

This can be rewritten immediately to give:

$$r_1 - \left(\frac{r_2^e + r_3^e}{2}\right) = \frac{3}{2}U_3^* \quad (U_3^* > 0)$$

This last expression indicates that r_1 is greater than the average of the expected futures short-term rates; or, put another way, a flat yield curve means that on the average short-term rates are expected to fall. Note that $R_2 = [(r_1 + r_2^e)/2] + U_2^* = r_1$ (flat curve). This implies that $r_1 = r_2^e + 2U_2^*$, or better for our purposes $r_2^e = r_1 - 2U_2^*$. In other words, $r_1 > r_2^e$. For $N = k$, we get:

$$r_1 - \left(\frac{r_2^e + r_3^e + \cdots + r_k^e}{k-1} \right) = \frac{k}{k-1} U_k^* \quad (U_k^* > 0) \tag{6.12}$$

The interpretation is the same as in the case where $N = 3$: a flat yield curve indicates that, on the average, short-term rates are expected to fall. Now for the case where the yield curve is rising. This means that generally we can write:

$$\frac{r_1 + r_2^e + \cdots + r_{k-1}^e + r_k^e}{k} + U_k^* > \frac{r_1 + r_2^e + \cdots + r_{k-1}^e}{k-1} + U_{k-1}^* \tag{6.13}$$

The next step is to break r_k^e/k out of the first fraction in Eq. (6.13). Simple manipulation will then yield:

$$r_k^e > \frac{r_1^e + r_2^e + \cdots + r_{k-1}^e}{k-1} + k(U_{k-1}^* - U_k^*) \tag{6.14}$$

The expression in the parenthesis in (6.14) is less than zero. Thus we have a situation where a rising yield curve means that short-term interest rate can, on the average, rise or fall.

If you have a problem with this, try a three period model, taking $r_3^e = 5$, $k(\ ) = -1$, $r_1 = 4$, and $r_2^e = 2$. Since we obtained (6.13) from a rising yield curve, when we use these numbers we see that not only is the yield curve rising, but the short-term rates are expected to rise: r_3^e is greater than the average of the short-term rates for the first two periods. But by changing r_2^e to 7, we still satisfy (6.13) — i.e. we have a rising yield curve — however now short-term rates are expected to fall: $r_3^e (= 5)$ is now smaller than the average of the short-term rates $(= 5.5)$ for the two preceding periods.

Let us sum up our conclusions: flat and downward sloping yield curves unambiguously imply that short-term rates are expected to fall. An upward sloping yield curve yields ambiguous results. A very steep curve means that short-term rates are expected to rise, but since we cannot designate *a priori* a boundary between rising and "very steep", we cannot say exactly when a rising curve means that short-term rates are expected to fall.

The last topic before the conclusion is called "riding the yield curve". It functions as follows. An investor purchases a security and holds it for a while. This means that, since it now has a shorter maturity, it will have a higher sales price. This higher sales price depends on the bid-offer yields in a fairly straightforward way; but what is not so straightforward is the return associated with the holding period. This return might exceed that which could have been realized if a security with comparable maturity had been initially purchased. Consider, for example, a market with the following posted returns on securities with the given maturities, where these returns are quoted on a given date:

Maturity	Yield (%)	
	Bid (Buy)	Offer (Sell)
30	12.0	11.9
60	13.0	12.8
90	14.0	13.75

Notice the widening of the bid-offer spread as maturities increase, which is a phenomenon noted earlier. Now let us examine some possibilities for riding the yield curve, if we are interested in buying a bond with a face value of 1,000 dollars for 30 days. Here we shall assume a year of 365 days.

(1) As a datum we can simply buy a 30-day security at the offer rate of 11.9%. Here we can say that we lock in a yield or return (on an annual basis) of 11.9%. This arrangement does not involve riding anything. (2) Buy a 60-day security, hold it for 30 days, then sell it as a 30-day security. We then have as the cost of a 60-day security:

$$\frac{1,000}{1 + 0.1280(60/365)} = \$979.39$$

Notice that this security is purchased at the offer (and not the bid) rate. Assuming no change in the bid-offer yields, it can be sold in 30 days for:

$$\text{Sale price} = \frac{1,000}{1 + 0.12(30/365)} = \$990.23$$

Notice that it is sold at the 30-day bid rate. The return (or yield) for holding this security is:

$$(100\%)\left(\frac{365}{30}\right)\left(\frac{990.23 - 979.39}{979.39}\right) = 13.4\%$$

In this example, riding the yield curve (for 30 days) provides a higher return than the simple purchase of a 30-day asset. But observe the assumption that there was no change in market yields! Actually, this might be unrealistic, however just as yield might change in such a way as to reduce the return to "yield curve riding", they might change in such a way as to increase the return.

Exercises

1. In the light of the discussion immediately above, consider the following strategy: buy a 90-day security, and after 30 days, sell it as a 60-day security — assuming again no change in the bid-offer yields. What is the calculated yield?
2. Use some numbers in Eq. (6.13) for a four period model so that you get expectations of a rise in the short-term interest rates. Change one or more of the numbers so that so that you get expectations of a fall. Discuss!

VI. Conclusion

Hopefully, most readers now have a good insight into some of the analytics of bond markets, but if you want to learn more, you will need a book that explains the rather special terminology of this market, and this is the kind of thing that you probably can obtain from a broker or dealer, although Mishkin (1998) is a good beginning. There are also many useful insights into bond markets in business publications such as *Fortune, Business Week, Risk, Forbes, Euromoney* and *Institutional Investor.*

Junk bonds have often been referred to in this book, but nothing as yet about the so-called Junk Bond King, Michael Milken. Milken was given a ten-year sentence for tax fraud, insurance fraud, and insider trading; however the charming judge who sentenced him suggested a pardon after three years, and Milken actually served only two years.

This caused Representative Robert Kennedy of Massachusetts to remark: "If you rob a 7–11 store, you get ten years in prison, while if you steal $1 billion, your sentence is reduced".

The problem is, however, that Milken never really stole anything: his trial and sentencing was a travesty of justice. Of course, he might or might not have known of his firm sponsoring an annual "junk-bond bash" (= party) where, it has been said, visiting tycoons were provided with attractive escorts who were brought in to "cozy up" the proceedings, and who were reputedly capable of discussing Freudian metaphysics if politely requested; however according to some reports, the only thing these tycoons were really interesting in discussing was how much money they had or would soon have. The opinion here is that Mr. Kennedy's comment was out of place, and that Milken's intelligence, income, sober life style, and self-satisfaction aroused a fanatic envy on the part of many pseudo-celebrities and "wannabees".

Something that you have not seen in this book is a long digression on the use of present value (PV) analysis in evaluating both physical and financial investments. According to Block (1999), analysts employed by mutual funds and bank trust departments use PV "frequently", while those employed by brokerage firms and investment banks do not. The problem here seems to be estimating future cash flows, and selecting an appropriate discount rate. An approach to obtaining a suitable discount rate is discussed briefly in Chapter 8, but obviously estimating future cash flows accurately is patently impossible much of the time.

VII. Appendix 1: Debt-for-Equity Swaps and Brady Bonds

These two very important matters are best approached in the context of the relations between the US and Latin America. We can begin by mentioning the program launched by President Bush in June, 1990, called "Enterprise for the Americas". According to the Chief Executive, he wanted to see a free trade area from Alaska to the Antarctic, or at least Argentina. At the time of President Bush's initiative, Latin America seemed to be in the process of turning its back on the socialist doctrines that were once so fashionable south of the Rio Grande, and caused so many temper tantrums further north. In addition, exports were rising, the banking system was growing in both size and efficiency, trade and non-trade barriers were falling by the wayside, and countries with long histories of antagonism seemed to be learning to work together. Undiluted optimism was prevalent in the conference rooms and offices of the Inter-American Development Bank (IADB), which functioned as a forum for the dissemination of new ideas on economic policy. The bank's director at that time was Mr. Enrique Iglesias, who was so enthused by his work that he ostensibly slept only four hours per night, which is the same amount reportedly logged by Mr. Jacques Attali — the former "conseiller spécial" to President Francois Mitterand — and president of the European Bank for Reconstruction and Development, commonly known as BERD. The latter institution was in the headlines in 1993 because of the outrageous luxury in BERD's London headquarters. That luxury was the direct cause of Attali's "demission"!

On the surface, all looked well. The problem was that the financial institutions of the industrial world were in possession of at least a half trillion dollars in non-performing (i.e. nearly worthless) loans, and most of them had a Latin American address. Getting these loans off the books without attracting too much attention became an important concern of the leading industrial countries, and particularly the US.

The first scheme that was advanced was debt-to-equity swaps. What we have here is debt being transferred to some foreign investor, who receives the local currency of a debtor country, and then uses this currency to buy equity in e.g. industrial installations. Looked at in somewhat more detail, we have the following.

1. A bank that is owed money by Ruritania decides to exchange some of its debt for shares in Firm X in Ruritania.
2. The chosen amount of loans are then taken to a broker in Ruritania. In some countries (e.g. Brazil) these loans are valued at a monthly debt auction, and this value often turns out to be a fairly high fraction of the face value of the debt. Otherwise, the loans might simply be valued by a public authority.
3. Through the broker, the value of the loan is exchanged at the central bank for an equivalent amount of the local currency. The broker is then paid a commission, while the central bank retires the loan.
4. The foreign bank, which now possesses a substantial amount of the local currency, can now buy equity in a local firm, or lend to a local or foreign investor. In theory, fresh capital would now be made available to this firm to expand production and exports.

It all appears very straightforward. For example, in May, 1987, Chase Manhattan Bank converted $200 million of its loans into (Brazilian) cruzados at face value, and then put these cruzados into a Brazilian–Argentine joint venture. But there were claims that these swaps could turn into a political nightmare some day, since people in the debtor countries were not particularly enthusiastic about the prospect of an excessive foreign ownership of domestic manufacturing capacity. It was also suggested that this scheme was inflationary, since it could involve central banks printing large bundles of the local currency. This criticism seems to have gone home, since not very much is heard about debt-to-equity swaps today,

Considerably more popular was the Brady Initiative. Launched by US Secretary of the Treasury Nicholas Brady in March, 1989, the purpose of this arrangement was to provide debt relief and encourage economic reform — where by economic reform Mr Brady and his friends meant extensive privatizations and the complete deregulation of capital markets. At the heart of the scheme are "Brady Bonds", which are bonds that in general are exchanged for outstanding bank loans, and which are at least partly backed by US Treasury collateral guaranteeing payment of the principal after 30 years. Brady bonds did not cover a country's entire debt, but it was clear that they provided a considerable economic boost because not only did they trade well, but they led to a more spirited trading of other debt. Brady bond yields were initially set as the US risk free rate plus the country risk premium (as, e.g. estimated by the IMF). These yields are also used as a proxy for risk-free rates in various Latin American markets.

It appears that the birth of the Euro is reviving the market for what has been called non-dollar Brady bonds. (Actually, this debt should be called Brady-type debt.) European banks have restructured the Latin American debt that they are holding, and used the bonds of European governments as a partial backing. For instance, the mark-denominated Brady-type debt due in 2019 is partially backed by German government bonds, and just now is trading for 501 basis points over the 30-year Bund. US banks have sold most of their Brady bonds, and written off the losses involved in these operations; but European banks have apparently kept most of their bonds, and now hope that they can find buyers for them, or even swap them for Eurobonds.

The on-and-off economic development that characterizes Latin America since the introduction of the above two initiatives seems to have moved debt issues out of the spotlight. True, Ecuador became the first country ever to default on Brady bonds (in 1999), but nobody has suggested that this default threatens the political or economic stability of the region. The international financial market seems to have taken the whole affair in its stride, and Washington, Brussels, and the IMF sit calmly in the ringside seats as individual creditors struggle to get the best deal they can from debtor countries. The best is not much better than the worst, but in the present environment of high profits and multi-bank mergers, there is no reason to believe that these creditors will be haunted by dreams of earlier bad decisions.

VIII. Appendix 2: Duration

What duration does is to adjust the maturity of a bond to account for the fact that with a coupon bond, some of the return comes in an earlier period and not just at the maturity date. The duration then is the average lifetime of a debt security's stream of payments, and if we were to examine this concept closely what we would find is that the greater the duration of a security, the greater its interest rate risk — i.e. the greater the price decrease of the security due to a rise in the interest rate.

The most common measurement of duration is "Macaulay Duration". This is given by the following equation:

$$D = \frac{1}{P} \sum_{t=1}^{n} \frac{tC_t}{(1 + r_m)^t} + \frac{nF}{P(1 + r_m)^n}$$

C_t is the coupon payment for period t (and these are of course usually constant for all t's), F is the face value, r_m is the yield to maturity (which in the terminology of this chapter simply means that $r_m = r$), and n is the time in periods to the maturity of the bond. P is the price of the bond (which, formally, is equal to the present value, calculated using the yield to maturity of the bond). Usually this formula applies to a bond with a single annual coupon payment, but adjusting to another payment scheme is perfectly straightforward. Note that for a zero coupon bond, the duration of the bond is equal to n: duration equals maturity. This comes out in an example below.

Pilbeam (1998) is a good place to get a stress-free explanation of duration. Among other things, he states that duration is extensively used by dealers and investment managers.

Now let us construct an example using the figures from page 164. As shown, this is a two-year situation in which $F = \$1,000$ and obtain r_m $(= r) = 10\%$. Let us examine three possibilities: lend $1,000 and obtain $576 at the end of the first and second periods (= interest + amortization); lend $1,000, and obtain $100 interest at the end of the first and second periods, as well as the face value at the end of the second period; and finally, the zero coupon arrangement, where $1,000 is paid for $1,210 obtained at the end of the second period. Note: in this last arrangement, the face value (F) is $1,210!

First, we can look at the zero coupon arrangement. Here the Cs are zero, and so $D = nF/P(1 + r_m)^n$, but $F/P(1 + r_m)^2 = 1$, and so $D = n = 2$: the duration of a zero coupon bond is equal to its maturity. What about the situation where we have two coupon payments of 100, and at the end of the second period the payment of the face value (= 1,000). The expression for the duration then gives us $[1 \times 90.91 + 2 \times 82.64]/1,000 + [2 \times 1,000/1,000 (1 + 0.1)^2] = 1.9091$. The duration has thus fallen from 2 to 1.9091. The first possibility mentioned above — two payments of $576 — is left to the reader as an exercise, but first the reader should check the above numerical result!

As explained in Mishkin (1998), we can also use duration to get an estimate of the percent change in the price of a security ($\Delta p/p$) due to a change in the interest rate (Δi). Taking i as the original interest rate, we can write $(\Delta p/p) = -D[\Delta i/(1 + i)]$. For instance, if the interest rate on a coupon bond rises from 10% to 12%, then $\Delta i = 0.12 - 0.10 = 0.02$ (2%). Using the coupon bond example above, where $D = 1.9091 \approx 1.91$, then we must have $(\Delta p/p) = -1.91[0.02/(1 + 0.10)] = -3.47\%$. It is obvious from the equation being used here, that the larger D, the larger the interest rate risk.

Finally, if we have a portfolio consisting of x% of bonds with duration D_1, and y% (= 1 − x%) of bonds D_2, then the duration of this portfolio is simply $D_p = xD_1 + yD_2$. This result can be extended to any number of assets. Note: x and y are in *decimal* and *not* percent form.

Exercise

1. Assume a newly issued 5-year bond that trades at its face value of $100. It has a coupon of $10, and a yield to maturity of 10%. Calculate Macaulay Duration! Now discuss what happens to duration when (a) the maturity of the bond increases, (b) the coupon payment decreases, (c) the initial yield decreases. Why would the initial yield decrease?

Chapter 7

Global Finance

This chapter is mostly involved with two subjects: covered interest arbitrage and financial swaps. Before beginning, however, the reader must be warned — or reassured — that the algebraic content of the chapter does not rise above that encountered earlier in this book.

By way of introduction, a few clarifications are in order. An *offshore deposit* is a bank deposit denominated in a currency other than that of the country in which the bank resides. For example, a dollar deposit in a London bank, or a yen deposit in a Geneva bank. Offshore deposits are often referred to as Eurodeposits, even if these deposits are in Singapore or Tokyo. An offshore deposit in the Bahamas or the Caymans does not usually require any special name, however. It is simply offshore.

Dollar deposits located outside the US tend to be called Eurodollars. It is here that we have a major source of confusion, and the confusion stems from the word "located". The creation of a Eurodeposit often — but not always — is a matter of a change in ownership: "The ownership of deposits with the US banking system is changed from a domestic to an overseas holder" (*Barclays Review*, February, 1980). For example, a European firm completes some business in the US, and thereby acquires dollars. This firm might then obtain a domestic currency or a dollar deposit (i.e. a Eurodeposit) at a Eurobank (e.g. Barclays Bank), however the dollars continue to reside in some bank in the US, only now they are owned by the Eurobank. They are Eurodollars, but they have not "escaped" abroad. No reduction in the US money supply is necessary in order to increase the quantity of Eurodollars.

Many distinguished observers seem to like the Euromarket because of its lack of official regulation. For example, Eurobanks are not generally subject to interest ceilings or reserve requirements on Eurodeposits, and what reserves they do choose to hold earn interest. Accordingly, these banks usually pay higher interest rates to depositers, while lending at lower rates.

Eurodollars may have initially come into existence in the 1960s as a result of the restrictions that the UK government imposed on the lending of sterling by British banks. (The pound is often referred to as the pound *sterling* because initially the pound was "backed" by silver (i.e. sterling) and not gold.) As a result UK banks began lending dollars, with many of these dollars supplied by the overseas branches of US firms. These firms were responding to the higher interest rates that UK financial institutions could pay on foreign deposits, and also such things as Regulation Q in the US, which placed a ceiling on the interest rates that US banks could pay depositors. (Another important regulation that I encountered when working in Geneva was the "interest equalization tax", which was designed to keep Americans from earning more interest on foreign than domestic deposits. Thus, there was a real incentive for American individuals and firms not to send dollars to the US if this could be avoided.) Once large enough quantities of dollars were available outside the US, the banks of other countries also took a fancy to them — as did US banks, which established record numbers of overseas branches.

Politics also had an important role to play in the forming of the Eurodollar market. In the 1950s, the Soviet Union and other Eastern European countries possessed dollars that they wanted to deposit in the "West" in order to finance trade. Unfortunately, political relations were somewhat strained between the US and what was then referred to as the Communist bloc; and in addition some financial assets that the Chinese government had carelessly left in the US had been frozen. In these circumstances, the Soviet government bypassed the Chase Manhattan and made substantial dollar deposits with their banking agent in France, the Banque Commerciale pour l'Europe du Nord. The bank's cable and telex address was Eurobank, causing the dollars deposited there to be called Eurodollars. At the same time some investigators insisted that it was Chinese dollars deposited in Europe that provided the impetus for the modern Eurodollar market.

I. Some General Background

Deregulation and advanced technology have led to an acceleration of the globalization of financial markets, and to a considerable extent the integration of these markets. For example, well over a thousand banks now participate in the Society for Worldwide Interbank Financial Tele-communication, commonly known as SWIFT. Banks wishing to make a transfer of funds send instructions to a regional processor, which then relays instructions to SWIFT.

In a similar vein, banks clear payments with each other through systems such as Fedwire, operated by the 12 Federal Reserve banks in the US, and CHIPS, the Clearing House Interbank Payments System, operated by the New York Clearing House Association. These institutions handle an average daily volume of at least a trillion US dollars in interbank settlements, with the majority of these settlements involving international markets and in particular Eurodollar and foreign exchange transactions. In addition, trading linkages have been directly established between financial institutions in different parts of the world. Two of the best known of these arrangements involve the American Stock Exchange and the European Options Exchange, and the Chicago Mercantile Exchange and the Singapore Monetary Exchange.

The second major topic in this chapter is swaps. Most financial swaps are agreements to exchange streams of payments over time. Currency swaps mean that if party A desires access to a certain currency, but cannot obtain it on terms as profitable as party B — but at the same time A has ready access to a currency that B desires — then these currencies can be "swapped" (i.e. exchanged), and perceived costs and/or risks might be reduced for both A and B. Interest rate swaps are based on the same principle: different conditions involving such things as fixed and floating interest rates are available to different borrowers, and as a result a swap might be possible in which everybody wins. What we have here is a variant of "the law of comparative advantage", in which a transactor borrows in the market where he or she has the best relative position, and then swaps into a market where his borrowing position is the weakest — relatively. If the swap is carried out with a counterparty whose relative position in the two markets is the opposite, then the position of both can be improved. As to be expected, arranging swaps has become an extremely lucrative business for financial institutions, since they can appropriate part of the gain accruing to one or both parties. At the beginning of the 21st century, the value of outstanding swaps was well into the trillions.

Foreign investment by institutional investors is now huge, and the great fear of many countries is that foreigners will precipitously decrease their investment. Two countries that are always mentioned here are the US and Japan. An interesting question now being posed is what will be the effect on financial market volatility of the creation of the Euro-bloc? What might happen is that smaller vibrations are damped, while larger ones are magnified. This is probably one of the many questions in economics without a really definite answer.

II. Currency Classifications and Seigniorage

In working our way toward a discussion of covered interest arbitrage, some terminology needs to be reviewed: key, vehicle, reserve, and intervention currencies; and also seigniorage. There is often a tendency to use the expressions key currency and vehicle currency interchangeably, and the same is true of key currency and reserve currency, but in truth these terms have unique meanings. Take as an example vehicle currencies.

It seems obvious that it might be difficult to find a market where e.g. New Zealand dollars are exchanged for Icelandic crowns. Instead, these and other currencies would be quoted against a single vehicle currency. Thus a bank in Reykjavik wanting New Zealand dollars will sometimes buy US dollars first, and then use them to buy New Zealand currency. At the same time it should be recognized that where this example is concerned, modern communication systems featuring low transaction costs have greatly increased the accessibility of most monies; and Icelandic crowns are one of the few West European currencies not habitually quoted on world financial markets. The South African rand is now in general circulation, but in

Scandinavia, a few years ago, it could only be obtained via a vehicle currency.

As for the expression key currency, this seems to be used in three ways. First, commercial transactions taking place outside North America, and not involving American firms, were often invoiced using a key currency (e.g. dollars). By the same token, oil prices are almost always quoted in dollars, and only under exceptional circumstances in something else. "Key" is also used to convey the idea that the US dollar is almost always universally acceptible in transactions of any kind, anywhere: dollars are the key that will open many doors in this old world of ours. In addition, a key currency is sometimes taken to mean a reserve currency, as in *key-currency systems*, where a reserve currency is a currency that is acceptable in payment of international debt.

Given this multiplicity of meanings, there is no doubt that a currency can be a key currency without being a reserve currency — both in fact and theory. Accordingly, the first meaning in the previous paragraph is most suitable for a key currency; and the reserve currency function is something that is fundamentally disparate. At the same time though it is clear that the dollar is a superstar where the means of payment is concerned, and will probably remain so as long as the US is acclaimed as the only superpower. Its role as an intervention currency is much less important than it was under the Bretton Woods System, but as long as other countries are concerned about the value of their currencies vis-à-vis the dollar, then they will find it necessary to possess dollars in order to obtain (i.e. buy) another currency — and thus drive down the price of the dollar; or to be prepared to accumulate dollars in case they want to support the dollar's price.

Finally, let us examine the term *seigniorage*, meaning the profits from issuing money. One way seigniorage comes about is as follows. A reserve currency country buys goods and services from a foreign country, and pays for them with its currency. If the foreign country takes this currency and stashes it with its other reserve assets (e.g. gold), then the reserve country is enjoying an interest free loan in the sense that its citizens do not have to give up any domestic goods and services in return for imports. With the flexible exchange rates introduced almost everywhere after the collapse of the Bretton Woods System, there was (in theory) no need for reserves, since if foreign exchange markets clear in the sense that supply equal demand, then reserves are unnecessary. This sounds good, however large reserves of dollars are held by many countries, because governments are not willing to remain passive in the face of waves of speculation that might be completely unrelated to fundamentals. As a result, it is impossible to avoid concluding that the US still obtains considerable benefits in the form of seigniorage.

III. Interest Arbitrage

Interest arbitrage is a favorite topic with many economists, but the opinion here is that it is often devoted too much time in conventional textbooks. Clearly, there are things here that we need to know, but it is not a good idea to overestimate the importance of the subject.

Suppose we begin by considering the simple "circuit" that is shown in Fig. 7.1, where someone at S_0 (meaning Sweden at time zero) is

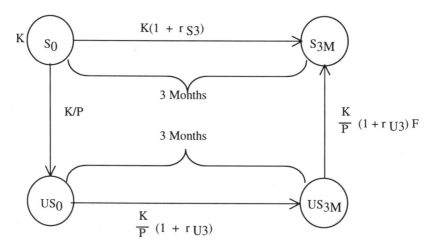

Fig. 7.1. Sweden–US Interest Arbitrage Circuit

wondering what to do with a sum of money amounting to K Swedish crowns. If we consider a three-month time horizon, the story is simple — in fact it's too simple; however it is one of those things that belongs in every book on global finance, because its absence would be noticed. Needless to say, the calculations that are shown below are carried out by simply punching exchange and interest rates into a computer. (I know of a case in the US many years ago where these calculations were carried out in the head of a mathematical "genius", with exchange and interest rates called out by traders. Had he been interested, John von Neumann could have done this kind of work, but probably not Einstein.) Unfortunately, with these calculations being done everywhere, having things turn out so that you can make some serious money is a matter of luck. But it does happen, I've heard.

The K Swedish crowns can be put into a Swedish bank, or used to buy a short term Swedish security, which means that in three months, it will become $K(1 + r_{S3})$, where r_{S3} is the 3-month interest rate in Sweden (expressed, of course, in decimal form). Another possibility is that the K crowns are turned into K/P dollars, and used to buy a US bank account or e.g. T-bill, which in three months will be transformed into $(K/P)(1 + r_{U3})$ dollars. Note that the exchange rate P has crowns/dollar for dimensions. The main point, however, is this. The dollars obtained in three months are immediately — at time zero — sold forward for a known quantity of crowns, F, where F is the forward exchange rate, and also has the dimensions crowns/dollar. The next thing is to choose which of these alternatives is preferable, although on strictly interest arbitrage grounds it might be judged that they are equally satisfactory, in which case no arbitrage takes place. As the reader will soon see, this no-arbitrage (or no money-movement) situation is regarded as an equilibrium. The model presented in Fig. 7.1 implies three possibilities. These are:

1) $$K(1 + r_{S3}) > \frac{K}{P}(1 + r_{U3})F$$

Swedes keep their money in Sweden, while Americans buy spot crowns, and sell forward crowns (i.e. buy forward dollars).

2)
$$\frac{K}{P}(1 + r_{U3})F > K(1 + r_{S3})$$

Swedes send money to the US, while Americans keep their money at home. Accordingly, Swedes buy spot dollars, and sell forward dollars (i.e. buy forward crowns). Finally, we have:

3)
$$K(1 + r_{S3}) = \frac{K}{P}(1 + r_{U3})F$$

This is obviously the no-arbitrage condition. We could, of course, have 1) and 2) and no arbitrage, because the difference between the left and right hand sides of these relationships is so small that, relative to transactions costs, arbitrage is a waste of time. But we might also have the same very small difference, and the arbitrageur attempts to do a couple of billion dollars worth of arbitrage. The investment bank D. E. Shaw might call that "finding the 100 dollars that costs 99.99 dollars". A billion dollars worth of these 100 dollar bills is well worth the few minutes that it would take to consumate this transaction, assuming that the person on the other side of the transaction does not balk at the proposed size.

Before changing the subject, let us manipulate the equilibrium relationship above to obtain what (Lord) Keynes called the *parity forward rate*. Continuing with a three-month horizon, we obtain:

$$F = \frac{r_{S3} - r_{U3}}{1 + r_{U3}}P + P \tag{7.1}$$

Probably a more useful version of this expression can be obtained if we introduce what Keynes called the *covered arbitrage margin* (CAM). We then have:

$$CAM = \frac{r_{S3} - r_{U3}}{1 + r_{U3}} - \frac{F - P}{P} \tag{7.2}$$

There are no mysteries in this expression: when we have an equilibrium, then CAM should be zero. Equation (7.2) is pedagogically useful because it shows that if, e.g. the interest rate in Sweden is higher than that in the US by a certain amount "x", then interest arbitrage will not take place if the forward rate (in crowns/dollar) is at a discount to the spot rate by a percentage amount (in decimal form) equal to "x". If both terms on the RHS of (7.2) are multiplied by 100%, they become percentages, in which case the CAM is also a percentage. This expression can be simplified by noting that for the small values of r_{U3} that would probably prevail, the first term on the RHS could be approximated by $r_{S3} - r_{U3}$, however with the computational technology now available, approximations are unnecessary.

Exercises

1. Discuss interest rate arbitrage with a numerical example.
2. Do the algebra involved in obtaining (7.2), and clarify the meaning of CAM in terms of this algebra!

Most of us know very little about what takes place in actual trading rooms, but having seen the film "Wall Street", and a few television soap operas about the financial world, I do not remember seeing anyone doing any algebra. Instead, the ladies and gentlemen in the trading rooms spend most of their time talking on telephones, and in fact it is this almost non-stop telephoning together with the non-stop searching of computer screens that enables investment banks to rack up a sizeable fraction of their multi-billion dollar profits.

In London, a few years ago, an investment bank hired as a currency trader an American who rode to work on a Harley Davidson, and kept his jeans and cowboy boots on during his long working days. That kind of attire was not encouraged at the time, however in his case nobody cared, because during his first nine months with the firm he reportedly accounted for $59 million in profits, and during his second year $70 million. His favorite expression was "buy them until your hands bleed". Eventually his luck turned, and consequently management elected to inform him that the bank had a strict dress code, which included a suit and tie.

That gentleman was in many ways typical of the sort of person that you find staring into the computer screens of currency dealing rooms. They are usually young, single minded, able to determine their currency position at all times (i.e. how much of various currencies they have bought or sold), and in theory they are capable of anticipating what is happening in the market so that they can react to new information in a split second. The last requirement is out of the question for many dealers, however they are kept up-to-date by analysts and other experts, who tell them what to watch for.

The screens of dealers — who are also called traders — also provide a great deal of information. These screens are fed with financial and sometimes political input by Reuters, Telerate, and other agencies that are specialists in finding and processing important economic information. The dealers receive price trends in chart and graph form, various short reports — to include some gossip, perhaps — and it is obviously technically possible for the currency positions of individual dealers to be displayed whenever they desire. Some dealers have screens which allow them to carry out transactions with other screen users by merely typing in prices and quantities, and then pressing a button. As the TV audience is probably aware, dealers also do a lot of shouting, because generally shouting is the quickest way to get information to colleagues in their own dealing room.

As to be expected, dealers begin the day by checking a spectrum of prices. Where prices do not seem to take into consideration the latest news, they are adjusted by the dealer in making his or her first quotations. The point is to take a speculative position that will result in a profit at the expense of another dealer. Establishing the first price of the day is thus a step into the unknown, because the dealer might have misjudged various economic and financial developments locally or in another part of the world. What often happens is that early in the day prices are quoted with a wide spread in order to provide some protection, but not so wide as to suppress interest. During the day, dealers will almost certainly modify initial quotations. Early mistakes can often be corrected, but it happens that a spell of poor trading causes some dealers to panic.

At this point it might be useful to construct an example involving The Bingham-Manhattan Bank (B-M), London Bank (LB):

LB: I'd like ten million dollars overnight. What is your rate?
B-M: Five point nine two (meaning 5.92 million pounds).
LB: That's expensive.
B-M: Take it or leave it.
LB: One moment, please.

The dealer at LB might then stand up and shout what he wants to his dealing room colleagues. Those colleagues talking on the phone will then ask the dealers they are talking to for a price, and when they get these prices shout them out. It might happen that our dealer will judge one of these prices to be advantageous, and he will tell his colleague to buy. Then LB sits down and tells B-M that there is no deal between them. (LB will simply say "No thanks".) But it might be that his colleagues cannot help him, and so LB rings another bank in the US — e.g. Soul Searchers Bank — and queries them:

LB: I need ten million dollars overnight. What is your rate?
SS: Five point nine five.
LB: No, thank you.

London Bank then resumes communication with B-M:

LB: I'll take it.
B-M: Ten million at five point nine two.
LB: Done

With luck, this operation was carried out in a few minutes, and our dealer immediately moves to the next transaction. Of course, it might take another call or two before a deal is struck, however it is by the process of calling and dealing that traders get a good feel of the market — which is something that may be lost in a regime of comprehensive electronic trading. At the same time, however, the practice is to limit the number of calls pertaining to a single deal to three or four, unless — money wise — the deal is something special.

It has been predicted that the way technology is developing, the shouting described above will be unnecessary, since all prices will be visible, but that day is definitely not here yet, as you would find out if you visited one of the major trading centers in the US on a day when bad news broke over the trading floor.

On these occasions you would find hundreds of traders going ballistic, screaming at each other with the special language used on trading floors all over the world. Palm out — sell! Palm in — buy! The quantity is obtained from fingers near the face, while fingers to the side of the body indicate price. Upright fingers signify one through five, while horizontal fingers mean six through nine. Single digits are counted on the chin; tens on the forehead. And so on and so forth. Electronic equipment is everywhere, providing a steady stream of information. So much in fact, that a large part of it goes unnoticed, because the only important thing for these ladies and gentlemen is being on the right side of trades, and doing everything possible to keep their positions from being decimated by the market. Most of them would hardly react if their own death warrants were to appear on one of the monitors, unless it were at the end of the day when all trading had ceased. Screen trading will undoubtedly change some of this behavior, and the attitudes behind it, but few of these people will forget that if you play to win, you cannot be half-hearted about it.

IV. Interest Rate and Currency Swaps

The value of outstanding swaps throughout the financial world in well into the trillions. Of course, this is to be expected of a procedure which has been called "that wonderful invention where everyone wins". Everyone? Well, sometimes. Certainly, what can be done is to exchange fixed interest payments for floating rates, and vice versa; to exchange interest payments in one currency for payments in another, or for that matter different combinations of these two. In fact, enthusiasts have claimed that there are as many swapping transactions possible as there are business agreements, and therefore firms in the process of borrowing money would do well to inquire into swap possibilities, regardless of how satisfied they are with the terms being offered to them.

The purpose of this section is to introduce readers to swap mechanics. A more extensive discussion of these matters can be found in e.g. J. Orlin Grabbe (1996), however I think it a good idea for all persons interested in this topic to attempt to follow the introductory materials below, and in particular to pay attention to the vocabulary.

The swap in its present form is probably an evolution of strategies developed in the UK in the 1950s and 1960s to evade currency regulations. For example, in the late 1950s, UK companies buying foreign currency often had to pay more than the going market rate outside the UK. As a result, the so-called parallel loan was developed. This meant that two firms in different countries lent each other an equal amount of money in terms of the domestic currencies in the two countries. These firms were often multinationals, and the loans would simply be passed to subsidiaries in each country. Naturally, this made a mockery of the concept of currency regulation, but it was quite within the law. The same was true of so-called "back-to-back-loans", where firms simultaneously borrowed and loaned currencies that were not readily available through normal channels.

Directly below I have constructed what I consider to be a very simple example of an interest rate swap, but for pedagogical reasons have excluded the intermediary from the analysis. However, until the advent of "screen swapping", the intermediary is the key element in a swap transaction, since they must find and evaluate the parties to a swap.

This can be a problem from time to time, since occasionally swap candidates are all on one side of the market. For example, there are periods when everyone seemed to want floating interest rates, and other periods — when interest rates seem volatile — that they want fixed rate arrangements. As to be expected, the need to tailor-make swaps to fit the needs of various clients, and also to find these clients, has tended to put a major part of the swap market into the hands of a comparatively small number of top financial institutions. At one time there was a fairly large number of second-rank participants, such as the larger of the London merchant bank elite, but if any of them are still involved in this line of work, the present era of bank mergers should eventually make it very difficult for them to continue.

Now for some algebra. To begin, we can assume that we have two firms, (1) and (2), and that each of them can borrow at a fixed rates of interest, or a floating rate of interest. Bank (1) wants to borrow floating, and can do so at V_1, while bank (2) wants to borrow fixed, and can do so at F_2. Figure 7.2 shows this arrangement, where the two fixed rates are F_1 and F_2, while the two floating rates are V_1 and V_2. The reader can also note in the diagram F and V. As will be explained later, these are transfers between the two actors: V is a variable rate going from (1) to (2), and F is a fixed rate going in the other direction. (Observe: the F's and V's are in percent.)

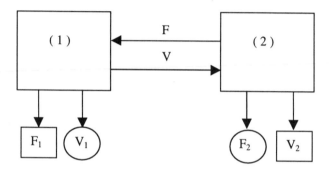

Fig. 7.2. An Interest Rate Swap

As it happens, however, a swap might give both of them better rates (i.e. lower costs). This would be true if we had:

$$V - F + F_1 < V_1 \tag{7.3}$$

$$F - V + V_2 < F_2 \tag{7.4}$$

From these inequalities we immediately get:

$$F_1 - V_1 < (F - V) < F_2 - V_2 \tag{7.5}$$

(7.5) could be manipulated to obtain our final result, however it is much simpler to write down the total gain as the gain to each transactor, or:

$$G = G_1 + G_2 = [V_1 - (V - F + F_1)] + [F_2 - (F - V + V_2)] \tag{7.6}$$

We rewrite this to obtain $G = (F_2 - V_2) - (F_1 - V_1)$, which in turn can be rewritten:

$$G = [(F_2 - F_1) - (V_2 - V_1)] \qquad (7.7)$$

The gain is now expressed as the difference in interest rates obtained by the two firms in the fixed interest market, or G_F, and the difference in interest rates in the floating interest market, which is G_V. Very often we find this gain written in terms of the absolute value of G, or $G = |G_F - G_V|$. (The absolute value means that e.g. $|-0.33| = 0.33$, or $|2.2| = 2.2$, etc.)

We can now peruse the first part of a numerical example. Suppose that we have $F_1 = 10.5\%$, $V_1 = LIBOR + 0.25\%$, $F_2 = 12\%$, and $V_2 = LIBOR + 0.75\%$. We notice immediately that (1) has an absolute advantage in both markets, but even so it can be shown that a swap is advantageous. According to the absolute value of (7.7) the advantage is $|(12 - 10.5) - \{(L + 0.75) - (L + 0.25)\}| = |1| = 1\%$. The total gain is 1%, and it will be divided between (1) and (2). This issue will be taken up below, but another piece of algebra might be useful first. This will involve returning to (7.6), because what we need to determine are the transfer flows F and V.

Continuing with the supposition that the floating rates are related to LIBOR (L), let us write $V_1 = L + x_1$, $V_2 = L + x_2$, and $V = L + \theta$. Then from (7.6) we get $G = [\{(L + x_1) - (L + \theta)\} + (F - F_1)] + [(F_2 - F) + \{(L + \theta) - (L + x_2)\}]$, with $x_1 = 0.25$ and $x_2 = 0.75$. Simplifying:

$$G = [(x_1 - \theta) + (F - F_1)] + [(F_2 - F) + (\theta - x_2)] \qquad (7.8)$$

If we use the numbers from the above example in this expression we get $G = [(0.25 - \theta) + (F - 10.5)] + [(12 - F) + (\theta - 0.75)]$. We know that the maximum gain is unity, and one way to get this is to take $\theta = 0$, and $F = 10.75$. Having done this, observe the contents of the parentheses. These are $G = [0.25 + 0.25] + [1.25 + (-0.75)] = 1\%$.

These calculations are not intuitive enough for my taste, and so let us make it clear that due to the transfers shown in Fig. 7.1, (1) did indeed obtain his floating rate loan, and (2) obtained her fixed rate loan. The cost of a loan to (1) is $V - F + F_1 = V + (F_1 - F)$, and using the numerical values we have as the loan: $L - 10.75 + 10.5 = (L - 0.25)\%$, which indicates that (1) did indeed obtain a floating rate loan. The saving for (1) due to the transfer was thus $(L + 0.25) - (L - 0.25) = 0.5\%$.

For (2) the cost of a loan was $V_2 + F - V = F + (V_2 - V)$, and using the numerical values this becomes $10.75 + [(L + 0.75) - L] = 11.5\%$: (2) gets a fixed rate loan! The savings on the fixed rate loan due to the swap is clearly $(12 - 11.5) = 0.5\%$! In this exercise V and F were arbitrarily chosen, but in the real world they are obtained via some kind of negotiation, which might begin by (1) and (2) going to the intermediary and inquiring if their borrowing costs could be reduced by a swap. The rest would be up to the intermediary, who would not forget to collect a fee for their services.

Swaps need not always involve fixed and floating rates. They may be between one floating rate regimen (LIBOR-based), and another (e.g. US prime rate based), or they can be between currencies, etc. Once the gains have been written down, as in the above, there is very little of an algebraic nature to do. A few problems follow. Readers should not have much trouble with them, and for the ambitious reader it might be worthwhile to simplify and/or systematize the algebra given above.

Exercises

1. Insert the figures given and obtained for the Fs and Vs in the example worked out above into Fig. 7.1.
2. Arrange a swap using the figures for F_1, F_2, V_1, and V_2 in the example so that (1) gets 0.6% and (2) gets 0.4%! Show your results in a diagram like Fig. 7.1! Can you arrange a swap so that both get 0.6%?

A swap arrangement that it will not be necessary to treat with algebra is the one shown in Fig. 7.3. Here we have a simple exchange between two counterparties of fixed rate interest in one currency in return for fixed interest in another. The reader will find an explanation for this arrangement immediately below the figure.

The fixed rate currency swap involves the three basic steps that are common to all currency swaps.

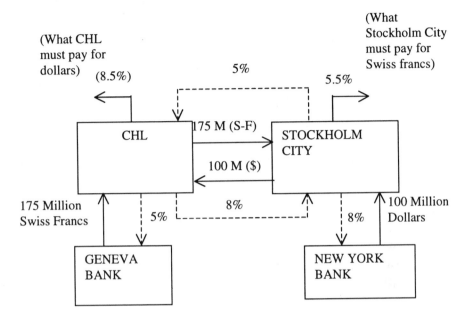

Fig. 7.3. A Currency Swap

1. *The initial exchange of the principal.* The counterparties — CHL and Stockholm City — exchange the principal amounts (100 million dollars and 175 million Swiss francs), at an agreed rate of exchange. Here this is $1 = 1.75 Swiss francs. Although this rate is usually based on the spot exchange rate, a forward rate set in advance of the swap commencement is also occasionally used. As shown in Fig. 7.3, CHL must pay 5% for Swiss francs, while Stockholm City pays 8% for dollars.

2. *Ongoing Exchange of Interest*: Once the principal amounts are established the counterparties pay interest on these amounts. As shown in Fig. 7.3, CHL will pay 8% for dollars (instead of 8.5%); while Stockholm City will pay 5% for Swiss francs instead of 5.5%. Thus the savings by CHL is 8.5 minus 8.0 = 0.5%, and the saving by Stockholm City is 5.5 minus 5.0%. Naturally, there is also an intermediary involved in this transaction, and this intermediary receives a fraction of the combined saving as a fee for supervising and coordinating the arrangement.

3. *Re-exchange of the Principal*: On the maturity date the counterparties re-exchange the principal. It should also be mentioned that the amount of the swap is called the "notional principal amount", which is $100 million in this particular example. Readers should refer to the glossary for a further elaboration.

As with the interest rate swap, the currency swap is capable of providing impressive savings in situations where the counterparties have a pronounced borrowing advantage in different markets. This includes the opportunity to gain relatively inexpensive access to currencies which normally are obtainable only at the highest rates. It is for this reason that some observers claim that swap markets are making a major contribution to the integration of the world's capital markets.

V. Swap Agreements

Swap agreements are a different matter from the swaps that we have discussed earlier. They are a device for financial institutions to obtain foreign currencies, and are usually presented as an alternative to spot and forward transactions. For example, suppose that Bingham-Manhattan Bank wanted 100,000 pounds for 30 days. They could borrow the pounds, and at the same time buy 30-day forward pounds in order to "lock-in" the price at which the pounds had to be repaid. Or they could enter into a swap agreement, in which dollars are traded for pounds now, and pounds for dollars in 30 days. The swap market is a largely interbank market in which banks swap, for a price, their different maturities of currency exposure on a sell now and repurchase later basis.

What we now need is the swap rate. In a purely academic context, this can be defined at the price at which swap transactions are carried out in the interbank market, and can be calculated from the interest parity conditions derived earlier in this chapter. Strictly speaking, the swap rate is not an exchange rate but an exchange rate differential. For instance, we know from Sec. III above that $F = P(1 + r_{UK})/(1 + r_{US})$. In this expression, F is the forward rate in pounds/dollar, P the spot rate (and also in pounds/

	Today	90 Days
B-M	−pounds (−100,000) +dollars (+160,000)	+pounds (+100,000) −dollars (−157,600)
London Bank	+pounds (+100,000) −dollars (−160,000)	−pounds (−100,000) +dollars (+157,600)

Note how this transaction functioned. B-M obtained pounds from the spot market at a price of 1£ = $1.6. A 90-day swap then took place in which London Bank obtained pounds for dollars, with the exchange again taking place at the spot exchange rate. Thus 100,000 pounds were swapped out for 160,000 dollars. In 90 days, however, when the transfer will be reversed, B-M will only have to pay 157,600 dollars for the 100,000 pounds that will go to the customer. This is because the reverse transaction is done at the interest parity forward rate (F), and as calculated above this was 0.6342(£/$). We thus obtain $157,600 ≃ £100,000/0.6342(£/$). Observe that 1/0.6342 = 1.576 $/£.

By obtaining F from the interest parity condition, arbitrage by one of the counterparties is precluded *at the time the deal is made*. In that sense F can be regarded as a fair price.

VI. Conclusion

When you reread this chapter, think about how you study calculus. Calculus is a magnificent subject, and if you are fluent in what may still be known (in the US at least) as College Algebra and Analytic Geometry (or perhaps Pre-Calculus), then you should have no problem with it.

The same is true here. An important and thorough book such as J. Orlin Grabbe (1996) — important and thorough except for pages 67–70 — is more advanced than the present book, and contains a large amount of valuable material; but if you are able to handle this book, and in particular the present chapter, then Grabbe's book as well as others on that level should be "a piece of cake". You should also take note of Grabbe's comment that international finance is a niche in its own right, and quite different from macroeconomics and corporate finance. Among other things, international finance is much more exciting to study, and some will find it extremely satisfying to know.

Exercises

1. It is April. You are in Chicago and on your way to Paris. However your thoughts are not on Paris, but on whether dollar or franc bank deposits are best to hold. Having read the first part of this chapter, you decide to do some algebra. If the present exchange rate is P($/fr), and you expect the exchange rate to be E(P) soon, then a dollar converted to francs and used to purchase a French bank deposit with an interest rate of r_F will yield an interest income of $[(1 + r_F)E(P)/P] - 1$. Explain! Now show how you go from this expression to $r_F + \{[E(P) - P]/P\}$! Hint: you may have to "drop" a very small expression! Finally, with the interest rate in the US equal to r_{US}, tell everybody the point of this exercise!

2. I once met a very rich oil man who told me that he never had any luck with futures contracts, even when he was hedging. Can you explain this?

3. The development of overnight loan markets seems to have led to commercial banks holding fewer reserves. Explain!

4. Why do junk bonds continue to be attractive, despite their (sometimes) above average default rate?

5. If the German mark is selling for 0.57 dollars, and the Japanese yen for 0.0088 dollars, what is the cross rate between the mark and yen?

6. How does a futures contract differ from a forward contract?

7. A well known analyst once claimed that a real bull market in bonds would not appear until his government found a way to reduce its deficits. What was his reasoning?

8. Electricity prices are extremely volatile. How do you feel about the survival chances of futures and options markets for electricity?

9. Do you feel that secondary financial markets are less important than primary financial markets?

10. Paul Erdman once said that "If the financial system goes, then we all go". Is this really true?

11. If you read in the Wall Street Chronicle that the experts expect stock prices to rise, should you rush out and buy all the stocks that you can afford?

12. Consider two bonds with five years to maturity. One is a discount bond, and the other a coupon bond with one payment per year. Suppose that they have the same present value (i.e. the same yield), which one has the shorter (effective) maturity, and what does this mean for interest rate risk?

13. In looking at some of the best professionally managed portfolios for the second quarter, 2000, average holdings in percent were 50% equities, 44% bonds, 6% cash (The Economist, July 8, 2000). Credit Suisse, though, had 35% equities, 45% bonds, and 20% cash. What was Credit Suisse thinking about? What did this cash consist of — could it have been notes and coins? Euro-denominated bonds were popular once, but they quickly became unpopular. Why?

14. It has been suggested that Russia's 30-year Eurobond — laucnched in 2000 — could challenge Brazil's capitalization bond as the emerging market benchmark. Explain! (Brazil's C-bond is the most actively traded emerging-debt security in New York, followed by Argentina's floating rate notes.)

Chapter 8

Risk, Uncertainty, and Financial Assets

This chapter consists of a brief discussion of risk and financial assets, with the accent on risk. It will be kept as elementary and as short as possible, because as alluded to earlier, much of the mathematical literature on risk and uncertainty does not seem particularly applicable to the operational side of global finance. Still, there are some aspects of this topic that we should *always* have at our finger tips if we desire to walk the walk and talk the confident talk of someone that friends, neighbors and the crowds passing by will immediately recognize as fluent in matters of international finance.

In our exposition, risk will simply be defined in terms of the volatility of potential outcomes, or the extent to which possible asset or portfolio values are likely to diverge from expected or predicted values, although there are undoubtedly other and more complex dimensions to this sometimes very disagreeable phenomenon. The position taken here is that risk and uncertainty should be taken into consideration whenever it is possible, because the majority of everyday situations in economics and finance are inherently uncertain. It makes little or no sense to approach the stock market from the point of view of the so-called omniscient consumer who has rendered such illustrious service to neoclassical economics. This might also be a good place to remember that earlier we distinguished between risk and uncertainty: with risk we can attach measurable probabilities to outcomes, while under uncertainty all probabilities are strictly subjective. What will be done here is to ignore the difference, and although uncertainty is definitely more prevalent than risk in the financial world, the term "risk" will be applied to both risk and uncertainty. The reason for this choice probably has to do with language: "risky assets" sounds more appropriate than "uncertain assets".

We will also find ourselves dealing with another definition of the "law of one price": asset prices should adjust until assets in the same risk class have the same price (per unit of expected return); and we will talk about two varieties of risk. The first is *non-systematic* risk, or diversifiable risk, which is risk that can be greatly reduced by careful *diversification* — i.e. acquiring a fairly wide mix of "uncorrelated" assets rather than just a few assets that may or may not be correlated. The other is *systematic* (or market or non-diversifiable) risk, and this is risk that cannot be diversified away. For example, when stock markets crash, they usually reduce the value of all portfolios, regardless of how skillfully individual portfolios are constructed.

The chapter begins with an elementary discussion of mathematical expectation, variance, covariance, and correlation. Here it should be noted that several concepts that appear complicated will be examined in a starred section that many readers may choose to skip. I feel obliged to remark, however, that the topics in this chapter are perfectly straightforward, and should be accessible to most readers. I would also like to reaffirm that these topics were chosen because they are interesting and, in some cases, fascinating to study and know; but in reality they may *not* be very useful in the everyday business of arranging your or your employer's portfolio. For instance, one of the weighty assurances provided us by mainstream financial economics is that obtaining a greater return generally necessitates accepting a greater risk, however the cave men undoubtedly knew this when they left hovel and hearth for the City and its many perils. (Note the word "generally". What this means is that you might be in an *inefficient* position: a position where greater returns are indeed possible for the same risk.)

I. Expectation and Variance

Let's begin by considering the tossing of an unbiased coin that has a 3 printed on one side, and a 4 on the other. A single toss gives us a 3 or a 4. Now suppose that we toss this coin twice. The *set* of possible outcomes are $\{(3,3), (3,4), (4,3), (4,4)\}$. If we consider the *ordered pair* (3,4), for example, 3 signifies the outcome of the first toss, and 4 the outcome of the second.

Now let us consider the number we get if we *divide* the sum of a pair of these numbers by the number of tosses (= 2). Still paying attention to ordering, that procedure gives us (3, 3.5, 3.5, 4). It may be that there is something significant about 3.5, and so let's toss this coin three times. The possible outcomes then are {(3,3,3), (3,3,4), (3,4,3), (4,3,3), (3,4,4), (4,3,4), (4,4,3), (4,4,4)}. This time let's divide the sum of the numbers in the parenthesis by three. This gives us (with a small amount of "rounding") the following eight values: (3, 3.33, 3.33, 3.33, 3.66, 3.66, 3.66, 4). The significance we saw in the 3.5 we can now find in the combination of e.g. 3.33 and 3.66 which, if they are added and divided by two, give us approximately 3.5. Dividing the first and last numbers by two will also give us 3.5. In fact, adding all these numbers and dividing by eight will give us approximately 3.5!

Finally, we can perform another operation. In the second experiment, when we tossed two coins, we had four outcomes; and if the coin was unbiased, then the probability of each outcome was 1/4. (Note that the sum of the probabilities is always unity.) If we multiply each of the outcomes (x_i) by its probability ($p_i = 1/4$), we get $\Sigma p_i x_i = 3(1/4) + 3.5(1/4) + 3.5(1/4) + 4(1/4) = 1/4(14) = 3.5 = \bar{x}$. This is a weighted average of the outcomes of this particular experiment — weighted by the probabilities!

Now we can do the same thing for the third experiment, where with an unbiased coin and three tosses, we have eight possible outcomes, and so the probability is 1/8 for each outcome. For our calculation of $\Sigma p_i x_i$ we immediately get $3(1/8) + 3.33(1/8) + \cdots + 4(1/8) \approx 3.5 = \bar{x}$.

There is definitely something magic about this 3.5, and in fact if we were to toss our coin any number of times, and go through the same procedure, we would obtain a similar result.

In the light of all this, perhaps we can reduce our exertions by defining something called the *mathematical expectation*. Noting that a random variable is the outcome of an experiment involving chance (e.g. flipping a coin), then if a random variable x can take on the values x_i with probabilities p_i, the mathematical expectation of x when there are N values of i is:

$$E(x) = \sum_{i=1}^{N} p_i x_i \qquad (8.1)$$

Our coin tossing experiment with two outcomes gives us $E(x) = 3(1/2) + 4(1/2) = 3.5$, where $N = 2$. This expected value is *not* the value that would occur on a single experiment — which is necessarily three or four — but it is the *average* value that we expect if we perform the experiment a large number of times: we obtain a string of 3s and 4s, mixed in some "random" fashion, and then divide the sum of these outcomes by the number of flips. Think of it in another way: as the single best representation of the outcome of this coin flipping experiment. An experiment in which the outcomes are random or stochastic (i.e. attached to a probability). In the first course in physics, we might use the expression "center of gravity".

A better known experiment is one involving two dice, where each has the number 1–6 on its six faces. There are 36 distinguishable outcomes, and if the dice are unbiased the probability of each is 1/36. The lowest value is two, and the probability here is 1/36; while the highest is 12, and the probability is also 1/36. The number with the highest probability is seven, since it can be obtained from the following distinguishable pairs: $\{(3,4), (4,3), (5,2), (2,5), (6,1), (1,6)\}$. The probability of a seven is then $6/36 = 1/6$, which is larger than any other probability; and if you calculate the mathematical expectation, taking into consideration all the possible outcomes, you get $\Sigma p_i x_i = 2(1/36) + \cdots + 7(6/36) + \cdots + 12(1/36) = 7$. If you entered a lottery which involved choosing only one number, from 2 to 12, obtained by rolling two unbiased dice, then your best bet would be to choose seven — assuming that you did not have to pay more to "play" seven than to play the other numbers.

We will now take a step back and see what the the situation is when we roll only one die. The outcomes now are 1, 2, 3, 4, 5, 6, and if the die is unbiased, the probability of each number is 1/6. Furthermore, if you calculate the mathematical expectation using the expression given above you get $E(x) = \Sigma p_i x_i = 1(1/6) + \cdots + 6(1/6) = 3.5$. This is close to the value that we expect to get if we roll the die a very large number of times (obtaining a string of random numbers from one to six), and then divide the sum of the numbers we obtain by the number (N) of rolls.

The expected values are the same, but the experiments are not really the same. It is obvious that the spread of possible results is much different. In one case we have {3,4}, and in the other {1,2,3,4,5,6}. If this were a gambling game with a great deal of money at stake, and with a given ante, most players might prefer the first arrangement, since you always get three or four; but some would undoubtedly prefer the second, where they might win five or six, even though there was a fairly large risk that one or two might appear.

The way that the spread of outcomes is approached is to compute something called the variance (Var). The variance — or its square root, the standard deviation (SD) — is often used as a measure of riskiness: the larger the variance or the standard deviation, the greater the risk. Designating the variance as "Var" or σ^2 we write:

$$\sigma_x^2 = \text{Var}(x) = \sum_{i=1}^{N} p_i (x_i - E(x))^2 \qquad (8.2)$$

The standard deviation (SD) of x is simply the square root of the variance, or σ_x. Everything considered, it is more appropriate for our work because of its "units": the units of the SD match the units for $E(x)$!

We can conclude this section by calculating the variances and the SDs of the above experiments. For the coin $\text{Var}(x) = 1/2(3 - 3.5)^2 + 1/2(4 - 3.5)^2 = 0.25$; and for the die $\text{Var}(x) = (1/6)(1 - 3.5)^2 + (1/6)(2 - 3.5)^2 + \cdots + (1/6)(6 - 3.5)^2 = 2.92$. The standard deviations (σ) are 0.5 and 1.71.

We have now arrived in mean-variance country, and for those of you who have studied some economics, what we do here is to ask for the utility (U) of a probability distribution of outcomes (x_i) with a utility function that contains expected outcome $E(x)$, and risk (σ^2). That utility function is thus $U[E(x), \sigma^2]$, and for the examples above we have $U_c(3.5, 0.25)$ for the coin and $U_d(3.5, 2.92)$ for the die. Mainstream theory suggests that the first is preferred to the second, and so $U_c > U_d$. This is fine, even if both you and I know that there are plenty of people who would prefer the second to the first because of the presence of higher outcomes — i.e. five and six. (Utility: measure of satisfaction from a good, service, portfolio, etc.)

Exercises

1. Calculate the expected value and variance of an unbiased three-sided coin that has 2, 4, and 6 printed on the sides! In the dice rolling experiments, what are the probabilities of obtaining a 4?
2. Suppose that you are holding a portfolio of shares, and you make the following (subjective) estimates of its returns and probabilities of returns: [(+20%, 0.15), (+10%, 0.45), (0%, 0.25), (−5%, 0.15)]. What is the expected value, variance, and standard deviation of this portfolio in percent?

The next topics are covariance and correlation. As Nobel laureate Harry Markovitz put it, the riskiness of a portfolio depends on the covariance of its holdings, and not on the average riskiness of the separate investments. Thus a collection of very risky assets may turn out to display a low risk as long as they are highly diversified in the sense that when the prices (or values) of some go up, the prices of the others go down, and vice versa. In other words, they have a negative covariance. Markovitz deservedly found a place among the greats because of this observation, although from a practical point of view his ideas on portfolio selection have done better in the Halls of Ivy than the Halls of Wall Street. The late Jan Mossin, for instance, once remarked that Markovitz's approach involved computing first and thinking afterward, which is not always recommended. If you can calculate a variance, then calculating the covariance is hardly more difficult. Algebraically this covariance σ_{xy} is:

$$\sigma_{xy} = \sum_{i=1}^{N} [x_i - E(x)][y_i - E(y)] p_i \qquad (8.3)$$

As you can see, the covariance is the average of two "difference" products over all relevant states "i". It is a measure of the average tendency of returns to vary in the same (positive) or in the opposite (negative) direction. Note how this works: in any state of the world "i", there is a value of x (= x_i), and a value of y (= y_i), and it is these two values that are put into the above formula together with the probability of their joint appearance.

Once we have the covariance, it is a simple matter to obtain the correlation coefficient (ρ_{xy}): $\rho_{xy} = \sigma_{xy}/\sigma_x\sigma_y$. What we are working toward is the "portfolio variance" and portfolio standard deviation, and for that the covariance is sufficient together with the individual variances; but the logic of the correlation coefficient is useful to know. It takes the covariance and constrains its value to between -1 and $+1$. -1 indicates that two assets move in the exact opposite direction, while if the correlation coefficient is $+1$, then the two assets are statistically clones. When the correlation coefficient is zero, then the two assets are completely uncorrelated. A further advantage of the correlation coefficient is that it is "unitless".

If we think back to earlier discussions in this book, it was suggested that Long Term Capital Management's bets were too highly correlated, and as a result they all floundered at the same time.

We are now going to calculate some values for $\text{Cov}_{xy} (= \sigma_{xy})$ that will be used to calculate the variance of a portfolio of two risky assets. Suppose that x and y are assets of some kind, while "1" and "2" are states of the world — e.g. summer and winter. The values of R in the schematic representation below signify expected returns, where e.g. $0.02 = 2\%$. We also need some "weights" that tell us what fraction of a given sum of money we would invest in each asset of a portfolio. In the discussion below, the weights are chosen as $w_A = w_B = 0.5$. (Weights always sum to unity.)

R_A \ R_B	R_{B1}	R_{B2}		R_A \ R_B	0.08	0.02		$\bar{R}_i = E(R_i)$
R_{A1}	P_{11}	P_{12}	P_{A1}	0.02	1/2	0	1/2	$\bar{R}_A = 0.04 = 4\%$
R_{A2}	P_{21}	P_{22}	P_{A2}	0.06	0	1/2	1/2	$\bar{R}_B = 0.05 = 5\%$
	P_{B1}	P_{B2}			1/2	1/2	1	

Before making the calculations, the reader should take note of the zeros in the table on the right. These occur because, e.g. when we have summer (1) or winter (2), it applies to both x and y. But later, when we look at a very elementary example of diversification, we will employ a slightly different scheme. We proceed with the calculations:

$$Var(A) = \sigma_A^2 = \frac{1}{2}(0.02 - 0.04)^2 + \frac{1}{2}(0.06 - 0.04)^2 = 0.0004; \ SD = \sigma_A = 0.02$$

$$Var(B) = \sigma_B^2 = \frac{1}{2}(0.08 - 0.05)^2 + \frac{1}{2}(0.02 - 0.05)^2 = 0.0009; \ SD = \sigma_B = 0.03$$

$$Cov_{AB} = \frac{1}{2}(0.02 - 0.04)(0.08 - 0.05) + \frac{1}{2}(0.06 - 0.04)(0.02 - 0.05) = -0.0006$$

These results can now be used to form the following table, noting that $Cov_{AB} = Cov_{BA}$; $Cov_{ii} = \sigma_i^2$, where i = A, B.

Security	$\overline{R}_i$	w_i	σ_i^2	Cov_{iA}	Cov_{iB}
A	0.04	0.50	0.0004	0.0004	—
B	0.05	0.50	0.0009	−0.0006	0.0009

From these data, we can calculate the expected return of the Portfolio (R_p) containing the two risky assets A and B. This, of course, is merely the (weighted) mathematical expectation of the components of the portfolio, and so we get $1/2(0.04) + 1/2(0.05) = 0.045$. Now for the portfolio variance σ_p^2. This will be obtained from a relationship that will be discussed in the next section. The expression is $\sigma_p^2 = w_A^2 \sigma_A^2 + w_B^2 \sigma_B^2 + 2w_A w_B Cov_{AB}$, and inserting the values from the above table the reader will see immediately that we have $\sigma_p^2 = (1/2)^2 0.0004 + (1/2)^2 0.0009 - 2(1/2)(1/2)0.0006 = 0.000025$.

We can also write down the standard deviations by taking the square roots of the variances. These are $\sigma_A = 0.02$; $\sigma_B = 0.03$, and $\sigma_p = 0.0050$. What we have now is a portfolio with a lower average return than the asset with the highest return — which is asset B; but at the same time a much lower risk. Many risk avoiders would find this portfolio superior to asset

B, because although return has been reduced somewhat, there is a very large reduction in risk.

We can also observe that although asset B *dominated* asset A with regard to both risk and return, asset A turned out to be useful in reducing the portfolio risk. This is a valuable observation and should not be forgotten! What we have said is that there can be risky assets with a comparatively low yield that, when included in a portfolio, can contribute to risk reduction. One final observation. In calculating the portfolio variance, we used the weights $w_A = w_B = 0.5$. There are obviously many possibilities here. Think of what the situation would be if we had three assets, or between 15 and 20!

Exercises

1. Do the above exercise taking as the weights $w_A = 0.4$ and $w_B = 0.6$. How do you "rate" this portfolio as compared to the one discussed above?
2. The exercise referred to above has two assets. Without filling in any numbers except those for the weights, construct a table for three assets, and discuss!

II. Some Statistical Observations*

Nothing will really be derived here. There is hardly any point in deriving relationships that are clearly expressed in the most elementary books on probability theory. However certain results need to be emphasized. The first of these will be used later, while the next was used above. A similar discussion is found in Bodie and Merton (2000).

Consider a portfolio consisting of a risk-free asset with a return r_f, and a risky asset with an expected return of r_x. The risky asset can be a single asset, or a portfolio of risky assets. For the time being it doesn't make any difference. Now assume that a fraction of invested wealth "w" is held in the risky asset, while the remainder $(1 - w)$ is held in the risk-free asset. The expected return on this portfolio is then:

---

*All discussions marked with an asterisk (*) can be skipped if the reader desires.

$$r_p = [(1 - w)r_f + wr_x] \tag{8.4}$$

Later the expectations operator will be used again to indicate expected values, but this introduction might be clearer if it is ignored. In looking at this expression, we see that when $w = 1$, $r_p = r_x$; and when $w = 0$, $r_p = r_f$. Now, let us obtain the variance of this portfolio, but before doing this let me note that if the reader feels frustrated with the next few manipulations, then he or she should simply skip to Eq. (8.6). From elementary probability theory we have:

$$\sigma_p^2 = \text{Var } r_p = \text{Var}[(1 - w)r_f + wr_x]$$

Some (perhaps not so apparent) manipulation will give us:

$$\sigma_p^2 = \text{Var}[(1 - w)r_f] + \text{Var}(wr_x) + 2w(1 - w)\text{Cov}_{fx} \tag{8.5}$$

The variance of the risk free asset is zero, which also means that the covariance between the risk free and the risky asset (x) is zero: $\text{Cov}_{fx} = \sigma_f\sigma_x\rho_{fx}$, where the last term is the correlation coefficient for these two assets. Since the variance of the risk free asset is zero, the covariance must also be zero, which leads us to the very important result:

$$\sigma_p^2 = w^2\text{Var } r_x = w^2\sigma_x^2 \quad \text{(or)} \quad \sigma_p = w\sigma_x \tag{8.6}$$

This last expression is crucial to what follows. Now we go over to using the expectations operator. First of all, we have $E(r_p) = (1 - w)r_f + wE(r_x)$, since $E(r_f) = r_f$. This is preferably written as $E(r_p) = r_f + w[E(r_x) - r_f]$. If we use (8.6), then $w = \sigma_p/\sigma_x$, and we get as the expected value of the portfolio $E(r_p)$, the simple expression:

$$E(r_p) = r_f + \sigma_p\left[\frac{E(r_x) - r_f}{\sigma_x}\right] \tag{8.7}$$

What this amounts to is an (expected) risk-reward trade-off line. The geometrical interpretation is a straight line intersecting the vertical axis at r_f, and sloping up to the right since $E(r_x) > r_f$. In case the reader is curious, Fig. 8.1(a) in the next section depicts this situation. The expression in the parenthesis can be called the *price of risk*. The explanation here is in the language: reducing risk by one unit means giving up an amount of expected return shown in the parenthesis. Of course, if you remember your calculus, then $\Delta E(p)/\Delta\sigma_p = [(E(r_x) - r_f)/\sigma_x]$; and if you remember your intermediate economics, then you should immediately recognize that the expression $\Delta E(p)/\Delta\sigma_p)$ is a price ratio.

Finally, it was mentioned above that the derivation of (8.5) is not particularly apparent, but it is obtained from a fairly simple manipulation of (8.2). In my lectures I never bother with this manipulation, which I regard as a sub-optimal use of valuable classroom time. Instead, I merely write down the general form for the variance of a portfolio having N elements. But first, as an exercise, consider the following double sum $\Sigma\Sigma a_i b_j$. If we have values of 1 and 2 for i and j, then we get from this double sum $a_1 b_1 + a_1 b_2 + a_2 b_1 + a_2 b_2$. In general we have for this double sum $a_1 b_1 + a_1 b_2 + \cdots + a_1 b_N + a_2 b_1 + \cdots + a_2 b_N + \cdots + a_N b_1 + \cdots + a_N b_N$, assuming that both i and j go from 1 to N.

Our final result is for a portfolio with N elements, and where ρ signifies correlation. Thus

$$\sigma_p^2 = w_1^2\sigma_1^2 + w_2^2\sigma_2^2 + \cdots + w_N^2\sigma_N^2 + 2w_1 w_2 \rho_{12}\sigma_1\sigma_2$$
$$+ 2w_1 w_3 \rho_{13}\sigma_1\sigma_3 + \cdots + 2w_{N-1} w_N \rho_{N-1,N}\sigma_{N-1}\sigma_N$$

In the most general form, this value of σ_p^2 is equal to:

$$\sum_{i=1}^{N}\sum_{j=1}^{N} w_i w_j \rho_{ij}\sigma_i\sigma_j \quad \text{or} \quad \sum_{i=1}^{N}\sum_{j=1}^{N} w_i w_j \text{Cov}_{ij} \tag{8.8}$$

Everyone who can should memorize these expressions!

Exercises

1. Write out both expressions in (8.8) taking N = 2!
2. Write out both expressions in (8.8) taking N = 3!
3. It was stated above that Eq. (8.7) slopes up to the right. Discuss this observation.

III. Portfolio Selection: The Mean Variance Approach

This section will look into the matter of selecting an optimal portfolio in a situation where there is a risk-free asset, as well as risky assets. A two stage approach of the kind suggested by Bodie and Merton (2000) and Bernstein (1992) will be employed: first construct an efficiency locus consisting of optimal portfolios of risky assets, and then use (Professor James) Tobin's *separation theorem* to select another portfolio containing both the risk-free and risky assets. By *efficiency locus* it is meant a locus (i.e. curve) where for any value of the risk, the maximum expected return is obtained. The risk-free asset is not always specified, but it is generally

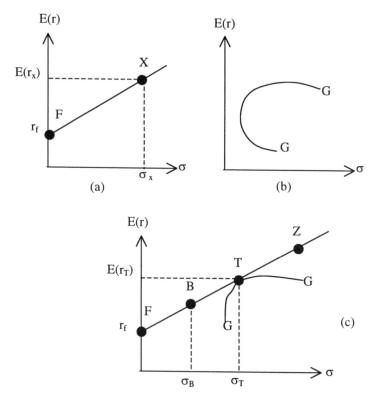

Fig. 8.1. Market Line and Efficiency Locus

thought of as bank deposits or perhaps government bonds, although it could be something like the low-risk liquidity funds referred to earlier. These funds are triple A-rated, and often consist of highly liquid money-market items that, at the present time, are outperforming bank deposits by 15 basis points.

This discussion requires Fig. 8.1. Figure 8.1(a) you already know about. It is merely a risk-reward trade-off (or "market") line. Expected return is on the vertical axis, while risk (as represented by the standard deviation of a portfolio) is on the horizontal axis. The important thing here is the intercept $E(r_f) = r_f$ on the vertical axis. Figure 8.1(b) is the efficiency locus referred to above, while Fig. 8.1(c) shows a tangency between the trade-off line and the efficiency locus. Once we have this tangency — labeled point T — we choose a point between F and T on the basis of our "taste" for risk. For instance, we might choose point F or point T. In the first case we have no taste for risk, and all of our investible wealth goes into the risk-free asset; while in the second case we do not invest anything in the risk-free asset. Instead we put all of our investible wealth into the risky portfolio corresponding to T, which has an expected return $E(r_T)$ and a risk that is represented by the standard deviation σ_T. Usually we choose a point between F and T, but if we want to borrow in order to assume more risk, we can attain a point to the right of T.

Now for a systematic approach to the choice of the optimal portfolio, beginning with the risk-expected return trade-off line in risk-expected return space. This can be written $f[\sigma, E(r)] = 0$. In Fig. 8.1(a), this is a straight line. We continue with:

1. The efficiency locus in risk-expected return space, which will be written $G[\sigma, E(r)]$. This is constructed from various portfolios of risky assets, and is shown as G-G in Fig. 8.1(b). Unless I am mistaken, the computational effort required to obtain a usable efficiency locus is enormous, and despite rumors I doubt whether it is carried out successfully very often.

2. Solving the two implicit equations (f and G) together would give us values for σ and $E(r)$ that correspond to the point of tangency between the "line" and the "locus". This point is shown as T in Fig. 8.1(c).

Associated with this point is an expected return $E(r_T)$, and a risk σ_T.

3. Each point on the risk-reward locus G-G represents a certain efficient portfolio having proportions $(w_1, w_2, \ldots, w_N)$, where N is the number of risky assets in the portfolio, and $\Sigma w_i = 1$. Therefore at T we can say that $[\sigma_T, E(r_T)] \to (w_{1T}, w_{2T}, \ldots, w_{NT})$.

4. We can now specify an optimal risk-return trade-off line, which in Fig. 8.1(c) is shown by FTZ. Since we have two points on this line we can write as its equation:

5.
$$E(r) = r_f + w[E(r_T) - r_f] = r_f + \left[\frac{E(r_T) - r_f}{\sigma_T}\right]\sigma \qquad (8.9)$$

6. Note that here we have used $w = \sigma/\sigma_T$: when we are at F, $w = 0$, and when we are at T, $w = 1$. In the previous section this was derived as (8.6), but with the notation $w = \sigma_p/\sigma_x$. Equation (8.9) is linear in $E(r)$ and σ, and so there should be no problem in using the separation theorem. This tells us that we can choose a point on the line FTZ that we prefer to all others, and for the purpose of this discussion I choose the point B. (Utility would be maximized at B.) Corresponding to that point is a value of expected risk and return $[\sigma_B, E(r_B)]$, and more important, we get from our relevant expression for w, $w_B = \sigma_B/\sigma_T$. This particular w ($= w_B$) refers to the situation on the (optimal) expected risk/reward line. Now we can get a division of the risk.

$$\text{Weight in riskless asset} = (1 - w_B)$$
$$\text{Weight in risky asset 1} = w_B w_{1T}$$
$$\text{Weight in risky asset 2} = w_B w_{2T}$$
$$\ldots\ldots\ldots\ldots\ldots\ldots\ldots\ldots\ldots\ldots$$

7. Eventually we arrive at the weight in risky asset N, which is $N = w_B w_{NT}$. Adding the weights for risky assets we get $w_B w_{1T} + w_B w_{2T} + \cdots + w_B w_{NT} = w_B(w_{1T} + w_{2T} + \cdots + w_{NT}) = w_B$, as to be expected. The total weight for the risky and the riskless asset is thus $w_B + (1 - w_B) = 1$, which at this stage of the game should not come as a surprise.

That concludes this part of the discussion. Frankly, I cannot see anything in this section that contradicts my intention to keep this book as easy as possible.

IV. Diversification

The next major topic in this chapter is the capital asset pricing model (CAPM). Of course, if you understood what has been said about the mean-variance model, the CAPM will give you little or no trouble.

But before we examine that construction, a few remarks must be made about diversification. Some of these are trivial, but diversification is considered one of the most important topics in financial economics. We can start with a situation where we have two risky assets that cost the same thing. We might call these assets shares of stock in the firms Consolidated Houses and Lots (CHL), and Purlace Entertainments (PE). For both of these shares "good times" (in their particular industry) will bring a return of four dollars, while "bad times" will mean a return of two dollars. Now suppose that we buy two shares of *either* CHL or PE. This results in a return of eight dollars in good times, and four dollars in bad times. These outcomes are shown in the following tables and frequency diagram, along with the specification that the probability of good times is 0.5, and the probability of bad times is also 0.5. (And note: two shares!)

State of the World	P	Outcomes	
		CHL	PE
Good times (X_1)	0.5	8	8
Bad times (X_2)	0.5	4	4
"Average"		6	6

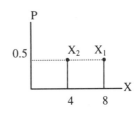

The "average" return, given the outcomes and probabilities, is as usual determined from $\overline{X} = P_1X_1 + P_2X_2 = 8 \times 0.5 + 4 \times 0.5 = 6$. This applies to both assets. We also find it useful to calculate the variance of these assets. For both the variance is: $\sigma(X)^2 = \Sigma P_i(X_i - \overline{X})^2 = 1/2(8-6)^2 + 1/2(4-6)^2 = 4$. The standard deviation of both assets is the square-root of the variance, or two.

Next, let us see what happens if we have a portfolio consisting of one of each shares, and assuming that the outcomes are independent. We then have for the pattern of outcomes:

	Purlace			
	"Good"	"Bad"		
CHL	8	6	"Good"	
	6	4	"Bad"	

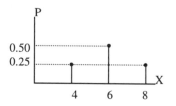

The expected value of this scheme is $\overline{X} = (1/4)8 + (1/4)6 + (1/4)6 + (1/4)4 = 2 + 1.5 + 1.5 + 1 = 6$, which is the same as the previous value of the "average" or "expected" return. Now let us consider the variance, which is $\sigma^2 = 1/4(8-6)^2 + 1/4(6-6)^2 + 1/4(6-6)^2 + 1/4(4-6)^2 = 2$, and the standard deviation $(\sigma) = 2^{1/2} = 1.414$.

Although the expected return is still six, the variance has been cut in two. This is the kind of non-trivial result that warms the heart of many economists. Note also that standard deviation is a preferred measure of variability, because it has the same dimensions (or units) as the outcomes. (Think about what we have here! If times are good for CHL, its share yield will be four; while if during the same period times are bad for PE, its share yield will be two. The combined share yield is six, and the probability of this situation is 0.25 (= 1/4), using the equiprobability rule that follows from assuming independent outcomes.)

We can now present, without prologue, a diagram which shows the most important aspect of diversification. On the vertical axis we have risk, while on the horizontal axis we have the number of different assets. The important thing in reducing risk is the heterogenity of a portfolio. What we see here is that as we increase the number of assets of different types, we

Risk

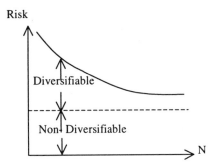

Fig. 8.2.   Diversifiable and Non-Diversifiable Risk

reduce the diversifiable (i.e. non-systematic) risk. It appears in fact that if we construct a portfolio of between 15 and 20 randomly selected assets, we have achieved a large fraction of the diversification that is possible.

Notice also that there is a part of the risk that we cannot get rid of. This is the non-diversifiable or systematic risk, associated with things like the business cycle. I have only seen one estimate of the amount of this risk, and it amounted to approximately 30% of total risk.

V. The Capital Asset Pricing Model

Going from mean-variance to the capital asset pricing model (CAPM) is mostly a matter of terminology. Instead of a locus of efficient points we are primarily concerned with one point, M, representing the *market portfolio*. Essentially what we have here is the efficient markets contention that if you are going to hold a portfolio of risky assets, then you cannot do better than "The Market" — or a portfolio that "effectively" replicates the market. M is then connected with a straight line to the risk-free point on the vertical axis to give a trade-off line known as the Budget Line (BL).

As in previous discussions, M is characterized by an expected return $r_m (= E(r_m))$ and a risk σ_m. The assumption now must be that the expected return of the market portfolio is actually measurable, since it has to do

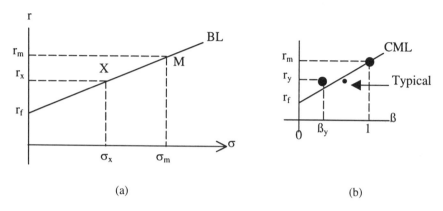

Fig. 8.3. Budget Line (BL) and Capital Market Line (CML)

with the present market, and this return applies during the period that we will be forming another portfolio consisting of the market portfolio and the riskless asset. We can now turn to Fig. 8.3.

How does this market portfolio look? One possibility would be the 30 "industrials" comprising the Dow Jones; or perhaps the collection comprising the Standard and Poor's 500; but probably a better choice would be the 15 or 20 randomly chosen shares from a prestigious index — in other words a subset of some prestigious index — since they would absorb most of the *diversifiable* risk shown in Fig. 8.2. (The CAPM says that in equilibrium any investor would hold risky assets in the same proportion as in the market portfolio. If we held 20 shares as our replica of the market, and the total market value of these 20 shares turned out to be $W_1 + W_2 + \cdots + W_{20} = W$, then if we decided to hold a risky portfolio of $50,000, we would invest $50,000(W_1/W)$ in share 1, $50,000(W_2/W)$ in share 2, and so on. (Obviously we have $\Sigma(W_i/W) = 1$.)

We can also pay attention to the fact that where in our discussion of mean-variance we had an arbitrary trade-off line, $E(r_x) = r_f + w[E(r_p) - r_f]$, we now have what is known as a *capital market line* (CML), or in algebraic form $r_x = r_f + \beta_x(r_m - r_f)$, where β_x is the famous "beta" that is the measure of the market-related nondiversifiable risk of a particular asset. For example, if we choose point "x" on the CML as the most desirable combination of the riskless and the risky asset (i.e. the collection of assets replicating the market), then $\sigma_x = \beta_x \sigma_m$. If we take the risk of the market portfolio as unity (i.e. $\beta = 1$), then if a stock has a beta of $+0.5$, it is considered half as risky as the market as a whole, and when the market moves by 10%, up or down, then it will move up or down by 5%. In other words, beta is a measure of how sensitive an asset or a portfolio of assets is to overall market movements. The following table might be interesting. It also contains the most conventional estimating equation for beta. Ostensibly, brokers and investment advisors are in possession of the betas of many stocks, and perhaps other assets, however many of these professionals are not enchanted by the emphasis placed on such abstract concepts as beta.

With the above table and our knowledge of the CML in the background, we can go to a discussion of the attractiveness of individual assets. $r_x - r_f$ is the risk premium on e.g. a stock "x", while $r_m - r_f$ is the risk premium of the market. Now, suppose that in Fig. 8.3(b) we had an asset y that is above the CML. In such a situation we have $r_y > r_f + \beta_y(r_m - r_f)$.

This is a good asset to buy, because when other investors discover it, they will bid its price up. With this taking place its return will fall, and it will descend to the CML. If, for instance, it is a share, and you bought it early enough, then you could sell it for a capital gain; and the same is true if it is a bond.

Table 8.1. Some Hypothetical Asset Returns (in %) and Betas

Asset	Good Times	Normal Times	Bad Times
Market	15	6	−2
High Beta	19	9	−8
Beta = 1	15	6	−2
Low Beta	6	3	2
Negative Beta	2	4	6
	Beta $(\beta_i) = \dfrac{\mathrm{Cov}(r_i, r_m)}{\mathrm{Var}(r_m)}$		

As many readers might suspect, it is much easier to discuss βs than to use them in portfolio selection, but before leaving this section it should be noted that the CAPM suggests a practical approach to selecting a discount rate when risk is present.

Without risk, the discount rate is r_f. For an asset "i", a risk premium reflecting non-diversifiable risk can be added to r_f to obtain the risk adjusted discount factor $r_i = r_f + \beta_f(r_m - r_f)$. If we use this r_i, and the discounted return on the asset is less than its cost, then the asset belongs below the CML with what Gordon Gekko called "dogs".

Very early in this book considerable care was taken to distinguish between nominal (or money) and real values of the interest rate. Before leaving this section we should perhaps inquire into the nature of discount rates. Should they be real or nominal?

The discounting rule is simple: if cash flows are in real terms, then the discount rate must also be in real terms; and if these flows are in money terms — as is usually the case — then the discount rate must also be in nominal terms.

In considering this matter, let us take the following example, with r as an interest (or discount) rate, in percent, and g the inflation rate. Assume that at time t, 100 dollars can buy 100 candy bars. If 100 dollars is saved (and therefore 100 candy bars abstained from), and if r = 10%, and g = 5%, then a year later (at t + 1) we have enough money to obtain 104.76 candy bars, taking the price rise into consideration. Accordingly, the real rate of interest is 4.76%. Put another way, the cost of the 104.76 candy bars that we can obtain at t + 1 is $104.76 \times 1.05 = \$110$, where 1.05 is the price at t + 1.

If we discount this $110 back to "t" using the real rate of interest, we get $110/1.0476 = 105$. The discounted value is greater than the actual sacrifice (= 100 candy bars), which is obviously unacceptable — since we did start our exercise with 100 candy bars — and so it is obvious that the correct discount factor should employ the money rate of interest, or 10%. Now try discounting the real value of our candy bars at t + 1 — or 104.76 — by the money rate of interest. This gives $104.76/1.1 = 95.23$. This is also a number that does not belong in the present discussion, because it indicates that

104.76 candy bars at t + 1 is not equivalent to 100 at time t — although we know that we generated the 104.76 by sacrificing 100. What should have been done was to discount the 104.76 with the real rate of interest. Then we would have had 104.76/(1 + 0.0476) = 100.

VI. Rational Expectations and Efficient Markets

Rational Expectations and the Efficient Markets Hypothesis (EMH) are in some ways closely related. This should become clear later, but we can begin with a pair of definitions. For the EMH, all available information is so rapidly reflected in stock prices that no single investor should draw the conclusion that he or she knows more than the market as a whole knows. As Richard Roll (1988) has pointed out: "In general stock prices are notoriously unpredictable, and financial economists have even developed a coherent theory (the theory of efficient markets) to explain why they *should* be unpredictable".

As for rational expectations, these are expectations that a market actor has no reason to revise up or down, even though they are not correct some of the time: in much of the elementary literature, the argument is that they are correct *on the average*. In addition, expectations will not differ from the optimal forecasts that are obtained when all available information is used. In this context, an optimal forecast can be thought of as the best estimate of the future value of the variable under consideration.

By way of elaborating on this topic, let us examine the daily journey to work of a certain rational citizen of Bergen, Norway, which is a city where, on the average, it rains almost 300 days per year.

Suppose Boris Buckaman rides to work on a bus that, according to the schedule, is "estimated" to arrive at his local bus stop at 8:56 every morning; and from which it will depart (on the average) in less than a minute. From Mr. Buckaman's house it takes, on the average, five minutes for him to walk to the bus stop. Sometimes he feels full of energy, in which case he runs, and as a result he reaches the bus stop in about three minutes. On other occasions his mind wanders, and he walks rather slowly; on those occasions he often finds himself arriving at the same time as the bus, and running the final 25 or 50 meters. On rare occasions he misses the bus. What he expects, however, is that his trip to the bus will take five minutes, and if he leaves home within a few seconds of 8:50, he will maximize his satisfaction where this bus-catching operation is concerned. But why leave at 8:50 and not 8:51? The answer is that by forecasting an arrival of the bus at 8:56, he ensures that even if the bus comes early, and his journey to the bus stop takes more than five minutes, he will still be in time for the bus on most occasions. (Also, if the bus is late, he will not be exposed to the eternal Bergen drizzle too long.)

Now let us point out the key issue being taken up here. The main thing is not the time that it takes to get to the bus: on the average this is five minutes. The key issue is maximizing Mr. B's satisfaction by, in this example, forecasting that the bus schedule is *on the average* correct, with the bus arriving *on the average* at 8:56, and consequently adopting a behavior (leaving at 8:50) so that if there are no changes in external circumstances, this behavior provides maximum satisfaction and does not have to be changed. It is here that we can speak of a *rational expectations equilibrium*! Furthermore, let us make sure we understand that on an ordinary day, Boris cannot predict whether the bus will arrive before 8:56, or after (on the average). In fact, if he could, he would (rationally) change the time he left the house.

Put more formally, the forecast error of expectations, $T - T_e$ (= the actual time of arrival *minus* the expected time of arrival) will — on the average — be zero, *and cannot be predicted ahead of time*! Once again, on a given day, Boris does not know whether the bus will be early, late, or exactly on time. This, incidentally, was why a forecast was necessary in the first place.

Something here sounds like an observation in the famous dissertation of Louis Bachelier "The Theory of Speculation" (1900), where he says that "The mathematical expectation of the speculator is zero … clearly, the price considered most likely by the market is the true current price: if the market judged otherwise, it would quote not this price, but another price higher or lower". When Bachelier speaks of a mathematical expectation of zero, he is referring to the possibility of outperforming the market. The rational speculator should not conclude that he or she is bigger than the market, just as a rational Boris would not try to outguess the bus timetable — i.e. try to guess how often (and when) it will be late or early (except for the cases mentioned below).

The reader should also appreciate once again that a rational expectation does not need to be perfectly accurate. What it should do is to make the best use of *all* available information. Often this last stipulation goes along with the expression "model-based", where the implication is that accomplished market "actors" are those who have learned the properties of some model that replicates certain mechanisms of actual economies, markets, or whatever. In particular, mechanisms that appear in the work of Professor Robert Lucas. It is here, of course, that this humble teacher of economics and finance feels obliged to part company with rational expectationalists, because making the best use of all available information, or "learning the properties of the model", is precisely what most of us cannot do. As Prime Minister David Lloyd George remarked after a battlefield catastrophe during the First World War: "Of course the people don't know. How could they know?" And by "people" he meant his generals as well as the newspaper reading public.

All this seems perfectly straightforward, but various complications can arise to plague the lives of hard working citizens like Mr. Buckaman. For instance, there might be excursions arranged for groups of small children living near the same bus line, and because of the problems involved in getting the children on the bus it might take an extra five minutes for the bus to arrive. By way of contrast, occasionally there will be holidays or "partial" holidays, in which case many commuters will not be using the bus, and it will arrive — and depart — early. How do these apparent exceptions fit into the rational expectations picture? On the one hand it might be argued that they do not fit in at all, since if Boris does not bother to find out about such things as excursions and holidays, he is not quite rational. However, according to many rational expectations adherents, such persons are few and far between. Furthermore, if for some legitimate reason Boris is initially unaware of certain highly relevant pieces of information, after a few uncomfortable experiences involving standing in the rain, he will make it his business to become cognizant of all factors having to do with getting to the bus on time. For example, on holidays he knows that the bus comes earlier.

Now let us sort out a few more of the key elements in the EMH. To begin, suppose that you are interested in buying a certain security. Naturally, you are concerned about the future prospects of this asset, and so the question arises as to whom you would consult about these prospects. One possibility is your finance teacher; or a well known and accessible consultant; or maybe even someone who claims that they can successfully pick stocks on the basis of what they read in tea leaves or the entrails of cockroaches. The EMH says that the place to find this information is the price of the security: this is the value that the market has set on it at the time, because investors everywhere go to a great deal of trouble to find out all they can about market conditions, and the information they (as a group) obtain — correct or otherwise — is promptly incorporated by comprehensive auction markets. In a loose sense, the price of the security functions in the same way as the "estimated time of arrival" on the bus schedule. Just as the bus may be earlier or later than the time of arrival given on the schedule, the security might increase or decrease in value in reference to the listed price; but you cannot tell which in advance.

(In fact, if this discussion were carried much further, what you would be told is that many equity managers with decades of experience, and the best contacts and information available, often alienate their insitutional clients through underperformance. As a result, many of their clients (e.g. pension funds) have gone over to passive index tracking. Of course, some of these funds are going in the other direction, and putting a slice of their assets in the hands of hedge funds, to include so-called "market neutral" funds that, supposedly, consistently outperform cash in both up and down markets.)

Continuing, suppose you think that the market is wrong and the price too low, so you buy the particular share. But notice that for you to be right, the market must agree with you: if the market does not validate your estimate of the "true" or "intrinsic" value at the time you make your purchase, then you could end up a big loser. Expressed another way, if you get rich it is because you bought ahead of the market. It is not because you know more than the market, but when buying a particular security you were fortunate enough to place yourself ahead of the queue. This is a wonderful thing, and you may feel that your rightful place is at the head of the queue, but you should be aware that all "scientific" evidence indicates that the individual investor buys too late relative to the market. The same thing is true of many experts. To paraphrase John Kenneth Galbraith, "financial genius is and always was a rising market". It takes exceptional luck or exceptional skill to be a big winner year after year, in bear as well as bull markets. There are persons who possess one or both of these resources, but most of us are not so fortunate. Now let us turn to the rational expectations equilibrium in Fig. 8.4.

Readers should note the use of the term *equilibrium*. As far as I am concerned, that word is used too often in finance, although I have no problem at all in calling the economics that I teach "equilibrium economics". However in the discussion that we are carrying on here, the concept of equilibrium has a meaningful role to play in the scheme of things. For example, we have a very good idea as to what equilibrium means to the gentleman waiting

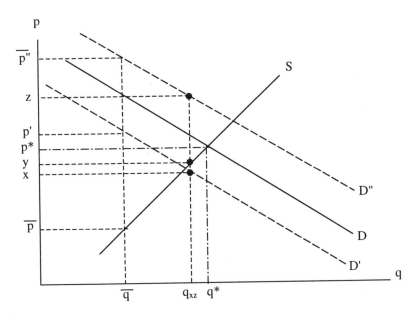

Fig. 8.4. Rational Expectations Equilibrium

for the bus, and often waiting in the rain, so let's look things over in the conventional manner, beginning with a simple textbook market that features a shifting demand curve that is shown in the figure as D.

Suppose that our market consists of a single supplier who, expecting a price of $\bar{p}$, chooses $\bar{q}$ as his profit maximizing production. As is obvious with our shifting demand scheme, price will vary between p' and $\bar{p}''$, as long as the quantity supplied remains fixed at $\bar{q}$. In these circumstances we cannot speak of an equilibrium in any sense. Conventionally, none of the expectations of our transactors are being fulfilled, while in the rational expectations sense we have not only underproduced, but there is no doubt that this condition prevails. We are facing a situation of the type experienced by our bus rider if he is always wrong.

Now suppose that our supplier shifts to q*. If the demand curve were not shifting, we would have an equilibrium (q*, p*) of the conventional type, with expectations fulfilled, and a stationary price and quantity. However, even with a shifting demand curve we can speak of an equilibrium in what might be called the rational expectations sense. The price does not stay at p*, but it varies around p* in an unpredictable (i.e. random or stochastic) manner, and in such a way that p* appears to be the average value of these price movements. Furthermore, if we decide to change production, what we find out is that our expectations are often unfulfilled, and unfulfilled in such a way that allows us to predict the type of unfulfillment. This is analogous to Boris deciding that instead of leaving home at 8:50, he will leave at 8:51. Now he finds that although he is mostly on time for the bus, and occasionally he will even be very early, he misses the bus more often — no matter how fast he sprints when he sees the bus coming. The mornings when he is very early for the bus are conspicuously fewer, and he is aware that he must run for the bus more often. He is also late an annoying number of times. (This last observation corresponds to q_{xz} in Fig. 8.3.)

The producer is occasionally right with q_{xz} (and price y), but he is often wrong. The forecast error of the price is not zero. We do not have the optimal forecast that is associated with "rational" transactors. Returning to Mr. Buckaman, he would no longer be making an optimal forecast of the time it would take him to reach the bus — or, put another way, given the speed at which he walks (and runs), he is not making an optimal forecast of the time of arrival of the bus.

In the present discussion, it is obvious that if we call an optimal forecast of the price p_o, then $p_o = p^*$, where p^* is the equilibrium price. This results in a q ($= q^*$) which does not involve systematic correctable errors in prediction. Thus, to really use the rational expectations *paradigm*, we need a market where we almost always see an equilibrium price. An example of this kind of market is an auction market — such as the stock market — where the structure of the market is such that out of equilibrium situations (involving supply not equal to demand) are almost immediately corrected by buying and selling. Looked at another way, in an auction market where imbalances in supply and demand are almost immediately corrected, the optimal forecast of the price is the price that we are viewing, the market price, which happens to be the equilibrium price. Thus, in the context of e.g. an auction market, rational expectations and the EMH are virtually the same thing.

VII. Value Additivity, and Conclusion

Readers of the mainstream finance literature are probably asking why there is no reference to the Modigliani-Miller (MM) theorem in this chapter. That question is easily answered, but before doing so let me remind readers that earlier I referred to Merton Miller as the leading academic financial economist, and I have made no secret of my belief that Franco Modigliani should have received his Nobel prize years before he was actually awarded this accolade.

More, however, I cannot do. Peter Bernstein concludes a chapter in his book by saying that "the bombshells are still exploding, and the world is still reverberating to them". He is talking about MM theory, and although my hearing is very good — most of the time — I seem to have missed these reverberations. He also tells us that the orginal MM presentation is a completely frictionless one: without taxes, transactions costs, and information problems, and corporations make investment decisions first and then worry about how to finance them. And so on and so forth.

This is not a bombshell, but a missile — a misguided missile. Bodie and Merton (2000) offer a very simple and fairly useful discussion of the MM model, but of course they do not go so far as to discuss its short-comings, which in many respects are the shortcomings of economics itself. I do not teach this kind of economics, but I do not make a point of interfering with what others teach or study. As a former heavyweight boxing champion of the world, Sonny Liston, once remarked: "Who am I to tell a bird how to fly".

In his approach to the MM theorem, Hal Varian (1993) employed something called "value additivity". Here we can call on Einstein's equivalence theorem: Varian's approach is "one way" to prove the MM theorem, and thus in its interior logic it must be equivalent to other "proofs". In obtaining the MM theorem from value additivity, Varian shows — at least implicitly — that the result is based on pure and simple arbitrage of the kind that *could* happen in the real world, but which — in the light of real world shortcomings — is highly unlikely.

Value additivity says that the value of a portfolio is equal to the sum of the values of its component assets. This sounds peculiar in the light of Markowitz's observations about portfolio diversification, where it is easy to get the idea that certain assets should be worth more if combined in a portfolio with other assets than if "standing alone".

But in Varian's well functioning, ivory tower securities market, where equilibrium reigns supreme at every hour of the day and night, to include Sundays and holidays, all assets are already located where their values are maximized. If not, their prices would be bid up as a result of a demand for them that originates with the desire to include them in various portfolios. As Varian points out, if these asset prices did not rise, then the portfolio manager finds herself being served a "free lunch", because the portfolio can be sold for more than its cost. Everyone knows that there are no free lunches in neoclassical economics.

The same reasoning is applied to the MM construction. If the firm could change its value by altering the cash flows that result from an initial makeup of equities and bonds — e.g. adopting a financial structure that gives more to debt holders and less in dividends — then any investor could make the same arrangement. Any value augmenting change available to the firm can be carried out by the investor, who buys or sells bonds and stocks in such a way as to obtain pure arbitrage profits. However if the market was efficient enough to eliminate arbitrage profits for individual investors, then it would eliminate them for the firm as well. Otherwise, since the whole (in value terms) is the sum of the parts, then the sum of the parts (stocks + bonds) remains the same, but not the whole. At this point I will repackage a comment that I made earlier. Arbitrage and equilibrium are wonderful tools in the classroom, but they are not always germane to what is taking place in the executive suite at Goldman Sachs or Bear Stearns.

John Maynard (Lord) Keynes, who was definitely one of the great economists of the millennium, once referred to the stock market as a "beauty contest", and he very definitely did not believe in "buying the market." I can understand where he's coming from. Keynes' approach was to read the most informative newspapers, and then drift through the best clubs in London, where the highest quality inside information was available for anyone who was interested in it — which was not the case with many London clubmen. Keynes increased the value of his own portfolio from £16,315 in 1919 to £411,000 in 1995, the year before he died. When taxes are taken into consideration, this is an annual rate of increase of 13%, which is not bad for a busy and versatile man who "did it his very special way". (Keynes, incidentally, did not believe in diversification.)

If he were alive today, however, he would probably take a different approach to this matter. As Gordon Gekko pointed out in the film "Wall Street", nothing is more important than information, by which he un-doubtedly meant inside information; and according to people who know about these things, there was never more of that in circulation than during the 1990s. The problem is that the snobbish Keynes would almost certainly find associating with Gekko and his friends infinitely tedious, and as a result he would probably settle for a "no brainer" — i.e. a collection of index funds — just like the rest of us.

Chapter 9

Into the 21st Century

Everything that was is no more.
Everything that will be is not yet.
— Alfred de Mosset

Someone has said that in the 21st century, screen based knowledge and information will be money; but before that happens, it might be wise for everyone interested in finance to obtain and read the books of Michael Lewis (1989), Nancy Goldstone (1988), and Peter Bernstein (1992). Mr. Bernstein is a finance insider of long standing, and his book is an easily read paean to some finance superstars, as well as being an important cog in what is sometimes known as the gossip machine. The other two authors enjoyed brief sojourns as traders at two of the leading New York investment banks, and in both of their books persons are mentioned — without being identified — who are more than traders or analysts: they are financial know-it-alls. This may not impress some readers, but the truth is that where finance is concerned, being a know-it-all is a great deal better than being the other thing.

The purpose of this chapter is to add a few passages that, hopefully, will round out the previous discussions. Included in this resume are some observations on the recent Asian Crisis. As I pointed out at the time (1998), the Asian economic miracle was and is exactly that, and what was achieved in Japan, South Korea, Singapore and Taiwan in the 20th century, will probably be duplicated in China in the 21st — assuming that this is what the Chinese really want.

A good title for this chapter might have been "The New Rules of Global Finance", but unfortunately *Fortune* used this title for the lead cover stories in its December 20, 1999 issue. However, after scrutinizing their version of these propositions, I am not sure that they are commensurate with the spirit of this overview. As far as the *Fortune* editors were concerned, the new international order for the 21st century will be predicated on the strong "consuming the weak — with relish". "There is no place to hide" That was the first rule, and my response to that is simple: you won't be consumed unless you open the door, and keep it open. This, incidentally, was what the rioting in the Seattle streets was all about at the most recent jamboree of the WTO: with globalization, led by multinationals, picking up speed, a backlash is coalescing. Prominent in that rioting were people who do not believe that they will benefit from an open-trading system; their targets are globalization and the deregulation that has made a runaway globalization possible.

As for the other rules, the less said about them the better, except that they reveal some toxic inadequacies of logic and imagination that could turn out to be the wrong paraphernalia to take into the 21st century.

I. Real and Paper Technology

As a first step in explaining what a country exports and imports, the basic course in international economics is predestined to invoke David Ricardo's principle of comparative advantage. In its original form, this reduces to a matter of examining the relative price ratios of the tradable goods being produced in various countries, where these price ratios are in turn explained by the productivity of labor in the production of different products. Although it was not made especially clear in Ricardo's work, from these relative prices (i.e. price ratios given in terms of goods) we go to absolute money prices. Knowing the direction of trade, and money prices, the law of one price tells us the rest of the story. Trade can be thought of as a kind of arbitrage that "evens out" prices, at least in its textbook version!

The Hecksher-Ohlin extension of this concept specifies that a country will export those products which require a high input of the factors with which it is liberally endowed, while importing those which utilize relatively large inputs per unit of output of factors that are comparatively scarce within its own borders. As neat as this may sound in explaining why Holland exports radios, and imports herbal products from the Golden Triangle area of Southeast Asia, it does not go very far in explaining trade patterns among many of the highly industrialized nations. A large portion of the products exported by these countries are skill-intensive to a degree that overshadows the primary inputs considered by Professors Hecksher and Ohlin, where the skill enters the picture directly via the training or education of the labor force, or indirectly through the sophistication of the machines being used, or both.

The "both" clause here, however, applies much less today than it did a few decades ago. The sophistication of machines has reached a point that machines manufactured in the highly industrialized countries by highly skilled technicians leave those countries, and are installed in low wage countries where, as a result of the lack of educational opportunities, skills are also low. However, this does not make any difference: the skills are in the machines, and thus employees in the industries using these machines are among the winners in this particular aspect of globalization. Furthermore, many of the technicians, engineers, and scientists in these low-wage, low-skill countries inevitably depart for the highly industrialized countries, while many of the comparatively low-skilled people in the industrialized countries find their incomes stagnant or falling due to the contraction of their country's industrial base. If we look at technology's promised land, the United States, what we see is a technological colossus growing even stronger because of the attraction it holds for the rest of the world's techno-elite, but at the same time a lopsided income distribution distinguished by a comparatively new phenomenon: large numbers of the working poor.

At the turn of the new century, technology shares made up 28% of the S&P 500. For example, Yahoo, the internet firm, was worth more than General Motors, and Nokia was about 70% of the capitalization of the Finnish stock market. These are absurd valuations, although none of us knows exactly when their absurdity will be revealed.

The theory here is that investors are buying tomorrow's stocks today, however the question is what will they buy tomorrow if it turns out that technology shares are grossly overcapitalized. These shares are perhaps the best example in modern times of a "blue sky" investment, where all the profits are far into the future. So far, in fact, as to nullify all the so-called logic embedded in mainstream stock pricing models, and thereby validating Phillip Coggans' brilliant observation that "almost any stock price can be justified" (*Financial Times*, December 9, 1999). Of course, as demonstrated in Chapter 6, distant earnings are highly sensitive to the discount rate, which is the (prevailing) risk-free interest rate plus a risk premium. Thus, when the interest rate moves up — which is inevitable — the technology stock boom will be over for the time being.

II. A Tale of Two Americas

In his Nobel Prize lecture given at Uppsala University on December 13, 1999, Professor Robert Mundell made another of his celebrated attempts to convince listeners that a one-currency world could provide the rising tide that former President Kennedy thought would raise all ships. Until that miracle happens, however, he was willing to settle for regional currencies. For example, he would like to see the US and Japan get together in a single currency union — which, as we all know, is a cultural impossibility.

But what about a single Latin American currency? That part of the world has just gone through a traumatic period of recession and crisis, although many of these countries should be among the richest in the world — Chile and Argentina, for example. If we ignore income distribution, the US has never had it better, while Latin America has experienced still another lost decade. Among the recurring suggestions for invigorating Latin America is resorting to a comprehensive dollarization. According to Argentine President Carlos Menem, "if the US dollar were the regional currency, we wouldn't have seen the Mexican tequila crisis or the Brazilian devaluation". Of course, in order to make this work, the Latin American countries would, in some sense, have to accept a common monetary policy, and in order to adjust to *that*, they would almost certainly have to set up some kind of joint central bank in order to at least give the appearance of independence from the US Federal Reserve. Despite the enthusiasm of people like President Menem for the dollar, it seems unlikely that the Fed would be willing to create a Latin American franchise for printing the greenback.

As will soon be discovered in Europe, a single central bank for a culturally heterogeneous group of countries has a touch of irrationality about it. Even worse, it could help to inflate the political extremism that is slowly gathering momentum in every country of the EU. A similar observation applies to dollarization. As Katherine Mann informed a US Senate panel, "Dollarization is like wiring your mouth shut if you're an obese person. It doesn't make you any healthier". She might have added: nor does it make you wealthier or wiser, especially on a continent (like Latin America) where an all-inclusive dislike of the US is never far away.

If countries like Chile and Argentina cannot get their act together, and become the Australia–New Zealand — economically speaking — of the Western Hemisphere, then what has made the difference for the US? History and culture are probably the two most important explanatory factors: "Nothing succeeds so well as success", as Tallyrand pointed out.

Especially if success means that the entire world stands ready to lend you money. The legacy of former president Ronald Reagan, for example, included a total increase in the real debt of the federal US government that was greater than the total real debt accumulated over the first 200 years of that country — to include the entire debt required to finance US participation in both world wars. In 1993, Fed Chairman Alan Greenspan said that it would take at least the remainder of the century to eliminate these debts, however he failed to say which century. Just now the US is borrowing hundreds of millions of dollars a day. The wherewithal provided by foreign savers has permitted US investors to carry larger financial market positions than would otherwise have been possible or, for that matter, thinkable. For instance, a single firm was able to raise $2 billion solely on the basis of its presence in a "hot" sector, after which it proceeded to lose $200 million a quarter with hardly a complaint raised from the true believers.

In the ideal world of learned journals, much of this money would have gone to the other America, with its vast natural resources and low wages. This might have meant a weaker dollar (since, ceteris paribus, the US securities purchased by foreigners strengthened the dollar), which in turn would have made US exports more attractive. Very likely, some of these exports would be bought by Latin Americans whose purchasing power was increased due to the physical capital installed with the money mentioned above, and this would be of considerable help in diminishing the veritable Alp of US debt. In this book a great deal of attention has been given financial diversification, but a similar approach might be appropriate for physical assets. The excessive use of investible funds to support North American consumption has probably impeded the optimal international allocation of industrial assets, which raises the likelihood of an international slowdown that could cause trouble everywhere. Of course, looking at this another way, if the US does not continue to receive its daily injection of loans, and experiences some withdrawal spasms, then Latin America — and everybody else — could be in deep trouble.

Although many quick-witted men and women who have purchased the right shares and/or real estate are having the time of their life, the IMF estimates that in the 1990s world output only grew 3%/year, as compared to 3.5% and 4.5% in the preceding two decades. If capital inflow to the US declines because investors lose their taste for US assets at present interest rates, or world growth continues to fall, or for that matter the US must begin to pay down its loans without the help of revenues from increased exports, then the carnival is over.

Something that has gone almost unnoticed is the adoption or proposed adoption by many emerging economies of inflation-targeting. This is a strategy that was pioneered in the early 1990s by Canada, Sweden, New Zealand and the UK. What it amounts to is the central bank publicly announcing a numerical target for inflation in the medium term, and then adopting the economic policies that will lead to the realization of this target: in other words, the fight against inflation is situated first on the economic agenda. According to *The Economist* (January 29, 2000), this means that the central bank must be "operationally independent", by which they mean independent of elected governments and politicians, who might become overconcerned with such things as rising unemployment. One of the reasons for the avowed popularity of this doctrine is the success of the Federal Reserve in the US, but whether this success can be duplicated in e.g. Latin

America — or even Europe in the long run — remains to be seen. When the New Economy and its advocates are history, many employees and voters will be less concerned with central bank credibility and City (of London) wine-bar gossip than avoiding the unexpected lay-offs and insecurity that have characterized even the recent years of high prosperity.

Another point worth mentioning, which was noted in the *Economist* article cited above, is that once inflation-targeting takes over, the exchange-rate regime is secondary. Logically, the exchange-rate regime — whatever that may turn out to be — that must be adopted is the one that will make the most beneficial contribution to the realization of the inflation target.

III. An Asian Crisis

The Asian crisis, which to a minor extent was also a global crisis, was probably inevitable, albeit at a lower level of intensity. Even the best managed economies display ups-and-downs. What happened this time — as, e.g., in North America and Europe in 1929 — was a huge financial implosion, followed by a sagging demand for consumer goods. With household confidence and job growth weakening, and inventories of all types of goods increasing, capital (i.e. investment) spending decelerated. Suddenly it became clear that producers were not only facing disinflation (i.e. a decline in the modest rate of inflation), but deflation itself was possible. Deflation is very bad news for profits, and once that eventuality was fully absorbed by the investment community, share markets began a long awaited correction, and unemployment began to climb.

Paul Krugman, who has been fully employed as a "guru" for the past decade, informed a number of important publications that the bad news from Asia could easily turn out to be the beginning of a Great Depression scenario, or worse. He was right in one sense: it could be a depression — or worse — if governments insisted on adopting behavior that would encourage a calamity to take place, which has happened before. But if they really desire another outcome, it is comparatively easy to arrange. The crash of 1987 was a meltdown of frightening proportions, but damage control worked its wonders, and the expected major depression did not materialize. It could have saved the situation in 1997 too if less pessimism had been generated. As Jeffrey Sachs pointed out: "There is nothing in the fundamentals of these economies that warrants anything like the declines they have suffered, other than a self-fulfilling withdrawal of short-term money".

The economies to which he was referring are Indonesia, Malaysia, the Phillipines, South Korea and Thailand. As part of the fundamentals, it should be noted that small and fairly small economies, like Singapore and Taiwan, and perhaps even South Korea and Malaysia, have the same opportunity to succeed in the international economy as e.g. Sweden and the Netherlands. If their exports carry the right price, the relatively small amount of them should ensure that they can fit into global markets, where total sales are gigantic.

Japan, the key country in the region, does not possess these "small-country" advantages, but perhaps they are not needed. Any tennis or boxing coach knows that a natural athlete with great faults can be turned into a great athlete once these shortcomings are corrected. My knowledge of the economic faults of the Japanese economy is unfortunately very limited, but I happen to believe that most of these faults can be eliminated in a very short period of time. And even if they are not eliminated, it may not make a difference. Japan is in position to play a major role in the development of China and Siberia, and they will almost certainly be well rewarded for their efforts.

The markets also believe this. Foreign direct investment into Japan reached record levels in 1999, and there was a temporary recovery by the stock market. Once it becomes clear that a serious restructuring of the country's corporate sector will actually take place, huge investments in the automotive, financial services and telecommunications sectors will become justifiable. The search for capital also resulted in a surge in equity issues, and it is obvious that there is going to be a sharp increase in merger and acquisition activity. Obviously, some "opening" of the Japanese economy is going to be necessary, but it will be kept to a minimum.

"Rich country, poor people", is the way many Japanese have described their situation, although in many physical respects Japan is not really rich, since it must grapple with enormous demographic and environmental problems. Their richness is in cultural resources, which is why many observers find it credible that not only will the "Pacific Rim" be the most important expansion area of the next 50 or 100 years, but that the sun that will warm this rim will rise over Japan.

IV. Apparently, the World is Not Enough

Prior to about 1997, the expression *financial architecture* was virtually unknown. Over the past year or two, it cannot be avoided, since apparently the spectre of unsound financial vistas and structures goes hand-in-hand with suggestions for keeping world financial markets on an even keel.

This book began with a non-technical survey, and it is ending on a non-technical note. The intention here is to touch on a few topics that would have been out of place in the previous four chapters.

Take the question of banking soundness. According to Stanley Fisher, the Deputy Managing Director of the IMF (1997), the international debt crisis of the 1980s threatened the health of major money center banks; while the US Savings and Loan crisis entailed a huge commitment of public funds into the banking sector. In the transition countries — i.e. the countries of East and Central Europe — large scale bank recapitalization is essential. Professor Fisher also refers to the eruption of major banking crises in Japan and, he says, the Scandinavian countries.

As far as I am concerned, there have been no banking crises worth noticing in the Scandinavian countries, and the other crises to which he referred were small beer as compared to the stock market meltdown of 1987, as well as the occasional turbulence that has been experienced in share and bond markets since that incident. The thing to remember here is that at the beginning of the 21st century, Americans have more of their wealth invested in the stock market than they had in their homes, and there are few — if any — countries in Western Europe where ordinary households are not dependent to some degree on what happens in the financial markets. A major stock market correction would entail more unpleasant consequences for these households than any imaginable banking crises, especially when we remember that an all-embracing bank crisis would invoke a massive central bank counter-attack. There is no longer any real chance of a banking crisis of the scope which caused so much damage in the early 1930s. IMF blundering aside, the "too big to fail" syndrome that Fisher speaks of in his important article will remain a reality unless — as has become the fashion in the Scandinavian countries — the politicians intend to sell out their constituents, or take leave of their senses.

I was once interviewed by a university publication, and asked my favorite "saying". I answered without hesitation: the wise man learns from the mistakes of others; while the fool must find out for himself. If I had been asked to name one of the great economic mysteries of the closing years of the 20th century, I would have cited the tendency for winners to attempt to learn from losers.

If we examine economic growth in the industrial countries for the 20th century — measured in real GNP (gross national product) increase per capita — we see Japan the the top, and Norway, Finland, Denmark, and Sweden in the first eight. Italy, Portugal, and Ireland are the remaining three, which, for all these eight countries, says something about where they were at the start of the century. The same observation applies to the UK, though in a different sense, because that country finished at the bottom of the 20 countries in the survey, although it must have been close to the top in 1900. Accordingly, if we stick to economics, it might be a good idea for the government and people of e.g. the UK, and other countries, to take a closer look at the culture and institutions of Japan and Scandinavia, rather than the other way around. (The exact ranking in terms of GNP/capita growth, 1900–1998, is Japan, Norway, Finland, Italy, Portugal, Ireland, Denmark, Sweden, Canada, Spain, France, Austria, Germany, US, Switzerland, Holland, Belgium, Austria, Mexico, and the UK. This list was compiled by the German IWD Institute, which is associated with the industrial association in that country.)

Very little has been said in this book about energy, which is probably due to my fatigue after recently completing a textbook on the subject. However an editorial in *Science* (July 30, 1999) says all that we need to know about the subject. "Affordable energy is the lifeblood of modern society. Without it, the networth of transportation, agriculture, health care, manufacturing and commerce deemed essential by many of the world's inhabitants, would not be possible".

Affordable energy is going to be a problem later in the 21st century. As was pointed out earlier, rising energy prices could have devastating macro-economic consequences for all except a few very rich countries. They will also have an enormous significance for the financial markets, with energy derivatives becoming a veritable gold mine for many traders and their employers. The poet Archilochus reputedly said "the fox knows many things, but the hedgehog knows one big thing". If hedgehogs decided to start talking about that one big thing, they would almost certainly focus their remarks on energy and the environment.

What about population? As I indicated in a book that I wrote 25 years ago, population was a problem that had to be dealt with at that time. This was not done, and now it is too late. In the last 40 years, population has doubled. Present estimates are that another doubling is unlikely to take place, but since the estimates were wrong 40 years ago, why should they be correct now? Of course, we should be optimistic and hope that something can be done to keep world population from reaching 12 billion, because hardly anyone really wants to experience a Malthusian scenario involving mass starvation, pandemics, wars, rumors of war and a greatly increased level of urban violence. There is also this matter of global warming that will be accelerated by the increased energy use associated with larger populations. The thing to remember here is that too many decision makers seem to have confused global warming with a global tour by some rap artist that you can avoid simply by not buying a ticket. With global warming, you get a ticket whether you want one or not; even worse, you have to use it.

Many of my international finance students at Uppsala University like to have important statistics available in case they encounter persons who are interested in important statistics, and a majority of the students in this country are interested or should be interested in the following. Globally, more than 250 million children are out of school at the primary and secondary levels; 840 million people are malnourished; 850 million adults remain illiterate; one billion persons have inadequate shelter, and 1.3 billion — most of them women — attempt to live on less than a dollar a day. This number is steadily increasing. Two billion have no access to electricity, and 2.5 billion lack basic sanitation. One third of the world's workforce is unemployed or underemployed, with what amounts to a below subsistence wage. Income inequalities are rising almost everywhere, and this includes the rich countries. Interior migration is producing unmanageable megacities, and cross-border migration is producing political extremism. Let me also note that figures do not always tell the entire story. Despite having a relatively healthy Gross National Product, Brazil is overpopulated, and its employment problem is often considered unlikely to get better. Instead, the presence of a fairly large and highly visible advanced economy creates appetites and aspirations that cannot possibly be satisfied.

What do these figures and comments have to do with financial economics? The best general answer is probably *everything*! As for the details associated with this answer, that will be the last exercise I give when I teach from this book, and will also be the first question on the final examination in the same course. In case the reader needs a hint, the following terms can be considered: anger, frustration, rage, and risk.

V. The Final Countdown: Two Final Observations on Financial Fact and Theory

Strictly speaking, in the world of finance there is no final countdown. For example, the bottom can fall out of the share market tomorrow morning, but even so the next day hundreds of millions of persons — or their representatives — must decide where to put personal savings, pensions, windfalls, etc until the time comes to consume or otherwise dispose of them. Similarly, countless decisions must be made as to where or how to borrow money.

Take the last item as it is applied to big-ticket borrowers. The first month of the new millenium, January 2000, was the busiest month on record for new issues in the *international* bond market. We are talking now of almost $160 billion, with multi-billion-dollar issues by the US Mortgage

Agency (Freddie Mac), The World Bank, Daimler-Chrysler, etc. The emerging economies Argentina, Brazil, and Mexico dived into the international market for a total of almost $6 billion, hoping to avoid expected interest rate increases. Fortunately for everybody, it appeared that investors were eager to do business. One explanation here is that the cash that had been hoarded to deal with any unwelcome surprises that might surface as a result of so-called "millennium bugs" did not appear, and as a result lenders were highly receptive to new issues.

Note something else here. We are only talking about international issues. Domestic issues involved many more billions. Is there any doubt then that investment banks the world over make sure that those departments dealing with the launching of new issues, and the trading of old issues, are always supplied with the best cerebral firepower available.

What this expression "the final countdown" (obliquely) refers to is providing readers — and especially non-technical readers — with another dose of the bread-and-butter issues of real-word financial economics. Remember that we can say the same thing about financial economics that Keynes said about economics: an easy subject that is difficult. Remember also that financial economists and other finance professionals are constantly in touch with "lay persons" of various descriptions who would be offended by such things as an ad-hoc lecture on the separation theorem: they want straightforward, unambiguous anwers that will enhance their capacity to participate in the management of their portfolios.

Stocks, Bonds, and the "New Economy"

Nothing characterizes the so-called New Economy as much as the stock market upswing in the US and a few other countries that began in 1990, and is now entering its second decade. The theory advanced by some observers is that this is more than an extended "bubble" — it is a paradigm shift. New technology combined with such things as changes in the tax structure, globalization, deregulation (and therefore changes in the distribution of income, since in e.g. industrial countries like the US, globalization will favor the wealthy and best educated, while causing problems for many others due to the decline of the industrial base) have supposedly created a brand new world: one whose material blessings will extend far into the 21st century. Obviously, the key factor at work here is the remarkable gains made by some technology and telecommunications companies that boosted the popular stock market averages, and the belief is that as the Internet and "dot-com" (= . com) revolution deepens in other parts of the world, all countries will benefit. For instance, the technology and telecommunications boom in the US brought large increases in wealth to some investors in e.g. emerging markets, as portfolio managers in these markets concentrated on these two sectors in their buying.

Personally, I do not buy a large part of the New Economy folklore, but it definitely is possible that now that the dot-com revolution has spread to Japan, it will provide a boost to equity markets everywhere, and thus compensate for any slack that may show up in the US expansion. The same holds true for the EU, whose population is larger than the US and Canada combined. However, people like Samuel Brittan of the *Financial Times* and myself are unable to understand how the growth in paper wealth can continue to greatly outpace the growth in physical wealth without something very unpleasant eventually happening.

Interestingly enough, it has recently been discerned that the technology-telecommunications euphoria may conceal a number of pitfalls. As these shares outside the US become more closely aligned with their counterparts in the US — where stock market capitalizations in some cases have reached what appears to be unsustainable levels — a downturn in the US could have a devastating backlash in other markets.

It is very definitely possible that by the time this book is published, or soon after, a major correction will have taken place in one or more large regional markets. Given this possibility, the question must be raised as to how the individual investor or fund should approach their investment strategy if they come to the conclusion that it may no longer be wise to buy every dot-com share in sight.

This question immediately takes us back to the previous chapters: how much risk is the investor willing to assume? There are a huge number of possibilities here, but the last time I asked a finance professional, his advice was 60% of a given investible sum in equities, 30% in bonds, and 10% in "cash". Of course, had I asked another professional for advice an hour later, she might have proposed a completely different allocation. (Worldwide, in the second quarter of 2000, some top funds averaged 50% equities, 44% bonds, and 6% "cash".)

For some years now it has been suggested that global diversification in shares is a good investment strategy. I supported this idea long before it became popular, and I still find it attractive. (Of late, however, some academics and investment advisers have claimed that it is a bad strategy.) In its simplest form, this amounts to no more than starting with the assumption that an investor's equity portfolio should be divided among the world's markets in a manner that is based upon each country's share of the global stock market capitalization. This, however, should *never* be regarded as more than the first move in what could be a very complicated process. The next step is extremely important. It involves deviations from this initial allocation. For example, some markets are obviously taboo for political as well as economic reasons. There is also this matter of currency risk: buying shares in a country where the value of the currency can change by large amounts in a short period can turn out to be a bad career move for a professional. (One of the arguments in favor of the EU is that currency risk between member countries will be eliminated.)

Similarly, *home bias* can be a major problem: portfolios should be scrutinized to ensure that after adjustment of the initial allocation begins, they are not overweighted in domestic stocks — which is a very usual phenomenon. By the same token, certain large portfolios should not be overweighted or underweighted in individual stocks. Purchasing the *right* individual shares at the *right* time can mean a free ride for a portfolio. For the last few years, dot-coms have often turned out to be the flavor of the moment, and a number of well placed professionals seem to be indicating that sometime in the not so distant future, health care shares may also carry this designation. One thing, however, is certain: it is here that top-flight investment advice is invaluable, and finance professionals who are able to identify this category of share can write superstar on their visiting cards.

What about bonds? Mainstream finance theory makes it clear that bonds are safer than shares — although the bond market blow-out in 1994–1995 caused many investors to completely lose their appetite for these assets. However, as pointed out earlier, there have been long periods in the not too distant past when a well constructed bond or bond fund portfolio would have meant a return of 10–12% a year.

After the turn of the millennium, strong aggregate productivity increases, together with an enormous amount of favorable advertisement for technology shares, led to a souring on bonds and bond funds in many parts of the world. (These productivity increases were expected to raise profits, and thus share prices.) This is only natural, because given the continued upswing in most international share markets, and the very heavy public and private bond issuance projected for the immediate future, the overall supply-demand balance shifted in such a way as to raise expectations of rising interest rates (and thus falling bond prices): as supply increases, prices fall, which is tantamount to interest rates rising. In these circumstances the correct strategy may well be to minimize bond holdings, as well as transactions in that market, and wait until yields rise to a point where they provide a nice annual return. With "riskless" yields on bank deposits now down to 2–3%, and in some countries lower, being able to lock in yields of 7–10% on medium-term bonds is something that many investors look forward to.

If a return of 7–10% is attractive, then what about average returns of 12%. Junk bonds (i.e. high yield bonds) have often been mentioned in this book, and a successful investor like Paul Erdman once said that they should be avoided like the plague. On the other hand, David P. Goldman (a strategist with Credit Suisse First Boston, and a very readable columnist with *Forbes*) is one of their greatest fans. He feels that these assets have a job to do — which is to pay borrowers a sizable risk premium above the yield on investment grade debt — and that despite a default rate that seems to average about 5%, the right kind of e.g. high yield fund can be a good bet. Goldman very definitely belongs in that category of financial economists whose advice cannot be disregarded, and as a result persons with time to study the entire range of investment possibilities, are likely to come to the conclusion that some high-yield debt is worth holding as a part of the bond component of a portfolio. Exactly how much, however, remains an open question. In the second quarter of 2000, investors seemed to lose interest in junk. In the US, there were only 66 offerings, as compared to 178 in the second quarter of 1999. The amount raised also declined to $7.5 billion from $32.2 billion a year earlier.

Finally, there is this matter of "cash". Ideally, cash would consist of something like the liquidity funds mentioned earlier in this book. These are funds holding "safe" assets such as short-term government paper, and which are as accessible as the money that ou can obtain at the nearest ATM. Many large firms have access to this kind of cash, but the rest of us often have to make do with low yielding demand deposits.

A Macroeconomic Aside

One of the things that I like about this book is the absence of macroeconomics. There were a number of superb macroeconomic books published during the last two decades of the 20th century, but not so excellent as to convince me that I could materially increase my knowledge of global finance if I were to become unduly immersed in the details of this sometimes fascinating subject.

Certain macroeconomic observations are inescapable, however. Both Wall Street and Federal Reserve executives agree that consumer spending has been driving the US economy during the prosperous 1990s — to include the US sharemarkets — and has also been functioning as a motor for the world economy. Functioning how? The answer here is via a huge US import surplus that is translated into a demand for foreign goods and services of all sorts, and from everywhere. (A good example here is Swedish automobiles and Finnish electronics.) There is also a tremendous wealth effect in operation. The increase in the value of their shares has (ceteris paribus) made US consumers more inclined to spend, and their spending on imports has driven up incomes and profits in foreign countries, which in turn has had a favorable effect on foreign stock prices. As noted by Samuel Brittan in the *Financial Times* (January 20, 2000), this wealth effect has escaped the attention of many analysts.

There is also a kind of miracle taking place, in that the almost decade long US expansion has *not* resulted in excessive inflationary pressures. This seems to be the core of the New Economy paradigm. Some persons believe — and perhaps correctly — that this is due to the central banking skills of Alan Greenspan. But even so, at the beginning of the new millennium, the ticking of the cyclical clock was unmistakably growing louder: where economic variables are concerned, it is very difficult to avoid the conclusion that what goes up comes down — with certain exceptions; and present thinking is that nothing will bring growth rates down faster than higher inflation.

Higher inflation, that is, reflected in higher interest rates. As has been pointed out in the first chapter of this book, this is due to investors demanding higher returns to offset expected increases in inflation. But in addition to this inflation premium, there is also a rate of interest that is directly attributed to supply and demand. For instance, the US demand for foreign money to support its present spending spree drives up interest rates abroad (due to the increased supply of US "paper"); but if it happens that growth is accelerating in these lender countries, then local interest rates will also usually be rising, which in turn pushes up US rates.

As Alan Greenspan pointed out, none of this should come as a surprise, because an excess of demand for credit over its supply causes an imbalance that is adjusted through "higher borrowing rates". Greenspan also reflected on the shrinking pool of workers in the US who do not have jobs, but who are interested in employment. He and others see this shortage of labor as the main inflationary threat, and implied that higher interest rates will be resorted to if they are necessary in order to slow down the rate of expansion, and thus keep the demand for labor from outrunning the supply, and pushing up wages to a level where they drive up prices by an unacceptable amount. Something else that needs to be pointed out here is that the labor supply in the US is as large as it is because the number of hours worked in the US is larger than in any other industrial country: e.g. almost 25% more than in Sweden.

The final subject in this section involves official as well as private debt, which has reached very worrisome levels in the two largest economies in the world — the US and Japan. According to many observers, the debt being carried by these two countries is approaching an unsustainable level, and sooner or later spending must be brought back into line with incomes.

How is this to be done? The answer given in *The Economist* (January 22, 2000) is that in order to borrow more, debtors must pay a higher rate of interest. The theory is that in the past 40 years no developed economy has had a ratio of public-debt to gross national product (GNP) of more than 135% without being forced by the financial markets to reduce its borrowing. Furthermore, even if markets do not react violently as this "limit" is approached, private-sector investment can be crowded out. There is also the matter of the "debt trap": higher interest rates (and thus interest payments) increase the government's budget deficit — and thus its need to borrow — even when spending is stabilized. (Here it needs to be noted that the yield on Japanese government bonds (JGBs) at the turn of the millennium was only about 1.785%. This came about because the Bank of Japan wants to implement a "zero interest rate policy", where it attempts to flood the market with enough liquidity to keep overnight rates around zero. This closes down an important investment option for lenders, and thus encourages them to buy JGBs.)

Japan's ratio of public-debt to GNP at the turn of the millennium was 128%. This is a serious matter, however Japan is the world's largest creditor nation — with 31% of its GNP, or $1.2 trillion, in loans; and it has a comparatively low tax burden — 29% of GNP, as compared to 39% for the other "rich" countries, and 42% for the EU. This means that there is a fairly wide scope to decrease or freeze the budget deficit by increasing taxes. In addition, Japan is still able to run surpluses on the foreign balance (i.e. larger exports than imports), in comparison to the other major debtors; and 90% of Japanese government securities are held domestically.

What we see if we examine Japan and the Japanese economy closely is a country that would be in the pink of good health if it could elect or employ the right kind of economic doctors: doctors that preferred prescribing healthy instead of dubious or unhealthy medicines for their ailing patient.

American voters, by way of contrast, no longer have any tolerance for government budget deficits. Instead, the colossal US debt can be credited to private borrowers. The ratio of US private sector debt to GNP now stands at 132%. There is an obvious danger here: with interest rates low, and the share market climbing, it seems shrewd to borrow instead of selling assets; but if the market fell, then many borrowers might be in serious trouble: certainly, if the Swedish share market collapsed, I would have a hard time justifying certain of my debts. In the US, expectations in the first months of 2000 were that the boom will last forever, and if necessary the debt that has been assumed by private individuals can be at least reduced by slicing off a small part of one's portfolio after it has swollen somewhat in size.

Returning to mainstream market lore to round out this discussion, in the chapter on the stock market it was pointed out that when judging the health of this market, it might be useful to examine the dividend yield and/or the earnings' yield on e.g. the S&P 500. At the turn of the millennium, these were deep in the danger zone — so deep, in fact, as to suggest that retreat is nearly impossible. Should it turn out, however, that the share market "law of gravity" has been repealed, and increased earnings and productivity gains will continue to propel the market into the stratosphere — even if interest rates increase — then many textbook authors and high-profile investment professionals will have to give the New Economy a much closer and detailed scrutiny, and perhaps pay more attention to conventional macroeconomics than they/we would have liked.

VI. Conclusion: A Word to the Wise

With all due respect to the readers of this textbook, and my former students, I have written a book that I think needs writing. From time to time I have attempted to advise readers on how to approach this topic, and in case they have forgotten, let me remind them that it is all in the rhythm. What was it that Louis Armstrong said: "It don't mean a thing if you ain't got that swing". They must learn a certain amount of economics and history, and a little algebra, and, ideally, ***they must learn these things perfectly***. Students who think that they can do less, but find a niche in global finance, are fooling themselves — even though there may be exceptions. Of course, the exceptions do not last long. This is perhaps the most competitive world of all, as salaries and bonuses suggest, but even so, there will always be a place in it for you — if you really want it!

It has been said that in the 21st century, and probably later, human (or "intellectual") capital will be more important than physical capital. Perhaps this has always been true. I was with the US Army in Japan before the Korean War, and in Germany afterward, and I cannot attribute the miracles that took place in those countries as being the result of anything other than hard work and a superior technical education, as well as what Gunnar Myrdal described as cultures that are "growth amenable".

It has now become common knowledge that high-quality traders, analysts, and various levels of executives are worth their weight in gold to top management and equity-owners. For instance, when Salomon Smith Barney — the investment bank component of Citigroup (of New York) — began its integration of Schroder (of the UK), about $250 million was earmarked as loyalty bonuses for 200 key staff members. Of course, some of these key persons turned up their noses as this offer, and scampered off to other establishments with healthy recruitment bonuses in hand, but I know how I would feel if Limberville U. were to buy or merge with Uppsala University, and I found myself being offered US$1 million to sign on for another tour.

There is something very remarkable about the market for finance talent. Thousands of economics and finance graduates apply for interviews at the major financial institutions every year, and a number of them possess some truly impressive credentials where such things as e.g. econometrics and stochastic calculus are concerned, but unfortunately a large majority of these neophyte rocket-scientists will never become candidates for the "loyalty" bonuses mentioned above, assuming that they are lucky enough to be hired in the first place. This is because investment banking as well as much of financial economics is an art as well as a science.

Of course, sometimes it is considerably less, with traders throwing telephones as trainees' heads, cursing analysts at the top of their voices, and where people like the investment banker Kay Swinburne once described her working environment as "juvenile and mean". (I can also mention that the activities at a certain New York investment bank only a year ago would hardly have been encouraged in some of the more infamous army or marine corps "boot camps" in the American South at a time when "hands on" management of trainees by the cadre was the rule rather than the exception.) No one, however, guaranteed aspirant finance professionals (or "masters of the universe" as they were labeled by Tom Wolfe) a lifelong billet in the perfect world that some of them experienced in the elite business schools. This is a place where big money inevitably means the big pressures that go with a long-hours culture, and where stress levels occasionally reach a point where even senior managers are prone to say and do strange things.

This does not mean, however, that members of this culture inevitably descend into madness, ruin, and bad language. More and more they are descending into new careers of one type or another at a fairly young age, with a very appetizing nest-egg from their first (finance) career carefully placed in the kind of highly reputable and, to a considerable extent, exclusive funds that are effectively off-limits to all except life's winners.

Exercises

1. A $9.5 billion sale of bonds in the US by Deutsche Telecom was split evenly among 5-year, 10-year, and 30-year securities. What would the MM Theorem say about that?
2. Open outcry is still the norm in US exchanges, while electronic trading predominates in Europe (and Australasia). I explain this with the help of Bill Tilden's "iron rule of tennis". Comment! According to the *Financial Times* (June 28, 2000) the most innovative and interesting derivatives business is to be found in the OTC market. Comment!
3. I make no secret of my belief that the electricity futures and options markets have their work cut out for them. Explain!
4. Practitioners and academicians have developed many adjustments to the Black-Scholes Model. Why?

Glossary

A la criée: French for open outcry.

Abschlag: German for discount.

Accepting: Signing a document signifying an agreement to pay. In the UK, "acceptance houses" accepted bills from exporters (for a fee), and later received money from importers.

Acid ratio: Ratio of current assets minus stock to current liabilities: a rough indication of solvency.

Actionnaire: French for shareholder.

Actions: French for shares.

Adaptive expectations: The formation of expectations in such a way that the expected value of a variable is taken as the average of the past values of the variable.

Adjustable peg: A system of exchange rates in which rates are regarded as fixed, but changes can take place when conditions warrant.

Adjustment mechanism: The method by which an economic system — e.g. the international economy — reacts to a disequilibrium.

Ad valorum tax: A tax on the price of a good or service.

Adverse selection: An arrangement in which those most likely to produce an outcome being insured against, are the ones most likely to purchase the insurance.

Agent: Someone who represents someone else: e.g. a fund manager is the agent of the owners of the fund (who are the *principals*).

Allocative efficiency: The efficiency with which a market channels capital into its most productive uses.

Alpha: The difference between the average rate of return on a security (or portfolio of securities) and the rate predicted by the capital asset pricing model.

American depository receipts (ADRs): These are negotiable instruments certifying shares of a foreign stock held by a custodian, and can be considered as an alternative to the listing of a foreign company's shares on an American exchange. The receipts trade on US stock exchanges instead of the actual shares.

Amortize: To pay off in stages over a period of time. (Fully amortized: Fully paid off.)

Animal spirits: A term introduced by Keynes to describe the willingness of entrepreneurs to invest in such things as machines and structures. (A non-quantifiable feeling based largely on intuition.)

Annuity: An asset (e.g. security) with a series of equal payments at regular intervals over a given time horizon.

APEC: Asia-Pacific Economic Cooperation Forum — ostensibly a prelude to a free trade arrangement involving goods and services.

Arbitrage: Strictly speaking, buying or selling a good in one market, while carrying out the opposite operation in another market, and thus locking in a riskless profit. (But this term is often applied to operations involving risk.)

Arms length pricing: Pricing that is acceptable to unrelated buyers and sellers.

Ask (= offer) rate: The rate at which an asset is being offered (for sale).

Asset: An item of value or possessing earning power that is owned by an individual, firm, or bank. Can be physical or financial — property or a bond.

Asset backed securities: Securities collateralized by assets — e.g. car loans.

Asset liability management: Adjusting the composition of a portfolio or balance sheet to attain the preferred risk-return combination.

ATM: An automatic teller machine that can be operated day or night.

At-the-money-option: The situation when the price of the asset (usually in the spot market) is equal to the exercise price of the option.

Auction market: A market conducted at a particular place (such as a traditional stock exchange) that employs some version of the auction process for trading.

Autarky: In international trade theory a situation where there is no cross-border trade.

Availability doctrine: An approach to monetary policy in which the central bank controls credit availability, rather than interest rates or the money supply (in order to achieve its policy goals).

Balance of payments: A book-keeping arrangement which accounts for the payments comprising a nation's international transactions. The balance of payments always balances, although this need not to be true of its component parts.

Balance sheet: The listing of the assets and liabilities (e.g. debts) of an economic organization or a household. Assets minus liabilities is equal to net worth.

Bank capital: The amount invested in a bank by its shareholders, plus the amount of retained profits (or losses) accruing to the bank over time. Often, in everyday usage, bank capital is considered to be the same thing as net worth.

Bank failure: A situation in which a bank cannot satisfy its obligations to depositors, and as a result must go out of business.

Bank holding company: A firm that owns one or more banks.

Bank notes: Paper money.

Bankers' acceptance: A (time) draft drawn on and accepted by a particular bank, that is paid by the maturity date given on the acceptance.

Bank run: A situation in which many depositors attempt to withdraw their money from a bank, usually because they believe the bank is about to fail. Often the prelude to a **bank panic**, which is generally taken to mean the simultaneous failure of many banks.

Barter: Trade in which commodities are exchanged for other commodities.

Base money: Currency plus commercial bank reserves (held against deposits). Sometimes called **high powered money**.

Basis: Usually defined as the spot price minus the futures market price of the same commodity.

Basis point: 0.01 (= 1/100)%. Sometimes referred to as "a point".

Basis risk: This is when the price movement of a hedge instrument (such as a futures contract) does not correlate exactly with the price of the underlying asset, particularly at the expiration (i.e. maturity) date of the contract. Geographical considerations might bring about basis risk — e.g. when North Sea oil is hedged using contracts written on East Texas (crude) oil.

Basket pegger: A country that maintains a fixed exchange rate with respect to a composite or weighted average of foreign currencies, rather than a single foreign currency.

Bearer bond: A bond that makes payments to the holder (or bearer) of the bond.

Beta: A measure of the portfolio risk associated with an asset.

Bid price: The price at which a transactor will buy an asset.

Bid rate: The rate of interest offered for a deposit (e.g. **LIBID**: The London Interbank Bid Rate).

Bill facility: An arrangement by a lender to renew (i.e. **roll-over** or reissue) a series of bills (i.e. loans). This creates a medium term source of finance for the borrower where the interest is determined each time the bills are rolled over.

Bill of lading: An agreement issued by a transportation company to carry goods to a specific point of discharge (e.g. a port).

Bimettalism: Two metals — usually gold and silver — serving as the backing for a particular currency.

BITS: The system for transferring large sums of money between banks that are members of the Bank Interchange and Transfer System.

Brady bonds: Named after US Treasury Secretary Nicolas Brady. These bonds are sovereign bonds that are (partially) backed by US Treasury bonds, and the actual repayments on the sovereign bonds are made by the relevant government. What these bonds amount to is a form of debt rescheduling. Ecuador became the first country to default on its Brady backed debt.

Brokers: Financial institutions or individuals who bring buyers and sellers of various assets together. The assets can be financial or physical, and often brokers act as middlemen.

Call bull spread: An option strategy that combines a long call with a low exercise price with a short call having a high exercise price.

Call option: The right to buy an asset (i.e. "call away"), at a specified price, on or before a given date.

Call rate: In some countries the rate paid on overnight bank deposits. In the Euro-countries it is called EONIA — Euro overnight index average.

Capital Adequacy Requirements: Under the auspices of the BIS (Bank for International Settlements, in Basle) the Group of Ten (G10) nations formulated rules for the capital backing that they must have for different classes of assets.

Capital Asset Pricing Model (CAPM): An asset pricing model that relates the required return on an asset to its systematic risk.

Capital-indexed bonds: Securities whose face value is indexed to the consumer price index.

Capital market: A financial market featuring the trading of longer-term equity and debt instruments (i.e. instruments having a maturity of one year or longer).

Capital (Financial) Structure: The mix of equity and debt, and the particular form they take, for financing the assets of a firm.

Central bank: The official bank of a government that is usually charged with overseeing the banking system, and usually has charge of monetary policy.

CHIPS (Clearing House Interbank Payments System): The Financial network through which banks in the US clear their financial transactions.

Clearing house: An establishment designed to organize the exchange of financial transactions involving such things as checks and futures contracts, and assigning net asset and liability positions to transactors.

Closed-end fund: A kind of mutual fund in which a fixed number of shares are acquired, and then traded in the over-the-counter market in the same fashion as a common stock or depository receipt.

Collar: A combination cap and floor: setting a band within which interest rates or currency rates, etc. will apply. Outside this band payments will be received or made.

Commercial bill: A short-term discount instrument where the drawer of the bill raises funds equal to the face value of the bill, suitably discounted (e.g. at the current interest rate). The acceptor of the bill, which is often a financial institution (e.g. an "accepting house") takes the responsibilty to redeem amount on the bill.

Commercial paper: Short-term securities issued to raise money. Can often be "bought" from a bank instead of "buying" a deposit. This asset can be traded in a secondary market.

Compensating balances: Bank deposits that must be held as a form of compensation to a bank.

Consol: A perpetual bond with no maturity date and no repayment of principal, that makes fixed coupon payments every period — where the period is usually once or twice a year.

Continuous quotation system: Market makers matching buy and sell orders as the orders arrive, ensuring liquidity in individual shares.

Convertible: A convertible bond can be converted into equity, or in some cases into a commodity.

Counterparty: The party on the other side of a contract.

Countertrade: The exchange of goods or services without the use of cash.

Coupon rate: The amount of the yearly coupon payment on a bond expressed as a percentage of the face value of the bond.

Coupon swap: A fixed for floating interest rate swap.

Coupon stripping: Removing the coupons from a bond, and selling them independent of the principal (which then becomes a zero coupon bond).

Covariance: A statistical measure of the degree to which two variables move together.

Covered interest arbitrage: Arbitrage that features buying or selling assets internationally, and using the forward exchange market to eliminate exchange risks.

Crawling peg: The exchange rate is pegged in the short run, but is periodically changed to reflect supply and demand pressures.

Cross hedge: A hedge in which the asset underlying the transaction is not the same as the asset being hedged (e.g. hedging crude oil with futures contracts on refined products).

Cum interest price: The price of a bond that provides the buyer with the next coupon payment.

Curb Exchange: See **Kerb Trading**.

Currency: Paper money and coins.

Currency union: A region — often involving a number of countries — in which exchange rates are fixed. The European Monetary Union (EMU) is often taken as an example.

Current yield: An approximation of the yield to maturity that is equal to the coupon payment on a bond divided by the price of the bond.

Daily resettlement: The daily marking-to-the-market. What it results in is the futures market clearing house requiring the holder of a futures contract that has lost value to deposit additional margin, in order to bring the total amount of margin up to the required amount. This additional margin is sometimes called "maintenance margin". In addition, the holders of contracts that have gained value can, usually, obtain this additional value either immediately or after a short delay.

Debenture: A medium-term fixed interest security that is usually issued in small denominations to buyers, and which often has a warrant or option (for the purchase of shares) attached. They are usually secured against specific assets of a company.

Debt-equity swaps: An exchange of debt for the debtor country's local currency, which is then used to buy equity positions in the debtor country. The debt being exchanged is (logically) "sovereign" debt (i.e. the debt of governments).

Deep market: A market with a large number of buyers and sellers, which makes it possible to trade at all times. (This is the opposite of a "thin" market.)

Depreciation: In finance usually a fall in the value of a currency due to market forces.

Derivative: An instrument whose value depends on the value of another financial asset (i.e. the "underlying"). Options and futures are the best examples of derivatives (or, as they are sometimes called, derivative products).

Destabilizing speculation: Speculation leading to changes in such things as exchange rates or commodity prices that are larger than would be the case if there was no speculation.

Devaluation: The setting (by a government or central bank) of the par value of a currency at a lower level.

Discount bond: A bond that is bought at a price below its face value, and which is repaid at the maturity date with the face value. These bonds do not make any payments before the maturity date, and are sometimes called zero coupon bonds.

Discount rate: In banking the rate charged commercial banks by the central bank for a (discount) loan. The loan is sometimes called an "advance". (This activity is also occasionally called "rediscounting".)

Discount window: The (US) Federal Reserve facility at which discount loans are made.

Discount (versus premium): The forward pricing of a currency at less than the spot price: the spot price is at a discount to the forward price. (The **premium** is the forward pricing of a currency at more than the spot price.)

Disintermediation: A reduction in the flow of funds in the commercial banking system in favor of such things as lending and borrowing via securities markets.

Diversification principle: The theory that by holding a carefully selected collection of risky assets, it is possible to achieve a reduction in the overall risk exposure with no reduction in return (or, better, perhaps a large reduction in risk with only a very small reduction in return).

Dividends: Periodic payments made to shareholders by the issuers of equities.

Dragon Bond: A Eurobond issued in Hong Kong or Singapore, and primarily intended for Asian investors.

DTB (Deutsche Termin Börse): German futures and options exchange in Frankfurt.

Economic exposure: The exposure of a firm or transactor to changes in such things as prices, exchange rates, and interest rates.

Effective return: The interest rate on e.g. a foreign debt instrument (to include a bank account) plus or minus the yield due to such things as changes in the exchange rate.

Efficient market: A market in which prices reflect (or transmit) and efficiently use all available information. Thus the prices in these markets are "fair" because they incorporate all the relevant information about the value of the assets being traded.

Emerging markets: Security markets in e.g. Eastern Europe and developing countries where these markets are just getting started.

EMU (European Monetary Union): The Monetary arrangements specified under the Maastrict Treaty. It involves "financial convergence" and the establishment of a European Central Bank (ECB). See "Maastrict Treaty".

Endogenous: Something that is part of or influenced by factors within a particular model or system. The opposite is exogenous.

Equity warrants: Equity warrants provide access to shares over the life of the warrant, and conventionally at an exercise price which is at a premium over the current share price. It is sometimes attached to a bond however, unlike a convertible, the bond itself continues to exist if the warrant is exercised. As a result, the bond tends to trade at a coupon that is somewhat lower than that for bonds of a similar quality.

Equities: The best example is common stock, signifying ownership in a firm.

Eurobank: A bank that accepts deposites and makes loans in foreign currencies.

Eurobond market: The market that engages in direct offshore borrowing and lending through the sale of bonds denominated in a currency other than that in which these bonds are sold. (They are sold in many countries.)

Eurodollars: US dollars deposited in foreign banks outside the US, or in foreign branches of US banks.

Euroequities: Share issues sold primarily outside the borders of the country where the issue is being made.

European Monetary System: The arrangement where exchange rates are fixed between participating countries, but float jointly against the rest of the world.

Exchange: A market — or better, an auction-type market — such as a stock (share) market or e.g. the London Silver Market (shown in operation in the film "The Silver Bears").

Ex-interest price: The situation where the price of bonds do not provide the buyers of these securities with the next coupon payment.

Ex-rights price: The price of shares which do not provide the buyer with access to a rights issue.

Exercise price: The price at which an asset may be bought or sold by the possesser of an options contract.

Expectations hypothesis: The hypothesis that the interest rate on a long-term bond will be equal to an average of the short-term interest rates that are expected to prevail over the life of the long-term bond.

Face value: Sometimes called par value. This is e.g. the amount paid to the owner of a coupon bond at the maturity date.

Facility: A (generic) term denoting a transaction — usually a loan — in one form or another: e.g. Eurocredit facilities.

Factoring: A business activity in which one company takes over the responsibility for collecting the debts of another.

Federal funds rate: This is the interest rate on overnight loans made by the US Federal Reserve institutions.

Federal Open Market Committee: The committee that determines the content of open market operations in the US.

Federal Reserve System: The authority responsible for monetary policy in the US, and comprising 12 district Federal Reserve banks.

Fiat money: Such things as notes and coins which have a face value greater than the intrinsic value of the item, but whose value is designated by the government.

Financial engineering: The process of innovation in which new financial products are created.

Financial innovation: The continuous change in the financial sector that, ostensibly, improves the quality and quantity of financial services.

Fisher effect: The effect of inflation on nominal interest rates.

Float: The issuing ("floating") of shares.

Foreign bonds: Bonds sold in a foreign country which are denominated in the currency of that country (instead of the currency of the home country of the issuers).

Forward cover: The forward purchase of foreign currency in order to meet future requirements for foreign exchange.

Forward discount: A forward rate that is less than the spot rate.

Forward market: The market for the trading of an asset that will be delivered in the future. *Not* the same as the futures market.

Forward rate agreement (FRA): An agreement between a borrower and a lender whose purpose is to fix the rate of interest at which a loan will be made. The agreement usually requires the party benefitting from the difference between the market rate of interest and the agreed rate to make a payment to the other party.

FRA (Floating rate note): A security on which the interest is determined by the floating rate.

Franchise agreement: An arrangement in which a firm (the franchisor) licenses its trade name, and usually its *modus operandi*, to other firms or individuals.

Funding risk: The risk that arises from having to finance assets with borrowed funds whose maturity is shorter than the maturity of expected receipts from the assets.

Fully funded: Pension plans are fully funded when the contributions to the plan and the earnings of the plan over the years are sufficient to pay out the defined benefits of the plan when they come due.

Futures: Futures are standardized contracts to buy and sell assets for future delivery that are traded on an exchange. Delivery is usually specified on the contracts, but the exchange is organized in such a way that delivery can be avoided by "offsetting" the contract. Futures should be compared to "forwards", which are not usually traded on an exchange, and where delivery almost always takes place.

"Gilts" (Gilt-edged securities): UK government securities of the highest quality. These are traded on the London Stock exchange. Occasionally these are in short supply due to the UK government running a surplus, and therefore instead of borrowing, previous debt is redeemed.

Global bond: A bond that trades in foreign as well as local markets.

Gold exchange standard: An arrangement whereby a currency is valued in terms of a gold equivalent (although it may not be possible to exchange the currency for gold). Under the Bretton Woods system the dollar was defined in terms of gold, and then other currencies linked to gold by being defined in terms of the dollar.

Gold Standard: A system under which the currency of a country is directly convertible into gold.

Gresham's Law: Supposedly discovered by Sir Thomas Gresham: Bad money drives out good money. In other words, given a choice, people will save or hoard what they regard as good money, and pay their bills with "bad" money.

Gross National Product: The value of all *final* goods and services produced in an economy in the course of a year.

Hedge ratio: The ratio of the amount on related derivatives contracts to the underlying risk exposure.

Hedger: A transactor who uses a market to obtain some form of insurance — generally price insurance. Derivatives are frequently employed for hedging purposes. Usually, the cost of this "insurance" is giving up part of the potential for gain.

Hedging: Generally taking a position in one market in order to offset the exposure to a risk in another market.

High powered money: Another name for the monetary base — usually currency *plus* the reserves of the commercial banks.

Historic volatility: The previous variability — as measured by e.g. variance or standard deviation — of an asset's price, profit, etc.

Implied volatility: The value of the volatility that makes the price of an option equal to the price that would be obtained if it were computed using the option pricing formula.

In-the-money-option: An option where the price of the asset exceeds the exercise price for a call, and the opposite for a put option.

Inflation tax: A reduction in the purchasing power of money due to a rise in the price level.

Informational efficiency: An expression relating to whether market prices are sufficiently efficient so that the true (or intrinsic) value of assets can be determined.

Institutional investor: An organization investing instead of an individual.

Interest-indexed bond: The coupon rate on this kind of bond is adjusted over time to keep pace with inflation.

Interest rate parity theory: The theory that real interest rates are the same in all countries, and if this is not the case then e.g. exchange (and perhaps inflation) rates will adjust in such a way as to obtain the equality.

Interest rate risk: The two major components are price risk — i.e. interest rates increase, and so bond prices fall; and reinvestment risk: short term assets must be "rolled over" at a higher rate of interest.

International banking facilities (IBFs): Facilities within e.g. the US that accept time deposits from foreigners, but are not subject to either reserve requirements or restrictions on interest payments.

International reserves: The holdings of a central bank of assets denominated in foreign currencies, gold, SDRs, IMF credit, etc. In other words, assets that can be used to pay international debt.

Intervention: The buying and selling of currencies by central banks in order to affect the exchange rate.

Intrinsic currency: The kind of money that has value in its own right, such as gold or silver.

Intrinsic value of an option: The value of an option if immediately exercised, given the exercise price of the option and the spot price of the underlying.

J-curve effect: Following a devaluation, an initial decrease in the balance of trade followed by an increase. Often this is attributed to low elasticities of demand in the short run, but high elasticities in the long run.

Junk bonds: Low grade bonds with ratings below BBB (or Baa) that have a relatively high default rate.

Kapitalanlage: German for investment.

Kerb trading: In the UK this is trading that takes place after the close of the official market. In the US the American Stock Exchange is known as the *Curb Exchange*.

Keynesian: A follower of John Maynard Keynes (i.e. Lord Keynes) who like Keynes believes that movements in aggregate real output can be brought about by movements in government spending, and who does not regard the economy as inherently stable. The point is that the economy can be efficiently managed.,

Law of one price: In a single market there can only be one price for identical goods — and this will be brought about by arbitrage. A weaker version says that identical tradable goods will sell for the same price worldwide when converted to a common currency, and when such things as transport costs are taken into consideration.

Lead Manager: The lead (or managing) bank in a syndicate selling an offering of securities.

Leasing: An arrangement in which a firm (e.g. a bank) purchases an asset and then rents it to another firm or individual.

Lender of last resort: Generally the central bank, which provides reserves to commercial banks in the event that they cannot obtain them from another source, and thereby prevents bank failure.

Letter of credit: A letter issued by a bank that obligates that bank to pay a specific amount of money to the seller of a good.

Liability: An obligation to make a financial payment.

LIBOR: Defined as the London Interbank Offer Rate: the interest rate on interbank deposits (i.e. loans) among the major London banks.

Liquidity: The relative ease with which an asset can be turned into a medium of exchange. (**Liquid assets** are assets that can be quickly turned into cash.)

Long position: A situation in which a trader occupies a "position" obligating him to take delivery on a commodity or asset at some point in the future. Or, similarly, buying a commodity or asset for delivery in the future.

M1: A measure of money that involves currency, travelers checks, and checkable (or transactions) deposits.

M2: A measure of money that adds "investment" deposits to M1. These investment deposits are usually defined as money market deposit accounts, money market mutual fund shares, small denomination time deposits, savings deposits, overnight repurchase agreements, and overnight Eurodollars.

M3: A measure of money that adds to M2 large denomination time deposits, long-term repurchase agreements, and institutional money market funds.

Maastrict Treaty: A treaty signed at Maastrict (Holland) by most — though not all — of the then member states of the European Community (EC). The intention was — and perhaps is — to work for a full economic and political union, with such things as a parliament, central bank, and a managing directorate.

Managed float (= "dirty" float): An arrangement in which the exchange rate is determined by demand and supply, but the central bank can intervene from time to time in order to obtain some desired exchange rate.

Margin: The amount of money a trader must keep on deposit with e.g. a broker in order to finance such things as futures trading or the purchase of shares. Is sometimes called a *"performance bond"*.

Margin call: Call for an increase in the existing margin deposit because e.g of unfavorable price movements of the underlying. (With a long position, the price of the underlying falls.)

Market maker: A transactor — usually a broker or trader — who is prepared to buy and sell certain assets (e.g. shares) at all times, and thus makes a market in them.

Matched sale-purchase transaction: An arrangement whereby the Federal Reserve sells securities, and the buyer agrees to sell them back to the Fed in the future. This is sometimes called a "reverse repo".

Matif: French Futures Exchange (Marché a Terme International de France).

Medium of exchange: Anything that can be used to pay for goods and services — e.g. money.

Mezzanine (financing): A financial transaction involving unsecured debt plus an option on some equity — i.e. an equity kicker.

Miller-Modigliani irrelevance hypothesis: If financial markets are perfect, then corporate policy (with regard to financing) is irrelevant. (See **perfect** below.)

Monetarism: The modern quantity theory of money to which is added a steady growth in the money supply in order to — ostensibly — bring about non-inflationary growth.

Monetary aggregates: The various measures of money used by a central bank.

Monetary base: Generally defined as currency in circulation plus the reserves of the banking system.

Money multiplier: The multiple represented by the ratio of the money supply over the monetary base.

Monetary policy: Managing the money supply and interest rates in order to achieve macroeconomic goals.

Monetizing the debt: A method of financing government spending by which the central bank buys outstanding government securities, and thus increases the monetary base.

Money illusion: An arrangement in which economic decisions are based on "money" rather than "real" variables. In Keynes' work, money illusion mostly had to do with wages.

Money market funds: Mutual funds that for the most part invest in short-term money-market securities.

Moral Hazard: A situation where the presence dof insurance leads insurance holders to take increased risk.

Moratorium: An agreed suspension of repayments on a debt that is spread over a designated period. This was quite a common practice during the "debt crisis", when various countries owned large banks huge amounts of money, after borrowing large amounts of "petrodollars" that had been placed in these banks by oil exporters. (This borrowing was sometimes called "the recycling of petrodollars".) Similar to **rescheduling**.

Mutual fund: An investment company that sells shares to individuals, who then own a designated portion of the assets of the fund.

NAFTA: North American Free Trade Association. An agreement allowing for the free movement of goods and services between the US, Canada, and Mexico.

NASDAQ: National Association of Security Dealers Automated Quotation System. A dealer market on which market makers post the prices at which they are prepared to buy and sell shares, and brokers — acting for themselves or their clients — choose among competing market makers to handle the transaction. This is usually considered an over-the-counter market, and compared to e.g. an "exchange" such as the New York Stock Exchange.

Net asset value: The value per share of a mutual fund, determined by dividing the total value of its assets by the number of shares.

No-load funds: Mutual funds sold directly to the public with no sales commissions.

Nonsystematic risk: Risk that is unique to a particular asset or portfolio, and which can be diversified away.

Notional principal: In e.g. a swap a principal amount that is only "notional", and is not exchanged. (Or **Notional Principal Amount**, which is the monetary amount upon which the payments of a transaction are based.)

Offer price: The price at which a transactor will sell an asset.

Open-end fund: The type of mutual fund in which shares can be redeemed at any time at a price that is tied to the asset value of the fund.

Open market operations: The purchase or sale of securities by a central banks. These are sometimes divided into defensive and dynamic. Defensive means open market operations that are used to offset changes in bank reserves or the monetary base created by outside factors, while dynamic open market operations are used to initiate a new monetary policy.

Open interest: Futures contracts that are open — i.e remain to be settled.

Operation Twist: A famous attempt by the Fed to combine easy money for domestic purposes with tight monetary policy for exchange rate purposes.

Opportunity cost of capital: The rate that could be earned on capital if it were invested elsewhere in assets in the same risk class.

Optimum currency area: A region where exchange rates are fixed between countries, but flexible between this region and countries outside.

Options contracts: Contracts on which the option holder has the right but not the obligation to complete the transaction.

Out-of-the-money option: The situation where the price of the asset is less than the option's exercise price for a call option, and the opposite for a put option. (Or, the situation in which an option is worthless if exercised.)

Over-the-counter market: A market without an exchange. Normally these comprise the various traders of a particular security who quote buying and selling prices. These traders are linked by electronic information systems and telephones. In the US, the shares of most smaller companies are sold and bought in this manner. Some observers consider them superior to exchanges, while others believe that exchanges offer better liquidity and transparency, and thus enable transactors to obtain better prices.

Par bond: A bond whose yield equals the bond's coupon rate. The bond trades at par.

Par value: The price at which an a security or asset is issued, and which may be greater or less than its market price.

Parallel market: A foreign market that exists as an alternative to the (regulated) official market, but which is legal. (A "black" market is not legal.)

Parallel loan: A loan arrangement in which a transactor borrows in the home country's currency, and then trades this debt for a foreign currency debt. In this way access to the foreign currency can be obtained.

Paris Club: A so-called "club" where creditors meet with (Third World) debtor nations in Paris to restructure debts.

Pension: Regular income that is received after a certain age, and usually after retiring from work, that is paid by the government and/or some private scheme. Traditionally pensions were pay-as-you-go arrangements in which current workers paid current pensioners, but because of the large increase in the number of pensioners relative to the number of workers, many countries are going over to pre-funded individual pensions, in which each employee has an account in which money must be saved, and in one sense or another invested, until retirement.

Perfect markets: Markets in which the law of one price holds; and where there is no friction or information problems, or uncertainty that cannot be hedged; and where investors and consumers are rational.

Pit trader: A trader in a designated space on the floor of an exchange, where prices are signaled and determined by "open outcry". Electronic trading has eliminated most "pits" in Europe, but this type of trading is still common in the US, although it is expected that in the long run pit trading will be liquidated.

Political business cycle: The hypothesis that monetary policy will inevitably be used to achieve political goals — e.g. to re-elect incumbent politicians.

Political risk: The risk that a sovereign government will change the rules by which it operates with respect to foreign investors.

Ponzi scheme (or pyramid investment scheme): An (often) illegal arrangement in which a portion of each participant's subscription is returned as profits to earlier subscribers. As long as new subscribers can be attracted, the pyramid grows.

Portfolio: The combination of capital assets, financial assets, etc. that a person or firm holds.

Position taking: Buying or selling, although at times it means buying in the expectation of a price rise, and selling short with the intention of making a profit by "covering" at a lower price.

Premium: In currency markets, the forward pricing of a currency at one point in time at more than the price at another. Also, the price of an option.

Primary market: A financial market in which new issues of a security are bought and sold.

Prime rate: The interest rate that banks charge their "best" customers. Corresponds in some ways to LIBOR.

Principal-agent problem: An arrangement where agents (for principals) do not make the same decisions that the principals would make if the principals had the same information as the agents, and were making the decisions themselves — e.g. shareholders and managers.

Private placement: The issue of new securities to particular investors (such as pension funds and insurance funds), rather than through a public offering. In some countries (e.g. Australia) there are limits on the private placement of shares.

Promissory note: A short-term discount security (or I.O.U.) that is issued by high-quality borrowers in their own name.

Proviso clause: The portion of a Federal Open Market Committee directive stating that a given policy should be carried out provided that another goal is not violated.

Purchasing power parity (PPP): *Absolute* — the law of one price, or the equivalence of the exchange rate to the ratio of foreign and domestic price levels; and *relative,* which means that the percentage change in the exchange rate is equal to the inflation differential (in percent) between two countries.Perhaps more clearly, PPP means that exchange rates adjust so as to maintain the same inflation-adjusted price of a (representative) basket of goods and services in different countries (or currency areas).

Put option: The option, but not the obligation, to sell a commodity or asset before a specified future date, usually at a specified price.

Pyramid investment scheme: See Ponzi scheme!

Quotas: Restrictions on the amount of e.g. goods that can be bought or sold.

Ramping: The purchase of shares for the sole purpose of increasing their price.

Random walk: The kind of movements (of a variable) where future changes cannot be predicted — i.e. are random — in the sense that given today's values, the variable in question is as likely to fall as rise.

Rational Expectations: A theory of expectations formation which says that expectations will not differ from optimal forecasts when transactors use all available information; and they will use all available information because it is in their interest to do so.

Real Bills doctrine: A once highly regarded doctrine for the conduct of monetary policy, which stated that as long as loans were made to support the production of goods and services, making reserves available to the banking system to make these these loans would not be inflationary. This policy was mainly employed by the Federal Reserve prior to the Second World War for its discount loans, and real bills was intended to mean the same thing as "sound" business loans.

Real interest rate: The nominal (money) interest rate minus the (expected) inflation rate.

Real options: An option or optionlike feature that is embedded in a real investment opportunity. For example, an oil firm might have the option of exploiting a deposit this year, or waiting to see whether the oil price rises or falls. This option has a value that can sometimes be calculated using conventional option theory.

Real time: An arrangement in which the generation of data (or information) and its transformation and/or processing takes place almost simultaneously. Electronic trading is a good example here, since prices and quantities are obtained as soon as deals are closed.

Redlining: The colloquial name of a procedure whereby a bank refuses to make loans to a borrower or a group of borrowers.

Refinancing: The exchanging of one loan for another. Often a borrower will refinance in order to obtain better terms.

Regulation Q: An arrangement in which the Federal Reserve System had the right to set maximum interest rates that banks could pay on savings and time deposits. Was in effect between 1933 and 1980.

Repurchase agreement (Repo): An arrangement in which a (short term) security is sold, but the seller agrees to repurchase it at a fixed price in a short period of time.

Rescheduling: Altering the pattern of interest and/or principal payments on a loan. See **moratorium**.

Reservation price: The minimum price at which an owner is prepared to sell, or the maximum price at which a buyer will purchase.

Reserve currency: A currency (like the US dollar) which is used by various countries to denominate the assets they hold to pay international debt, where these assets can be called international reserves.

Reserve requirements: Central bank regulations specifying the reserve ratios for financial institutions.

Revaluation: Changing the par value of a currency so that it is more expensive with respect to other currencies.

Risk adjusted discount rate (= market capitalization rate): The return that investors require in order to invest in a risky asset or project. This return is often given as a "spread" over a high-quality asset such as a government security.

Risk premium: One important example is the spread between the interest rate on default free bonds, and bonds with a default risk — or for that matter bonds whose future price is highly certain, and therefore likely to fall by a large amount.

Savings and loan associations: In the US these are financial intermediaries that specialize in making mortgage loans. One of their most unfortunate characteristics turned out to be the practice of lending long while borrowing short. This forced many of these institutions into near bankrupcy.

Schatzobligation: German for treasury security. Similarly, **Schatzwechsel** is a treasury bill, and **Schatzbrief** a savings bond.

Securitization: The process by which a financial asset or a number of financial assets are transformed into marketable capital market instruments. For example, mortgage loans can be formed into a single bundle/package and sold as a security. It also means the substitution of securities for bank loans: a bank may purchase a bill of exchange etc instead of lending to a customer.

Seigniorage: The difference between the real resources acquired by issuing a national money, and the cost of issuing this money.

Short position: A "position" where a transactor has the obligation to deliver an asset or a commodity at some time in the future, and often at a previously agreed upon price.

Smart card: A plastic card containing a microchip. (Invented in France, where they are known as cartes a mémoire.) They can be used as money, and when "run-down" can be recharged by the issuing bank. Can often be used at ATMs.

Smithsonian Agreement: An agreement signed at the Smithsonian Institute in Washington which meant that the dollar was officially devalued, and that currencies would be allowed to fluctuate within a band of 2.25% around the new parity (or par) value.

Soft loan: A loan made at below the market rate of interest.

Sogo shosha: An expression that applies to some very large corporations in Japan. Recently there have been some problems in Japan with so-called "**sogo banks**", or banks specializing in mortgage credit.

Sovereign debt: The debt of governments. In the period 1997–2000, there were debt defaults by Russia, Ukraine, Pakistan, Ecuador, and Ivory Coast. (Ecuador defauted on Brady Bonds in 1999.)

Special Drawing Rights: Sometimes called "paper gold", these are an IMF created and issued asset that are designed (like gold) to serve as an international reserve — i.e. an item that can be used to pay foreign debt.

Specialist: A dealer-broker/market maker who operates on the floor of an exchange, and is supposed to maintain "orderly trading" in the set of securities for which he or she is responsible.

Specie: Money in the form of coins (often gold or silver).

Spreadsheet: A grid or matrix showing large amounts of financial or other data. (See, e.g. Bodie and Merton (2000).)

Sterilization: Central bank operations designed to offset undesirable changes in international reserves. Sterilization generally involves open market sales of domestic securities in order to prevent a rise in the monetary base.

Stock parking: Selling shares with the understanding that they will be sold back at a time and price favorable to the initiator of the transaction. This is often done for tax purposes, and generally it is illegal.

Stop-loss order: A *limit* order to buy or sell which operates only when a given price is reached.

Store of value: An asset which allows wealth to be stored over time without diminishing. For example, a good store of value would be something like a government bond that was indexed to the inflation rate.

Strike price: Also called the exercise price: the price at which an option can be exercised.

Sunk cost: A cost that is usually irrelevant once an investment is made.

Supply side economics: Policies whose purpose is to increase output *and* decrease inflation by shifting the supply curve outward (i.e. to the right). Supply side theorists want this done by decreasing taxes.

SWIFT (Society for Worldwide Interbank Financial Transactions): The network through which banks can conduct their international financial transactions. It is operated on a non-profit basis from Brussels, and the system comprises almost 1,600 banks.

Synthetic loans: These are loans that have been modified by being combined with futures contracts. Variable rate loans combine a fixed rate loan with a long position in interest rate futures, while a synthetic fixed rate loan combines a variable rate loan with a short position in an interest rate futures contract.

Systematic risk: The part of an asset or a portfolio's risk that cannot be eliminated by diversification.

T-account: A balance sheet in the form of a T that shows assets and liabilities.

Term structure of interest rates: The interest rates on bonds of different maturities, beginning with short maturities, and proceeding to long maturities. The term structure can be falling, rising, or flat.

Thin market: A market with only a few buyers and sellers, where the sale or purchase of large amounts of a commodity or asset might cause large price changes.

Time preference: The preference for present as compared to future consumption.

Time value (of an option): The difference between the (market) value of an option and the option's intrinsic value.

Tombstone announcement: An announcement advertising the successful raising of a syndicated loan, and usually naming all the menbers of the syndicate.

Transactions cost: The cost — in time and money — of buying and selling.

Transactions deposits: Deposits on which checks can be written without prior notice, such as demand deposits and various checkable deposits.

Transfer price: "Internal" prices that are charged a subsidiary or a department in a firm for the intrafirm transfer of goods.

Transparency: In economics transparency is interpreted as the ability of transactors to compare the characteristics of goods and services. In finance it mostly means knowing which assets are available. For instance, if you want to buy bonds, you want to know what they are offering in Pago-Pago or Guadacanal — assuming that they are offering something.

Treasury bill (T-bill): A short-term security issued by the treasury of the United States.

Underfunded: A pension arrangement where earnings are estimated to be insufficient to pay out promised benefits. This is one of the reasons for the enthusiasm — on the part of governments — for pre-funded arrangements, in which employees must save in special accounts for their own pensions.

Underground economy: Also called the subterranean or black economy. That part of the economy where economic activity is unreported to the authorities.

Underwriting: The process in which a financial institution (or a broker) guarantees the price on securities to a corporation, and then sells these securities to investors.

Unit of account: The monetary unit in which value is measured.

Universal bank: A bank that is engaged in both commercial and investment banking activities. Examples are Deutsche Bank, UBS, HKSBC, etc.

Unmatched Swap: A swap in which the intermediary (e.g. a bank) assumes the role of counterparty

Vault cash: Currency in the physical possession of banks that, unconventionally, is stored in vaults at night.

Velocity of money: The average number of times per year that a dollar "turns over" in an economy, where the usual measurement is the GNP divided by the money supply.

Wealth: Wealth in money terms is financial and capital assets minus total liabilities. Wealth in real terms is money (or nominal) wealth divided by a price index.

Wire transfers: The telegraphic transfer of money to other banks and to customers.

Working capital: The difference between a firm's current assets and current liabilities.

Yield curve: A graphical representation of the yields on default free government bonds with different terms to maturity.

Yield to maturity: The interest rate that equates the present value of payments received from a financial instrument (e.g. a bond) with the price at which it is being traded.

Zaibatsu: Large interlocking groups of companies in pre-war Japan. These were more or less outlawed by General Douglas MacArthur in the late 1940s. They have been more or less replaced in present-day Japan by the *keiretsu*, which have often been described as trade associations.

Zero-coupon bond: A bond that pays no coupon income, but is issued at a discount to its face value. In Australia, Treasury notes fit this description, and the same is true in the US and many other countries.

References

Aggarwal, Reena and James J. Angel (1999), "The rise and fall of the Amex Emerging Marketplace", *Journal of Financial Economics* 11(26): 22–33.

Amram, Martha and Nalin Kulatilaka (1999), *Real Options*. Boston: Harvard Business School.

Bachelier, Louis (1900), *Theory of Speculation*. Paris: Gauthier-Villars.

Banks, Ferdinand E. (2000), *Energy Economics: A Modern Introduction*. Dordrecht and Boston: Kluwer Academic Publishers.

——— (1998), "Real and unreal in the Asian Crisis", *Petromin* 12(22): 54–58.

——— (1977), *Scarcity, Energy, and Economic Progress*. Lexington and Toronto: D.C. Heath and Co.

Bernstein, Peter L. (1992), *Capital Ideas*. New York: The Free Press.

Block, Stanley D. (1999), "A study of financial analysts practice and theory", *Financial Analysts Journal*, July/August.

Bodie, Zvi and Robert C. Merton (2000), *Finance*. Upper Saddle River: Prentice Hall.

Campbell, John Y. (1995), "Some lessons from the yield curve", *Journal of Economic Perspectives* 9(3): 129–152.

Congdon, Tim (1988), *The Debt Trap*. London: Basil Blackwell.

Cornell, Bradford (1999), "Risk, duration, and capital budgeting", *Journal of Business* 16(24): 33–43.

Davis, L.J. (1982), *Bad Money*. New York: New American Library.

Easton, Thomas (1999), "Investment rules that have stood the test of time", *Forbes* 2(26):158–159.

Erdman, Paul (1987), *What's Next*. London: Bantam Books.

Faber, Marc (1989), *The Great Money Illusion*. Hong Kong: Longman Group (Far East).

Fama, Eugene F. (1968), "What random walk really means", *Institutional Investor* April.

Ferris, Paul (1984), *The Master Bankers*. New York: New American Library.

Fisher, Stanley (1997), "Financial system soundness", *Finance and Development* 34(1): 14–16.

Galbraith, John K. (1975), *Money*. London: Penguin Books.

Goldstone, Nancy (1988), *Trading Up*. London: Pan Books.

Grabbe, J. Orlin (1996), *International Financial Markets*. Englewood Cliffs: Prentice Hall.

Graham, John R. (1999), "Do personal taxes affect corporate financing decisions?", *Journal of Public Economics* 22(8): 24–38.

Hanke, Steve H. (1999), "Euroflop", *Forbes* 2(26):25.

Hong, Han Kang (1990), *Financial Management*. Singapore: Butterworth.

Hunt, Ben and Chris Terry (1993), *Financial Instruments and Markets*. Melbourne: Thomas Nelson.

Kennedy, Paul (1995), *Preparing for the Twenty First Century*. New York: Random House.

Leeson, Nick (1997), *Rogue Trader*. London: Little-Brown.

Levinson, Marc (1999), *Guide to Financial Markets*. London: Profile Books.

Lewis, Michael (1989), *Liars Poker*. London: Hodder and Staughton.

Malkiel, Burton G. (1985), *A Random Walk Down Wall Street*. New York: Norton.

Melvin, Michael (1992), *International Money and Finance*. Harper Collins: New York.

Miller, Merton H. and Charles W. Upton (1974), *Macroeconomics: A Classical Introduction*. Homewood Illinois: Richard D. Irwin.

Mishkin, Frederic S. (1998), *The Economics of Money, Banking, and Financial Markets*. Reading Massachusetts: Addison-Wesley.

Modigliani, Franco and Merton H. Miller (1958), "The cost of capital, corporation finance, and the theory of investing", *American Economic Review* 48(3): 655–669.

Moffit, Michael (1984), *The World's Money*. New York: Simon Shuster.

Montbrial, Thierry de, (1974), *Le Désordre Economique Mondial*. Paris: Calman-Levy.

Morishima, Michio (1984), *The Economics of Industrial Society*. Cambridge UK: Cambridge University Press.

Naylor, R.T. (1987), *Hot Money and the Politics of Debt*. London: Unwin.

O'Hara, Maureen (1995), *Market Microstructure Theory*. Oxford: Blackwell.

O'Rourke, P.J. (1998), *Eat the Rich*. London: Picador.

Pilbeam, Keith (1998), *Finance and Financial Markets*. London: MacMillan Press Ltd.

Reich, Robert B. (1989), "As the world turns", *The New Republic*, May 1.

Roll, Richard (1987), "R^2", *Journal of Finance* 35: 1073–1104.

Sachs, Jeffrey D. and Felipe Larraine (1993), *Macroeconomics in the Global Economy*. Englewood Cliffs: Prentice Hall.

Sampson, Anthony (1981), *The Money Lenders*. New York: Coronet Books.

Schwager, Jack D. (1989), *Market Wizards*. New York: New York Institute of Finance.

Sherris, Michael (1991), *Money and Capital Markets*. Sydney: Allen and Unwin (Australia).

Shiller, Robert J. (2000), *Irrational Exuberence*. Princeton: Princeton University Press.

Smith, Adam (1988), *The Roaring "80s"*. New York: Summit Books.

Tobin, James and Stephen S. Golub (1997), *Money, Credit, and Capital*. New York: Irwin/McGraw Hill.

Valdez, Stephen (1997), *An Introduction to Global Financial Markets*. London: MacMillan Press Ltd.

Varian, Hal (1993), "A portfolio of Nobel laureates: Markowitz, Miller, and Sharpe", *Journal of Economic Perspectives* 7(1): 159–169.

Wachtel, Howard M. (1986), *The Money Mandarins*. New York: Pantheon Books.

Walmsley, Julian (1991), *Global Investing*. London: MacMillan.

Warburton, Peter (2000), *Debt and Delusion*. London: Penguin Books.

White, Lawrence H. (1999), *The Theory of Monetary Institutions*. Malden Massachusetts: Blackwell.

Winstone, David (1995) *Financial Derivatives*. London: Chapman and Hall.

Index